For Jennifer
With Love & Best Wishes
Keith Porter (Grandpa) Tappy
and Grandma "P" too!

ME, MYSELF AND I, INC

For Jennifer, Russell, Nathaniel and Emily,
our next generation of explorers.

Me, Myself And I, Inc

10 Steps To Career Independence

Shirley Porter
Keith J. Porter
Christine Bennett

IMPACT PUBLICATIONS
Manassas Park, VA

ME, MYSELF AND I, INC: 10 STEPS TO CAREER INDEPENDENCE

Library of Congress Cataloging-in-Publication Data

Porter, Shirley, 1943-
    Me, myself and I, Inc : 10 steps to career independence / Shirley
Porter, Keith J. Porter, Christine Bennett.
        p.   cm.
    Includes bibliographical references and index.
    ISBN 1-57023-093-5 (alk. paper)
    1. Career development.   I. Porter, Keith J., 1942-
II. Bennett, Christine, 1963-   III. Title.
HF5381.P666   1998
650.14--dc21   98-9771
                                                                   CIP

For information on quantity discounts, Tel. 703/361-7300, Fax 703/335-9486, or
write to: Sales Department, IMPACT PUBLICATIONS, 9104-N Manassas Drive,
Manassas Park, VA 20111-5211. Distributed to the trade by National Book
Network, 15200 NBN Way, Blue Ridge Summit, PA 17214, Tel. 800/462-6420.

Contents

Preface

W hy are you reading this book? Probably because you work, or want
to work, and are concerned about your future. Perhaps you've had
one of these thoughts:

"Why can't I just get a normal job with good benefits and security?"

"I have one of those 'good' jobs, but the benefits and security are
fading before my eyes."

"I'm expected to do more with less, and have a good attitude to
boot, while others around me get the ax."

"I'd like to have a work-life balance, but the pressure at work only
gets more intense."

"I'm looking for a job, but it seems that the rules and techniques
have changed, and no one told me about it."

"I'm concerned, confused and angry about my work—it's not
supposed to be this way."

Maybe you're a long-term employee with a company, or a graduating
student looking for a first job. Or you're a temporary or contract worker, or
someone considering re-entry into the job market. Whatever your situation,
what is it that brings you to a book called *Me, Myself and I, Inc: 10 Steps
to Career Independence*? Is it your hope that there's life after downsizing,

restructuring and employment upheaval? Or your search for a way to not just survive, but prosper in the changing work environment? If so, you've come to the right place!

Why the title *Me, Myself and I, Inc*? The idea reflects the fact that each of us will have to change the way we look at ourselves at work. The changes in the world of work are forcing each of us to become more of an independent economic entity, thinking and acting more like a business. Why this is true and what it means for you is the subject of the book; the 10 Steps to Career Independence are the way to make it happen.

What Can The 10 Steps Do For You?

This book can literally transform you from workplace victim into someone who knows what they want, and how to get it. You'll get answers to your questions about what's happening in the work environment. You'll learn about the vital skill of incorporating your right-brain, inner abilities and knowledge into a more successful relationship with your work and into a balanced life. You'll learn how to create a secure, prosperous future for yourself as an important part of the workplace economy. You'll learn how to prepare a comprehensive personal plan for taking the reins of your future into your own hands.

One client told us, "I just want to get the right job, not plan my whole life." The problem with this outlook is that fewer and fewer traditional jobs are available, which means you need to take a different approach. Instead of looking for a job, you need to actively develop and find your own best position, or *niche*. By thinking of yourself more as an independent economic entity, you can take charge of your own work (and life). And that's equally true whether you're employed now, looking for work, or planning to be self-employed.

How To Use This Book

You can take advantage of *Me, Myself and I, Inc: 10 Steps to Career Independence* in two different ways. On the one hand, a quick read can be very helpful in finding the key issues with immediate payoff for you if you're faced with an imminent crisis in your work life. On the other hand, when you're ready to step up and take full charge of your future, you'll find thought-provoking suggestions and questions to guide you through a step-by-step, comprehensive process for planning your work future. You'll get the most benefit by following the Steps in sequence, and thoughtfully considering each suggestion or question, making notes or writing answers to the questions in a notebook or journal. Make the material your own, based on your unique needs and wants, using it in the way that's most comfortable for you. When you do, you'll end up with a very powerful personal tool for direction and motivation as the uncertain future unfolds.

What's In The Book?

Me, Myself and I, Inc: 10 Steps to Career Independence is organized so that each of the first ten chapters focuses on one Step:

Step 1:   Understand the Changing Work Environment
Step 2:   Create Your Vision
Step 3:   Define Your Product
Step 4:   Develop Your Livelihood
Step 5:   Create Your Niche
Step 6:   Create Your Competitive Advantage
Step 7:   Develop a Financial Strategy
Step 8:   Market Yourself
Step 9:   Integrate Your Work and Your Life
Step 10:   Create and Implement Your Plan

The closing chapter is called "The Bridge: Putting the 10 Steps to Work." The Bridge will help you apply the 10 Steps in the actual process of your employment search—getting the position. Each chapter except the last closes with case studies, relating the stories of four real people applying the 10 Steps to their own work lives.

Who Are The Authors?

The three of us who wrote this book have several things in common. We have each personally experienced the turmoil of today's changing work environment. As a result, we formed a family business in 1995 to help people make sense of what's happening to work and to find a way to respond creatively. Using our combined backgrounds in career management, business management, and education, we developed a three-day seminar to lead working people through a step-by-step, interactive process to find security in their work, with or without traditional jobs. After leading these seminars for 18 months, we put the concepts into the form of a book in order to reach a wider audience. *Me, Myself and I, Inc: 10 Steps to Career Independence* will give you the same opportunity to benefit from the concepts and experiences that have worked so well for others.

Over time, we began to see the ten-step process as a navigational tool to guide the search for prosperity and fulfillment at work. In the 18th century, before the sextant was invented, seagoing explorers used the astrolabe to navigate through unknown, treacherous waters. The parallels between the hazards faced by 18th century explorers and those faced by workers today in the chaotic job marketplace are strong. Therefore, we chose the astrolabe as a symbol for the 10-step process of finding safe waters at the end of a successful journey.

ME, MYSELF AND I, INC

Get Ready For
Career Independence

This book has a simple goal: to help you see the reality of the new work environment and formulate a creative response to it that enables you to survive and prosper. Using this book, you'll master 10 Steps which will assure that your journey into the new work future is successful. You'll prepare for your journey in a way that will make you aware of both the speed bumps and the vista points you'll find along the way.

10 Steps to Career Independence

The 10-step process outlined in this book will be useful to everyone who works for a living: managers and "doers"; new workers and old hands; the self-employed and the still-employed; part-time and full-time workers; those happy with their work and those who feel unfulfilled; those who have been personally affected by downsizing and re-engineering, and those who haven't (yet). Since the work environment itself is in such a massive transition, no one who participates in it is unaffected. And all of us can use ideas and guidance for figuring out how to survive and prosper despite (or because of) the changes that are occurring.

If you happen to be one of the few lucky ones who still haven't been touched by change in the workplace, standby! Unless you're just about to retire and leave the workplace completely, we can safely predict that change

1

is in your future. The question for you—in fact, the question for all of us—is: "Are you ready for it?"

A Mini Reality Check

Take this quick quiz, which is modeled on tests designed to see if a person is ready to be an entrepreneur:

Success Factors Quiz

YES	NO		
____	____	1.	Do you have a passion for your work?
____	____	2.	Do you have a clear and inspiring vision of where you're going?
____	____	3.	Do you know (and can you describe) exactly your product?
____	____	4.	Do you have a current and expanding network of contacts?
____	____	5.	Do you have general expertise in accounting, word processing, legal issues, marketing and business planning?
____	____	6.	Have you developed a financial plan to get you through dry spells and transitions?
____	____	7.	Have you set clear goals and do you have a method to measure your progress toward them?
____	____	8.	Are you prepared to be "out there" marketing yourself and your ideas?
____	____	9.	Have you developed a complete, yet flexible, business plan?
____	____	10.	Are you ready to move from the known and comfortable into the new and untried?

So, how did you do? You may have answered some questions "yes," but probably have doubts about others. So you're not cut out to be an entrepreneur, right? Guess again! The new title for this quiz is "Success Factors for the Twenty-First Century Worker." In today's world of work, every one of these success factors will be required for the most successful workers—*including employees.*

If you marked 8-10 questions "yes," you're already thinking like someone with success potential in the emerging world of work; the 10 Steps in this book will offer you hands-on techniques and information to improve your strategic position. If you marked 5-7 questions "yes," you're on your way to developing the necessary attitudes and skills for prosperity; the 10 Steps will help you accelerate your progress on your path. If you marked fewer than 5 questions "yes," don't worry; you're not alone. Most of us who are working today will have said "yes" to fewer than 5 questions. But take heart! Every one of these success factors is something you can learn to do—well. And in the course of this book, you'll make great strides toward getting the expertise you need in each of these areas for success. This book is designed especially for you, so read on.

The End Of Your Career And
The Beginning of MMI, Inc

"The end of my career? Aren't we supposed to be talking about success in the future, not the end of my career?" you ask.

The answer is: "Yes, we are talking about success, and that means we have to set aside some old ways of coping with work and look at things from a new vantage point. From this new vantage point, we can see that the concept of a career is obsolete." Here's why.

A career is something that can be traditionally managed in one of two ways. The first way is to go for help to someone like an employment agency when you need a job. Let's call it the *flat-tire* approach, because the goal is to get the immediate problem fixed—now. This is a short-term and narrowly focused view of the work world—you're not changing cars or directions, just getting back on the road—but it's exactly what you need if you're out of work and searching for immediate help. This approach typically involves little reflection or creativity; it's all busy activity, consisting of job searches, phone calls, resumes, interviews, and salary comparisons. The flat-tire approach is *not wrong*, especially if you need money! But what's been done to help make you "future-proof?" Not much.

A second approach to managing a career, perhaps the approach taken during a traditional career counseling session, is more sophisticated and often more helpful in the long run: the *fork in the road* approach. This strategy involves using the change that has occurred—whether you've lost a job, realized that you can't continue to tolerate a bad job, or are in transition from school or child-rearing into the job market—as an opportunity to evaluate who you are and where you're headed. Making a decision at a fork in the road involves, first, realizing that there are options, and then spending some time choosing among the possibilities. With the greater investment of time, energy and thought, this approach involves some reflection and creative planning. But it's still mostly activity (research, testing, resumes, applications), and the goal is to change your career, which is still based on an outmoded view of the work place.

In this book we're talking about an approach to work which could be called *cross-country*. In this approach, you are no longer dependent upon already created paths. Instead, you have the ability to diverge, turn back, or take a previously unexplored direction; your options are limited only by your personal strength and ability. Armed with the right motivation and preparation, you can explore the terrain to see what's coming and what's right for you: you can scale a mountain to see far and wide, or climb a tree to look further down paths to see where they lead. This approach also involves a balance between reflection (finding motivation, choosing a direction) and activity.

In taking the cross-country approach, you may be asking these questions: What do I need to be aware of in my job and in the work environment *before* my income is at risk? Is a job necessary or desirable for me? What other possibilities exist: start a business, become self-employed, work as a consultant or contractor? Are there ways I can continue working creatively in my old workplace by finding a unique niche, bringing creative, fresh ideas to my work and thereby changing the situation so that I can remain there and enjoy it? What am I really good at? What do I really want? And what do I need to do and change personally that will allow me to create my own best situation? The primary goal for this approach is to find a creative way to change my relationship to work, including looking realistically at both the environment and what I bring to the work equation.

This approach to work is so different and new that it can't be called career management at all—it's something fresher and more renewable than a "career," and it's more contemporary and responsive than "management." It will take reflection, thought, information, and planning, but when you've learned to approach your work in this new way, you will become something different than a worker seeking a job. This new you needs a new name— beyond your job, beyond your career, able to roll with the punches and rise to the top—**MMI, Inc.**

MMI, Inc stands for *Me, Myself and I, Inc*. It's symbolic of moving away from an old, outdated view of yourself, at the same time using what and who you are to create an *independent economic entity*. The idea of *you* as an independent economic entity—self-reliant, adaptable, prepared for the future—is the opposite of our everyday sense of *you* in the workplace: an employee, in a position, tied to a job. At the same time, recognizing **MMI, Inc** as only one aspect to be balanced with the rest of your life will help keep work in perspective.

By the way, the final action of last resort in traditional career management is often the outplacement of employees—off the payroll! Outplacement has become the default way for big employers to fix—or cause—a career flat tire. The real benefit of learning how to work as **MMI, Inc**, using a cross-country approach, is to do what's best for you *before* the tire goes flat.

So, are you ready to use this book to change your life? If so, start your engine; the road awaits. And it's a lot safer to start your journey now than to wait unprepared for the changes that will sooner or later occur in your work life.

Step 1

Understand the Changing Work Environment

Elena, a 35-year-old Registered Nurse: *After ten years as a nurse, I hardly recognize the field. Between the rise of HMO's, responsibility shifting to nursing assistants, downsizing, and hospital closures, there's a huge increase in job responsibility and a huge decrease in security. Every nurse I know is looking into other jobs, but what else can we do? Talk about low morale— that's us in a nutshell.*

It may have happened to you already. If it hasn't, it probably soon will. Eventually we'll all experience some form of work dislocation— downsizing, re-engineering, diminished benefits, economic downturn, or job obsolescence. The changes in the workplace occurring around us every day present each of us with an opportunity: take creative measures to find a new, more secure relationship to our work, or . . . or what? We don't know exactly what the "what" is for each of us personally, but we all know "it won't be pretty."

In contrast, moving ahead successfully can be seen as embarking on an individual journey toward redefining yourself in relation to work. This book will make that journey more attractive and ensure that it becomes a successful journey from the *unsustainable* present into a *prosperous* future.

The psychological impact of starting a journey, necessary or not, comes from the knowledge that you're consciously heading out in a direction without knowing exactly what's ahead. It's great to be in a place where one can look forward to "movin' on" as an interesting, attractive proposition.

But like most of us, you've probably had times when dealing with present circumstances was just about all you could handle. When the winds of change present themselves at such a time, it can be overwhelming. And maybe you've been so immersed in change, so abused by its demands or so freshly hurt by the consequences, that it seems impossible that you'll ever again find anything exciting or enjoyable about "movin' on."

Whether you wish for change, enjoy it or fear it, need it or are overwhelmed by it, the realization that change is nevertheless occurring brings with it two important questions.

1. How can you make the demands for change seem less imposing and more manageable?

2. How can you ensure that you make the right choices in response—choices which will lead to a successful outcome?

This book will help you answer these two questions as they relate to the way you make your living.

Where You Are Now, and Why It Isn't Working

The Challenge

Here is the heart of the matter: *in the employment market of today jobs are going away, and those of us who are going to survive and be successful in the future are going to have to change the way we make our livings.*

You can look at the demand for change as negative and oppressive, the initial, natural response of most people. But go back to the first question above: "How can you make the demands for change seem less imposing and more manageable?" You can start by looking honestly at your negative emotions and feelings, and acknowledging their validity. Once you've dealt with that, you'll discover that you can find the positives (or at least the possibilities) that exist, and develop a creative response.

The 10-step process laid out in this book will enable you to answer the second question: "How can you ensure that you make the right choices in response—choices which will lead to a successful outcome?" By clearly understanding yourself and your chosen field, and by developing a precise, individualized road map, you equip yourself for a successful venture into the new work environment.

For example, think about Elena, the nurse from the beginning of this Step. She clearly (and rightly) sees the changes around her as oppressive; hence her negative emotional response, which is normal and healthy—as long as she moves through it. After admitting and dealing with some of her feelings, she was able to think ahead creatively and to develop her own successful path into the new world of work. You'll have a chance later in this Step to vent some of your own feelings.

The Molecular Marketplace

We call the new work environment the "molecular marketplace." Why? Because work life is becoming a marketplace for everyone; not just employers or big companies, but workers as well. Seeing the workplace as a market is a good first step toward thinking of yourself as an independent, business-like economic entity—**MMI, Inc** (Me, Myself, and I, Inc). The word molecular represents the smallest entity in this rich economic stew, and is also symbolic of the constant interrelationship between all the pieces.

You'll create the road map you need for your journey into the molecular marketplace by working through the 10 Steps in this book, and building your own Portfolio Development Plan (PDP) as the final Step. If you're going to fully master the 10 Steps by completing your own personal PDP, apply the 10 Steps to your individual situation.

Your personal journey into the molecular marketplace will be different from anyone else's, but it will have at least one important thing in common with every journey—the fact that it is a movement into the unknown. Anyone facing the unknown is well advised to start with a sense of vigilance. *Pay attention to what the environment is telling you.* On a strange highway, it can be a big mistake not to read the road signs. Here's a look at some of the signs you'll see on the road to the molecular marketplace.

Even Change is Changing

There's nothing new about change—it's inevitable. What's truly new now is the *speed and magnitude* of changes around us. Perhaps the most obvious example of this "change in change" is in computers—as opposed to human generations spanning 20 years, a new generation of computers is created every two to three years. And as we move into the information age, the sum of human knowledge now doubles every 18 months. Clearly the new millennium will bring as-yet unimagined possibilities.

So let's look first at the broadest perspective on change. Just as the way we work is changing, so we find that this is a time of re-definition in many fields: science (the merging of disciplines and new fundamental ideas); health (HMOs and managed care); computers (processing speed and networking); money (debit cards and instant access to information); shopping (services going "on-line"); family (both its definition and its role); and even morality (assisted suicide and the "right to die"). Things we have felt comfortable with are being turned upside-down and inside-out. Although, on one hand, many of these changes seem exciting and innovative, taken together they seem for many to signal an endpoint. The resulting anxiety about what's coming next can cause stress, frustration and anger.

When so much that forms a society is in transition, a conflict inevitably arises between revolutionary forces advocating change and reactionary forces demanding to go back to the "good old days." The molecular marketplace is no exception, with simultaneous excitement over possibilities as well as longing for lost security and tradition.

YCDBSOYA (You Can't Do
Business Sitting On Your Assets!)

The environment of the workplace in America today is sending all of us—workers and employers alike—a strong message: things are changing, so a different approach to work is required. More and more jobs are being "lost" as larger businesses downsize or re-engineer. Even government, the "employer of last resort" and (we often thought) a safe haven, is reducing the public payroll—witness the military base closures across the country.

The good news is that very often the "lost" jobs are actually just transferred somewhere else as functions or work groups are "outsourced." But the bad news—which may be very bad for you personally if you lose your job—is that something has changed. The role the individual worker once had is going, or gone, to be replaced by something or someone else, somewhere else, in another town or country, in another group or company. Usually the displaced worker is left with no option but to move with the work or try to prepare for doing something else, often less rewarding work at less pay. Psychologically there's been a clear shift among workers from feeling "taken care of" to feelings of "they're out to get us". Two employee comments from a US News and World Report article on Kodak sum up this change. A laid-off computer operator says of pre-downsized Kodak, "It was truly a family. Times were great, and we'd find any excuse to celebrate." In contrast, a still-employed material supplier says that now, "You start wondering, when are they going to take my job?"

The journey each of us must make to keep up with, and get ahead of, these work changes goes right to the heart for most of us. Where you work, and what you do at work, not only supports your economic survival, it may very well be the main way you identify yourself. As Faye, a long-time administrative worker, put it: "I'm afraid of losing my job—it's who I am." The thought of changing your livelihood, or of *losing* your livelihood, can be distressing. So moving to a new relationship with work is usually painful to contemplate, and even more painful to actually start.

The rewards are compelling—economic security, freedom from want, fulfillment in work, being in charge of your own destiny. But the down side of where you find yourself today may well be that, like most others, you have no choice: like it or not, the environment is going to require you to change. The change will require moving away from the employment relationship that you're used to today, under the threat of being displaced, marginalized or cast off from society's economic activities.

So your task now is to be vigilant in looking for the clues which will help you find and move toward your chosen destination. And once you understand the problem and the solution, you'll have to reach down and find the motivation and resources you need to prepare yourself thoroughly. The rest of this book will guide you through the necessary process of reworking your relationship to work.

A Critical New Skill Set: BE and DO

Changing your relationship to work is a very big task, and it will take the resourcefulness and power of all of your faculties to figure out how to respond to what's going on around you. Really using "all of your faculties" means you need to have the skill—new for most of us—of balancing the two aspects of yourself: BE and DO.

The BE aspect of a human being is the foundation of who you are—your inner, true self. The DO aspect is the active part, which expresses itself in what you plan, build, and execute. They are separate but interconnected; each requires the other. The BE aspects of ourselves have been called the "right-brain" expressions; the DO aspects are identified with the "left-brain." These associations are based on research that seems to show that they are linked with activity in the right or left hemisphere of the physical human brain. For example, your sense of beauty or artistry is usually located in the right hemisphere, while analysis of mathematical equations and language generally occurs in the left hemisphere.

There's a growing awareness of the value of the "right-brain" in many fields, including education, health, and business. Several recent business and career books have taken an emphasis on BE as their central thesis: *The Heart Aroused*, *Your Signature Path*, and *The Re-Invention of Work*, to name a few. In another example, the importance of one's emotional maturity, or "EQ," has recently been developed and popularized by Daniel Goleman. He wrote in *Emotional Intelligence* that a person's emotional abilities are more reflective of future success than standard measures of intelligence. Some of these emotional abilities include things we often associate with the BE side, such as empathy and optimistic response to a setback.

A few years ago, the phrase "high-tech, high touch" came into vogue. This term describes the growing trend in our society to attempt to reconcile technology with human relationships, whether in computers or counseling. This is one more piece in a growing body of evidence that integration and understanding of the BE aspect is becoming a critical skill in our new environment.

Yet in our culture, and particularly in work, we have traditionally emphasized DO and neglected BE. Think of what's typically rewarded at work: drive, long hours, and accomplishment. How many traditional workplaces have encouraged creativity, play, or music as part of the work environment, much less considered employees' needs to take care of family or emotional problems? While this connection to inner resources has not previously been considered important in work, it's actually emerging as a key success factor in the molecular marketplace. And the most important factor in developing your BE abilities is to become familiar with and use them.

These two threads—BE and DO—are interwoven throughout this book, as in life; and as you master the 10 Steps, you'll spend time working with both. This will help you think in terms of balancing the two aspects of yourself, to be more vigilant and better understand both what's going on around you in the world of work and who you, yourself, really are.

The ancient Yin and Yang symbol represents the way two opposites—such as BE and DO—interrelate as a single whole: Each side contains a portion of the other, each the complement to its opposite. When applied to a person, the symbol portrays how an individual is completed through a balanced emphasis on both aspects of life.

What Would You Do If...?

Let's warm up the BE side of your intellect and lay some groundwork. Do you remember the TV show from the Fifties called "The Millionaire?" A wealthy man got pleasure out of making someone an anonymous gift of $1 million, tax free, and watched to see what happened. Of course, some recipients were wildly successful at meeting their dreams, and some failed miserably. But what we want you to do is imagine—or brainstorm, if you like—what you would do if someone handed you $1 million, tax free, right now. But wait, there are conditions!

First, you have to use the million to start a business or enterprise, some sort of economic activity. Second, this should be something that *you* want to do or be, not something someone else might want. Third, it can be a profit-making venture, but it doesn't have to be; you can do something charitable if you want, but you can't just give it away. Finally, the money has to be used to *start* something, not just be given to someone or something else. For example, you can use it to start a school, for profit or non-profit, but you can't just give the money to an existing school.

What would you do with this money? Of course it isn't real that you're going to get the million, but what is very real about this exercise is that it can help you focus on what is really of interest and value to you. You've also given your imagination a good stretch. Don't underestimate the power of imagining what you would really love to do—that's the first vital step toward doing it. When this exercise is done with groups, it often gets very animated, and the responses people give are unique and often surprising. You may find it interesting to compare notes with someone you know on how both of you answer the question.

Now let's switch over to the DO mode, and try to think about what would be needed—besides money—to actually start the enterprise you imagined. What things would you need to buy? What information would you need? What services would you have to get from others? What personal skills or capabilities might you need that you now lack?

Here are two example lists of "needs" that have been developed by others who have done this activity; one is for a service-based business, and one applies to opening a store or shop.

Consultant to a non-profit agency:

time
computer, fax, telephone
insurance
accountant
network contacts
billing process
achievement-oriented resume
regular involvement with
    agencies
model consulting contract
memberships in associations

research
office (home or outside)
licenses and permits
marketing plan
knowledge of grants
complete an MBA
skills:
    self-confidence
    planning
    financial management
    writing proposals

Book Store/Coffee Shop:

time
store site
insurance
accountant
book distributors
pricing
furniture/fixtures
delivery van
buy or make food items
look into franchise options

research
cash register, fax, telephone
licenses and permits
advertising and promo materials
knowledge of world of books
know the competition
point-of-sale systems
attorney
skills:
    people management

Notice that, although some general things apply to all situations (like "time"), the lists quickly become very individualized. For that reason, use these lists to expand, but not limit, your thinking; you may have good ideas that aren't on these lists, and many of these items may not be right for your situation. The point is, there's a *lot* to think about as you get started. The dream is a necessary starting point, but remember Thomas Edison's formula for success: "Genius is 1% inspiration and 99% perspiration."

So what's the point of this exercise? To help you begin to identify, first, what **MMI, Inc** might look like as an independent economic entity, and second, what you may need to actually create it. In Step 10, when you create your plan for **MMI, Inc**, you'll look back at this list to help you be sure you've thought through all the issues you'll be facing.

Let's be sure one point is clear: the 10-step process is *not* just for people who are going to become entrepreneurs and start their own businesses. The path to each of our employment futures will be unique, and finding a traditional job with a business, or staying in a job you now have, may be precisely the best thing for you. What *is* clear is that *as the molecular marketplace continues to develop, each worker will need to think of him- or herself as though they were a business*—that is, an independent economic entity.

For many of us, this journey toward creating **MMI, Inc** sounds a bit interesting, certainly different, and more than a little daunting. You may be thinking: "It's okay for some of those entrepreneurial types, but I'd just like things to go back to the way they were!" Let's take a deep, sobering look at the changes occurring in the work environment, and at why they *require* a new response from each of us, whether we're ready or not.

Why Is The Earth Shaking Around Us?

"Widening Income Gap Divides America" (*USA Today*)

"47% of 18- to 24-year-old US workers hold full-time jobs that pay less than a poverty income!" (*The Futurist*)

"The rate of job loss hit a peak of 3.4 million a year in 1992 and has remained nearly that high ever since, even while the economy grew and the stock market boomed." (*NY Times*)

"Organizations institute layoffs to cut costs and promote competitiveness, but afterward often find themselves worse off than before. All they have gained is a depressed, anxious, and angry work force." (*Healing the Wounds*, David M. Noer, 1993)

There are two very clear reasons to discuss the changing environment. First, *there is not (and never will be) the "same old" to go back to*; and second, as a result, *trying to work in the "same old" way will result in frustration and failure for most working people*.

In February of 1996, the *New York Times* ran a week-long series of front-page articles entitled "The Downsizing of America," in which they chronicled this ongoing trend. The writers at the Times didn't create, nor were they the first to examine, the issues around downsizing, but those articles certainly highlighted the increasing consciousness that downsizing and re-engineering are having a sizable impact, and that they're here to stay. For example, the *Times* writers looked at the evolution of the terms "downsizing" and "layoff." The word "downsizing" was coined in the 1970's to describe the process of making smaller, more energy efficient cars; however, today we've accepted this euphemism for companies shedding workers. Likewise, a "layoff" used to mean a temporary break in employment with an expected return; now, it implies a permanent end of employment.

The Birth of New Work Issues

Along with these new, yet all-too-familiar, phrases, we've seen the birth of new workplace issues. For example, there is a growing recognition of "survivor syndrome" as it applies to the remaining members of a downsized workgroup. While those who leave deal with pain, frustration and embarrassment, sociologists and companies are beginning to realize that those who remain also bear a burden—of guilt, overwork, and blame. As David Noer says, in his groundbreaking study *Healing the Wounds*, more and more companies are trying to function with "a whole building full of angry, unproductive employees."

There's also a new dynamic between employees and employers which can be called the "Conspiracy of Ignorance." On one hand, the boss feels that he or she can't offer the employees support in making the transition to career independence "because they'd all leave." On the other side, employees who realize all too well that they have to do something try, with limited resources and no support, to discover the best way to respond— "but don't let my boss know."

For example, Martin, who owned a small business helping tutor students for exams, was invited to a seminar on helping prepare his employees for the future work environment. In declining to attend, he said, "Your ideas are interesting, but my employees know they're staying for life." Later in the same day, Leanne, one of his key employees, said: "Sign me up for your seminar. I'm out on my own as soon as I can manage it, but don't tell Martin I said so." This atmosphere of secrecy and denial leads to distrust and betrayal for both sides, and escalates work tensions. More importantly, it denies the transition which we all face.

These changes in terminology and issues are symptomatic of a *sweeping shift to a molecular marketplace*. You can certainly see the trend in the work environment from the old clearly-defined model—get a good job with a stable company, move up the ladder with regular salary increases, and retire with a pension—to the mish-mash of multiple careers, job categories disappearing, increases in the number of contractors and temporaries, and underemployment (meaning that one still has a job but is getting a smaller salary than one's education or experience should command).

At the root of many of these new work issues is the transformation of what can be called the "employment contract." This contract isn't a sign-on-the-dotted-line, written agreement; instead it's the common understanding in our society of the relationship between employer and employee. It's usually not stated outright, but rather implied and learned by experience with the workplace culture. And, as with any contract, it carries implications for both involved parties.

The old, traditional employment contract dates back to the industrial revolution, when the modern concept of a job—a worker employed in the service of someone else—was born. In return for worker loyalty, productivity and commitment, an employer would provide long-term employment, salary, security and benefits such as a pension, and maybe advancement. While each employer had a unique take on the details, the fundamentals were pretty universal, and both parties felt like they knew where they stood. But as a result of shifting demands in the workplace, employers are less and less likely to stick to this old employment contract, as many workers have discovered to their shock and dismay. Instead, the new contract implies (or sometimes states outright) that employers expect career self-management, ongoing added value, and a "happy to be here, but ready to go" mentality.

As this change occurs, the most interesting question is, what's the flip side of this new employment contract? In other words, what does the employee get? The logical consequence of the employers' new expectations is that an employee will get greater challenges and authority, more resources and skill development, and compensation in line with performance. But the rub is, how? It comes back to the idea of being self-directed: in this new environment, the pressure to equalize the contract must come from a motivated, productive and market-oriented worker—**MMI, Inc**!

If you're still not convinced that this shift is as real or as big as it sounds, here are some statistics that might surprise you. First, who do you think is the largest private (non-government) employer in the US? The answer is ManPower, the temporary help/employment agency. Second, for the first time in history, loss of jobs among workers with some college or a college degree is greater than jobs lost among those with high-school diplomas or less; even the demographics of unemployment, and work, are changing. Third, a recent New York Times poll found that nearly three-quarters of all households have had some personal experience (family, friends, or neighbors) with layoffs since 1980. Finally, *less than 50% of American working adults are employed full-time*.

Three Environmental Trends

Another way to clarify the magnitude of this change is to examine some of the fundamental and permanent changes taking place in the workplace. Looking at these three trends can also suggest what skills and approaches might lead to success in the molecular marketplace. Here are three broad categories of change in the workplace today:

1. Technology: None of us can escape the phenomenal effects of technological change in every field. Witness the explosive growth in the power of, and availability of, machines like faxes, modems, Internet/e-mail, cellular phones, etc. A great example is long-haul trucking, that last great bastion of the independent "cowboy" type job. Yet with trucking mergers creating a demand for optimal efficiency, and satellite tracking providing the technological tool, most truckers can no longer function independently. Someone, somewhere knows where that truck is every minute. Though the image hasn't yet changed, the reality is far removed from tales of side roads, long layovers and breakneck convoys.

Also, smarter, faster computers and other office machines are able to do more and more of the analytical, repetitive tasks that have traditionally made up most jobs. Many workers have found themselves asking, "Where does this leave people?" Often the practical result is that employees are needed more on a contingency, or project, basis. However, author Harry Dent, in his book *Job Shock*, suggests a further ramification of this change in the nature of jobs available. His thesis is that people who develop strong right-brain (BE) skills such as relationships, communication, synthesis, and intuition will have an edge and enhanced value in this newly emerging work environment, since those are tasks not easily delegated to machines.

2. Interconnection: Creating networks, whether of individuals, computers or corporations, is the name of the game right now. Mergers at the high end produce fewer, but bigger companies, as seen in the recent merger mania in banking, telecommunications and pharmaceuticals. The business environment seems less attuned to specific companies, and more attentive to the "ecology" of whole industries, whether shrinking (such as defense and traditional health care) or growing (such as mobile services and home health care). Of course, computer and communication networks link remote people and places with ease. And improved travel, increasing information and real-time communication seem to be making a reality of globalization. It really IS a small world, Walt!

Beth, an at-home mother of a two-year-old toddler, exemplifies how pervasive interconnection really is. As the sole independent US representative for a piece of technical German software, she works part-time out of her home selling software by referral and on the Internet. In the 18 months she has been successfully marketing the software to clients around the world, she has yet to physically meet either her superiors in the German company or a single customer—but you can bet she knows their phone numbers and e-mail addresses!

It's this interconnection category of change that inspired the "marketplace" half of the term molecular marketplace: vast yet accessible, allowing options for mixing and matching never before possible.

3. Customization: This is another trend in today's corporate America; there's a growing understanding that focus is vital for business success. Think, for example, about the push in corporate giants toward shedding sideline enterprises and strengthening "the core business." From a corporate perspective, the use of temporary and contract workers allows internal customization without making long-term, expensive commitments. In addition, corporations try to encourage customization by moving away from corporate hierarchy and set job descriptions to teams, projects, and "quality circles."

Another offshoot of this trend is that small companies (not to mention individuals) often have a lot of flexibility and creativity, so they can compete as effectively, if not more so, than the big guys. Bill, for example, is an exterminator with a difference. His company, Animal Gidders, specializes in removing unwanted medium-sized animals like skunks and raccoons from in, under, or around the house. With his unique can-do approach to pest management and 24-hour availability, Bill runs a thriving small business. The most telling indication that the "little guys" like Bill are successfully competing in the current marketplace is the fact that the vast majority of jobs being created in the US today come from businesses employing 20 or fewer people

It's this customization category of change that lends the "molecular" piece to molecular marketplace: the growing importance of small, mutable entities changing, interacting, and impacting the system.

One small-business owner embodies all three of these trends in her work. A veterinarian in a medium-sized city, she has an established practice but is looking for ways to grow personally and professionally. Her discovery of on-line services, in particular using the Internet (technology), is very exciting to her. She finds that she can communicate with an interest/ professional group of other vets both to talk about issues and difficult cases and to keep up-to-date on what's happening in the world of veterinary medicine (interconnection). At the same time, she discovers a niche market—working with the local animal protection society—that fits her particular interests and talents, making her particular office more competitive and flexible (customization).

Likewise, an accounts receivable clerk with a large utility company works there part-time as a contractor (customization). He uses a networked computer (technology) to gather information from a number of sources (interconnection) in order to process bills and send on-line late payment information (technology) to the outside vendor used for collection (customization).

It's evident from looking at these trends that they are large-scale, permanent, and current. We definitely aren't going back to the traditional way of doing business, though we haven't entirely left it behind. And furthermore, there aren't any formal classes in "how things are changing"; rather, individual workers are required to find their own ways to keep abreast, both of what the changes are and how to best adapt to them.

View From the Ivory Tower

So how can we begin to make some sense of these changes, especially from a historical perspective? Author William Bridges, in his book *JobShift*, argues that the present change in work is a transition of the same magnitude as the agricultural or industrial revolutions. In fact, the shift that's going on today is sometimes referred to as the "information revolution." The industrial revolution caused an overwhelming shift: from people working on whatever tasks needed doing at their own pace—a farmer or a blacksmith—to doing what we think of as a "job." In fact, jobs as we know them were invented at that time—they didn't *exist* before the late 18th century! People then had to get used to working for someone else more wealthy and powerful than themselves, working indoors, doing a repetitive task as demanded by a machine, by the clock, when and how someone else said to do it. This caused huge, widespread trauma; workers had a hard time and complained; and many rebelled or refused to change.

It's particularly interesting to note that the same three fundamental trends of change in the present transition also played key roles in the Industrial Revolution: technology via the steam engine and the advent of accurate timekeeping; interconnection in terms of interdependence between factories and suppliers of raw materials; and customization, with each factory creating a single product.

Bridges, along with other thinkers, argues that the present upheaval in work results from a similar shift, but this time *away* from jobs. For the past 200 years we have gotten used to having a boss, a time clock, and a paycheck. Whether we like it or not, we've become accustomed to the idea that the employer holds all the economic cards, while the worker is a supplicant, ceding power to the employer in return for protection and compensation.

Now the molecular marketplace is dictating that jobs are too structured or too long-term, and that shorter, less binding work arrangements function better for companies. People are being required to hold different positions or tasks for shorter periods of time, and again it's traumatic. Loss of benefits and security, financial instability, and loss of job identity are just some of the issues that result. These changes, as they shake the foundation of the work environment, require a reinvention of the individual worker. Hence the idea of **MMI, Inc**: every economic entity, large or small, even the individual, is a vendor in the molecular marketplace.

In his book *BreakPoint and Beyond*, author George Land suggests that our current atmosphere of change more closely parallels the Agricultural Revolution in that it represents a total shift in mindset. Think of all the aspects of human life impacted by the shift from hunter/gatherer to farmer: shelters became permanent, fire was made and kept at hand, clay and metals were worked to make implements, roads and transportation came into existence; indeed, civilization became possible. Land says that our society is at a crossroads of similar magnitude now, and because of this old approaches and models not only don't help, they hinder progress. One example of this is trying to do "business as usual," emphasizing the bottom line and devaluing people; the result is fragmentation, disillusionment, and lowered productivity. In Land's words, we must now be "pulled by the future" rather than "pushed by the past."

Cognitive Dissonance

As these fundamental and light-speed changes occur, each of us feels the effects. One such effect is the sense of "cognitive dissonance." This is a fancy term for the tension we feel between old ideas we hold or were taught, and the new reality. For example, a family consists of a father who works, a mother at home, and 2.3 kids, right? Not necessarily, but that's still the image many of us hold. Try reconciling that image with this statistic: between 1980 and 1995, there was a 30,000% increase in the number of American women leaving their husbands for another woman!

David Noer, in *Healing the Wounds*, cites a number of examples of cognitive dissonance among corporate survivors of downsizing. He quotes one field employee's reaction: "I have no idea whether or not to trust them [the company] any more because of what you hear positive [from them] about the state of the company. The next day you come in to work and it's 180 people out. You can't believe what they say. My key word is that I've lost trust."

Trying to live with cognitive dissonance without reconciling it leads to anger, denial, blame, illness, and other negative side effects. You can hear the emotion in Elena's words in the opening quote of this Step. It is possible, however, to reconcile the opposing ideas that cause cognitive dissonance, given two necessary conditions: first, a clean, clear look at what's really happening in the environment; and second, the development of new models. One goal of this book is to help you create those two conditions; however, developing new models can be a challenge in a transition time when the models are still being created. It requires creativity and flexibility, as well as a willingness to look beyond examples from the past and imagine something new.

Volleyball, Anyone?

Let's explore how the model for working has changed. The old model often worked in ways similar to a football team: clear, inflexible positions; strong coaching from above; move the ball in one direction. By contrast, a possible new model could be a volleyball team: fluid field positions; think and act in real time; not directed from outside, but by the changing situation; no pauses; it doesn't matter who hits the ball as long as it gets over the net. You may not have seen this shift in your own work environment, but the environmental road signs certainly point to increasing flexibility and personal responsibility in successful enterprises.

Do I Have to Like It?

Understanding the context for these environmental changes can be exciting, but it's not easy or fun to deal with in the midst. In fact, it's often frustrating and can bring up lots of feelings and issues. But experience has shown that people can't really begin to think and plan for the molecular marketplace until they've acknowledged the negative feelings stemming from work dislocation.

As you think about the changes occurring in the workplace, what comes to your mind? Does your list include words like these?

fearful	unloved
stressful	psychosomatic illness
guilty	without direction
insecure	under pressure
out of control	loss of self-esteem
angry	victimized
useless	lethargic
loss of confidence	anxious
rejected	lost
unvalued	trampled
worried	pushed down
betrayed	off-balance
grief	used and abused
adrift	"what happened?"
loss of identity	confused
failure	unable to plan
embarrassed	no time to deal with changes
shock	facing the unknown
frustrated	resigned
unfair	have to do more with less
in a financial mess	resentful
abandoned	burdened
relationship problems	no connection with performance

Group brainstorming about negative feelings resulting from changes in the workplace generally builds up so much momentum that it's hard to stop, and often ends up with what looks like justification for years of psychotherapy! But these reactions are completely natural when you're being forced into a new, untried situation. Once people begin venting, they feel how important it is to deal with the negative feelings; only then can you begin to look for a creative solution.

Finding a Niche

Once the emotions have been acknowledged, it's clear when you think and read about the new environment that it also offers lots of room for innovation and initiative. In fact, there are some great examples of positive, creative approaches to it, especially when someone discovers the right "niche."

Essentially a niche involves creating a unique and suitable spot for yourself, rather than trying to fit into someone else's job description. Creating the right niche is so important to the success of **MMI, Inc** that it's the sole focus of Step 5. For now, here's a preview of a successful niche in action.

John was an unhappy insurance salesman looking for a new career. One day he happened upon a lost and found ad in the newspaper offering a

$1,000 reward for the return of a lost dog. He felt attracted to the idea of becoming a professional pet-hunter, and after researching the market, discovered that this was uncharted entrepreneurial territory.

For several months after officially launching his pet-search service, John felt like a failure because his success rate was lackluster. But then two things turned his business around: he came up with the clever name "Sherlock Bones"; and he realized that his most effective niche was not doing the actual search, but providing pet owners with advice and expertise on effectively hunting for themselves, from making eye-catching posters to unmasking false reward-hunters. His enterprise eventually got the attention of the media, and after a stint on *Good Morning America*, John's business took off. In addition, he looks forward to going to work rather than dreading it. If the environment is dictating a change for all of us, then developing a niche is basically taking the initiative in creating the environment that's best for you, and for **MMI, Inc**.

Elena, whose story begins in the opening quote of this Step, found that her niche took her out of hands-on nursing and into nursing education. She had always enjoyed teaching, and was able to continue her own education to qualify as a nursing instructor in her local community college. Teaching has been a great change of pace for her, providing a stable income, some time off between terms, and the opportunity to spend two or three days each month working vacation relief shifts in the hospital to keep her practical skills up to date.

At this point, you may feel overwhelmed by the new demands on you and your work. It is important to see and accept these changes for what they are—big, potentially devastating, and present-tense. Bear in mind, though, that the purpose of this book isn't to focus on dire future consequences; on the contrary, it's about your understanding the changes *in order to make a constructive, prosperous response*. This Step has created a map of the sometimes scary territory through which you'll travel on your journey to **MMI, Inc**; the rest of the book will help you personally get in shape for making that journey a success.

It also helps keep things in perspective to know that you're not alone. Let's meet four real people who have written about their experiences on their own version of the journey you're starting. In their case studies, which continue after each Step, you'll find information and insights about how they've applied the concepts which may be useful for you.

Case Studies

1. *Shannon [27 years old, single, has had many varied short-term work experiences; now trying to decide what she wants to do long term, and how to balance work with the rest of her life]:*

    I have the dubious honor of being the "gypsy" of my family. I've always had more interests than time, and never had much interest in really focusing on just one activity or idea for too long. Does that derive from my nomadic childhood (eight schools from kindergarten through high school)? Does it reflect an unwillingness to "settle down" and make a commitment? I don't know for sure, but it's definitely been a lifetime pattern.

    And my approach to work has been no exception. As a job has fit my talents, hooked my curiosity or kindled my competitive spirit, I've tried it out. From my high school beginnings as a private piano teacher, to advertising, to physical therapy assistant, to tutoring, I've lived the portfolio lifestyle—often to the dismay of my bosses and family.

    The best chance I had for a "real" job was in the technical writing group of a major manufacturing company. When I turned down the promotion, the reactions of my former colleagues ranged from vicarious delight—"I wish I had the guts"—to shock—"Do you understand what you're giving up?" Somehow, even then, walking away from a drab cubicle and uninspiring work didn't seem like much of a sacrifice.

    So it's with a sense more of relief than regret that I enter the molecular marketplace. The fact is that most people of my generation don't *expect* a lifetime job, and actually, many of us don't *want* it either. Perhaps understanding that mobility and flexibility are useful traits, and not an excuse for shirking responsibility, can help my generation find its working place, and even claim this new work environment as our own.

2. *Brent [36 years old, main support for family of four, trained as aeronautical engineer and worked in defense industry, moved into civilian electronic engineering when defense job reductions began]:*

    As far back as I can remember, I heard that the single goal of one's employment was security. My father moved his family to California in search of the sacred Steady Job, and he found it: a government job at an Air Force base. He told me what was important in one's career: security, benefits, and salary—in precisely that order. I first used his teachings to decide to study engineering because I was sure engineers made good money and had secure jobs.

While attending college I learned that the engineering job market was fiercely competitive. I decided to get two engineering degrees: one in aeronautical engineering just wasn't enough, so I added one in mechanical engineering at the same time. As luck would have it, the aeronautical engineer got a job at the same Air Force base where my father had worked for decades!

I found there was a dark side to job security. Security breeds complacency; in an environment where it seemed to take a signature from God to get fired, some workers found their jobs were so secure that they didn't need to do a thing to stay employed. I found myself taking on the responsibilities of others (like hoarding spare parts under my desk) to get the job done effectively, and I began to resent it.

I quit my job and my parents were appalled. I sent my resume out and was promptly snapped up by the second company I spoke with. That experience changed my life—I learned that flexibility is more important than stability in the modern marketplace; as a result, I've held five different jobs at four different companies since that first Air Force job, including two as a contract employee. My latest job move is a stretch—after ten years, I left the shrinking aerospace industry for the burgeoning electronics industry—and from it I've learned that my skills and talents are far more transferable than I'd expected ten years ago. I've found that my father's values—honesty, hard work, reliability, a willingness to help, and the drive to do your best—were his real keys to security, and have been mine as well.

3. *Emily [45 years old, college educated mother and community volunteer, finishing up studies for a counseling degree and planning to enter the professional workforce:]*

Like many women of my age, I decided when I had two young children to fully focus on their upbringing, rather then pursuing a career. Like many of my friends, I had a spouse who went to work every day bringing home a pay check that very adequately met our financial needs. We were not in a position where a double income was required simply to make basic ends meet, as is often the reality for today's young families.

Not being burdened with the need to participate in the family financial support, when the two children were old enough to go to school, I found myself with the freedom to choose more altruistic interests, like looking for "meaning in life." Eventually I settled within the welcoming embrace of a community of people traveling a spiritual journey, and began to understand more about the inner dimension of myself.

Two important elements of my spiritual evolution were first to learn how to DO the things needed to help sustain life in a positive way: e.g. develop and practice good family relationships; take right actions to help sustain the environment, such as recycling; and provide high quality experiences for my family so that we would be exposed to the rich diversity of life. The second was to practice the BE side of life which wasn't quite as easy. I've learned that imagination exercises open me to a part of myself that I knew very little about, but I was delighted to get to know better.

Now that my children are grown I want to go to work, to earn some money of my own and to make a difference in the world. I feel a little like the world of work has bypassed me and I need to catch up, both to actually know what it's like to hold a job and to share what I've learned with others.

4. *Forrest [53 years old, worked in a single large corporation for 30 years, and then as a consultant for the last three years; now plans to start his own small consulting business]:*

My work environment changed drastically about twenty years into my life as a manager in a big business. The stable, "Ma Bell" environment I'd lived with for years was becoming agitated under the influence of growing competition on my company. Jobs, work groups and whole departments were eliminated. People were forcibly reassigned and sometimes relocated. The intake of new employees dried up, and total employment was dropping. Early retirements and other incentives were offered to employees to leave the company, and for the first time in anyone's memory, significant numbers of people were departing before "normal" retirement age. It was new and strange, and it shocked all of us.

It wasn't entirely predictable, or at least I couldn't predict, just who would end up having the new skills and be winners, and who would be inflexibly tied to the old ways and end up losers. Some lost in big ways. I watched people, including a couple of good friends, lose their purpose for living as soon as they left their job, dying soon after from over-drinking, suicide or lack of a reason to live on. Others, some of whom I thought would struggle, did surprisingly well. They figured out how to make something more out of what could have been a very negative experience.

Watching all of these changes unfold in my employment environment kindled my interest in doing something different. My "wake-up call" came in the form of an early retirement incentive package offered by my company. At age 50, I eagerly accepted.

I don't regret a moment of my 30 years with "Ma Bell," especially the opportunities to learn about work, management, people and their behavior, and myself. But freedom to chart my own course toward work fulfillment and relief from energy-sapping bureaucratic limitations were a breath of fresh air for me. I decided to set out on my own, and never looked back. I put in three years as a consultant—the money's been pretty good, and I now have the basic financial security to make a move into what could be the final phase of my work life.

Step 2

Create Your Vision

Mark, a 52-year-old Architect: *I've never before felt like I needed to look very far ahead. Even though I'm a professional, the pressure has always been to produce and bring in revenue today. Now, there are many younger architects out there who are hungry and will work for less, and I need to figure out what this means for me. Who and what do I really want to be for the rest of my working life?*

To know where you are going means you have to be clear about your destination. That leaves you with two possible approaches: you can either make a conscious decision about the specific destination that makes sense for you, or allow yourself to be overwhelmed by circumstances, forced by a crisis to make inappropriate and unfortunate decisions. If you choose not to make a conscious decision about your work future, you're playing a very dangerous game.

For example, Mark, who's quoted above, could have drifted along until a bright young architect was awarded Mark's most lucrative account. Then he might have stormed into his boss' office to give the ultimatum: "It's her or me!" The result could easily have been finding himself out of a job in the twilight of his working life. Instead, Mark took a good long look at himself, and decided on a future that was right for him. He gave up some of his current income to have more personal time, and took on a role in his firm as a backup and mentor to the new, younger staff architects.

If you think there are risks in drifting along without a worklife direction, you're right—and it's true for every worker. It truly can be disastrous to face the journey into the molecular marketplace unprepared. But with events overtaking us, each of us must set out on this journey if we want to be successful. What does this require of you? It means you will need to take the initiative and create a meaningful personal vision for **MMI, Inc** which will enable you to lay a course *to* something positive, instead of simply moving *away* from something threatening.

This Step will provide the opportunity for you to discover your unique destination, which will embody your hopes and dreams for **MMI, Inc**, and which will lead to your vision. Make your vision concrete by setting it down in a clear and concise statement which will inspire and guide you on your journey. Your vision will serve as a beacon during the inevitable times of stress and uncertainty and as a reminder of the dreams you hold most deeply for yourself.

Your Take On Things

Before you actually begin to create your vision for **MMI, Inc**, it will be helpful to understand your own background and how it contributes to your unique perspective on life. This perspective is the foundation upon which your personal vision for the future is built. It can be called your "frame of reference."

Mark initially swore that, although everyone else might have a frame of reference, he didn't; he saw things clearly and realistically, without any particular bias. This is a common first reaction, so the first thing to understand is that each of us does indeed *have* a frame of reference! Every time we look out of our eyes, touch with our hands, or think a thought, what we perceive is filtered through multiple layers of experiences. With all the filtering, modifying, and checking with past experience, the way we see reality can become diluted; it's no wonder that we see and respond to things so differently from one another.

The Art of Being an Artist

Lucy, an aspiring sculptor, had just set up her materials for her next project. Leslie, her roommate, saw the clay and asked harshly: "What's this pile of mud doing on the table?"

Lucy, somewhat taken aback, replied: "I'm starting a new project for my sculpture class. It's going to be a mother and child. I can already imagine how it will look. See? The mother's torso ..."

Leslie interrupted: "All I can see is the big mess in my clean dining room. Don't you remember that Brad and Lisa are coming over to dinner in an hour and a half?"

Lucy seemed surprised, and said sadly: "Oh, no. I totally forgot. I was so involved in deciding what the piece would look like, I lost track of the time."

Leslie saw how Lucy's enthusiasm had been crushed, and said kindly: "If you'll move your work into the garage, I'll clean up the table and floor."

The difference in perception between Lucy and Leslie stems from the fact that each one has a completely different frame of reference. The ability to see that the clay has potential comes from one perspective, or frame of reference, which sees the final shape embedded in the clay, waiting to be released by the artist's skill and vision. Lucy's frame of reference enables the clay to become something greater, while Leslie's frame of reference, which emphasizes another form of beauty—a spotlessly clean house—allows no such possibility. To bring it closer to home, think about your own frame of reference—would you be more like Lucy or Leslie?

Here's an opportunity for you to begin to explore your own frame of reference more fully.

Imagine the following scene: you are walking down a street in your neighborhood. As you turn a corner, you see that there has been an accident. Several cars are in disarray and there are injured people. A policeman is arriving at the scene. At a quick glance you see that a big, expensive car is pulled over at a strange angle by the side of the road; that a motorcycle is overturned in the middle of the street, with a person wearing black leather biker clothes and a black helmet lying nearby; and that a small child, out of your field of vision, is crying. Without any additional information and without taking much time, what's your first impression about what happened at this accident site?

After you've identified your first impression, try to expand your ideas to encompass other possible stories. It might be that the biker was at fault, since you certainly can't trust those "black leather types" to drive responsibly. Or it might seem obvious that it's the fault of the person in the expensive car, because they always think they own the road and can do whatever they want. On the other hand, maybe the child was responsible in some way because parents these days just don't have enough control over their kids!

Whatever immediate conclusion you come to, it is totally determined by your frame of reference. Your own set of filters, developed through your personal experience, determines the way you perceive this scene. And this process of perception and interpretation occurs so quickly and comes from sources so deep that when the actual truth surfaces, you may find it hard if not impossible to believe.

Of Flat Planets and Round Women

Some other examples of differing frames of reference include the Flat Earth Society, a group which insists to this day that the earth is flat. This is a deeply-held belief derived from some inner sense of what is right. And there are people who insist that humans didn't actually walk on the moon—that the Apollo missions were staged in a huge warehouse in New Mexico. Again, this group holds on to their idea militantly in spite of contradictory information. Or consider the frame of reference of Renaissance artists who painted what they considered the ideal female body, a physique we now see as plump compared to our current version of beauty as expressed by tall and impossibly slim models. Do we need lower taxes or better government services? Are the Dallas Cowboys better than the San Francisco 49ers? These are all examples of the impact of frame of reference. Indeed, we all *do* have a frame of reference, and for the most part we don't want it messed with in any way, shape or form.

Where Does Your Frame Of Reference Come From?

It's critically important to understand that you have a frame of reference, and so does everyone else. It determines who you are, how you act and, very importantly, how you interact with others. It can be difficult to see and acknowledge your own frame of reference, because it is second nature, the ground from which all of your responses to the outside world spring. But success in the molecular marketplace will require some understanding of both your own and others' frames of reference. To begin to understand what makes up and influences your own frame of reference, let's look at the four categories of experiences that interact to create a frame of reference: personal, family, social, and cultural.

The first category, personal experiences, is especially influenced by your early childhood, and it particularly affects how you perceive yourself. Did you have an ideal childhood, with Mom always home in an apron, baking cookies, and Dad coming home every evening to play with you? Were you dropped off at a baby-sitter's because Mom worked? Were you raised by a grandmother or an aunt? When you got your first bicycle, did you sail down the street with ease? Or did you fall off in the presence of friends? If so, did they support and encourage you, or did they laugh at your lack of coordination? Do you remember believing in the tooth fairy? When, and why, did you stop believing? These types of early experiences helped to set attitudes about yourself. As a result, you made deep unconscious decisions about how much you were willing to risk, how much you were willing to trust, and in general how you perceived the world.

Our frame of reference is also influenced by family experiences. Did you feel securely loved, just tolerated, or even abused? Were you the oldest or youngest of several children, or an only child? Were you a little princess or prince, the adored child, your parents' hearts' desire? That may have left you feeling even today that others ought to bow down to your every whim. Or were you neglected, left with a feeling even today that you have to fight for what is rightfully yours? Were your parents not physically affectionate with each other or with you, so you now feel that intimacy is frightening, something you are unwilling to risk? Whatever your family experience, it has had great impact on your frame of reference about the world.

Social experiences also contribute to your view of things. Were you pretty or handsome and popular in school? Or an insecure late bloomer, perhaps critical of those people who would do anything to be "cool"? Did you make a lot of friends easily, or did you have one or two deep attachments? Were you proud of your parents when your friends came over, or embarrassed by them? Were you sexually adventurous or restrained? Were you successful in your first paid working experience, moderately accomplished, or downright awful? These social experiences continue to add to your view of what life should be, and of how relationships work.

The last category of factors that makes up one's frame of reference is cultural experiences. Were you aware of your ethnicity as you grew up? Is it a factor now? Were you and your family part of the dominant culture in your community, or part of a sub-culture that was discriminated against? How does your culture differ in its expectations for men and women in terms of work? Have you traveled abroad and experienced truly different environments, people, languages, food? Do you accept and enjoy differences in people, or stick with those similar to you? Although their effects are sometimes less clear, your cultural filters contribute strongly to your frame of reference.

How Your Frame Of Reference Limits Your View

You can visualize your frame of reference as the windshield of a car. Imagine driving on a rural road on an autumn afternoon, when the sky darkens and a thunderstorm hits. The windshield already had a few bug spots; now it's quickly covered with drops of water, and you start the wipers. It becomes more difficult to see where you're going. Do you focus on the drops of water on the windshield and the action of the wipers? An experienced driver knows better. You focus through the windshield and beyond it on the road so that you can maneuver, avoid dangerous situations, and get home safely.

Your frame of reference, like the windshield, is what you look through to see the world with your eyes and your other senses. It's always there, and it's not perfectly transparent. Your experiences have left a lot of "stuff" on your windshield, which can sometimes get in your way of seeing reality, but which also makes you uniquely you. This mixed blessing can't be eliminated any more than the bug spots, water drops or wiper blades. To navigate safely, the trick is to learn to focus beyond your frame of reference, just like looking past the windshield, to see the reality out there for what it really is, not what you imagine it to be.

Just as in driving, expanding your focus plays a vital role in successfully living with the limitations of your frame of reference. If you concentrate exclusively on one aspect of your life, you run the risk of missing important road signs or opportunities. For example, after an argument with your partner you find yourself preoccupied with "I should have said," or "she just doesn't understand," or "I'll get even." You might continue with the basics of your normal functioning, but want nothing to do with relating to other people. By refusing to open the front door when someone knocks, you lose out on your $6 million check from Publisher's Clearinghouse! Or, perhaps more realistically, you miss out on the chance to spend a creative and affectionate evening with your kids. Like someone with raindrops on the windshield, looking at a broader field of vision ensures that life's experiences aren't distracting you from, or even blinding you to, the larger reality.

Russell and the Unions

During Russell's childhood, his dad delivered produce for a local supermarket chain and was a strong union advocate. Russell heard endlessly about how the management was always trying to "jerk around" the union membership to keep them from making any gains, and generally treated them with disrespect. As a result of his father's ideas, Russell's own frame of reference—his windshield—was colored with an anti-management sentiment.

With this limited perspective, Russell has had a very difficult time adjusting to the current work changes in which individuals must learn to fend more for themselves, not relying on union leadership or management to provide the level of benefits and support workers have had in the past. He can't get rid of the drops on his windshield that came from his father's attitudes because they are deeply ingrained, but if he chooses to take into account the broader picture, he will be able to find a successful niche for himself. For example, he might choose to work at a forward-thinking automobile manufacturing facility, where teamwork and communication are emphasized over traditional boss/employee relationships.

Removing The Blinders

Seeing beyond yourself in order to realize that you have a frame of reference, and to observe how your own frame of reference interacts with the rest of the world, can be difficult.

In the Spring, 1995 issue of *Parabola Magazine*, artist John Biggers said it this way: "If you are so bottled up with personal problems, or if the environment causes you to retreat within yourself, your horizon is your own self. You don't look out there, because you're not free to let your eyes rest gently on the horizon, to consider this limitless space you are in. You don't own limitless space if you are a prisoner of problems that might be social or political or physical. And this determines, to a great extent, what kind of mind or personality you have, whether you are able to see a far-off horizon."

The BE Stuff

After drawing his frame of reference windshield, Jerry, a self-employed construction contractor, had this reaction : "So what does this concern about better understanding my frame of reference have to do with the changing world of work? Don't I really just need to go out there, get some more current skills like working with a computer, and then go get a better job? That's what my friends and I have been doing all along and we're doing okay so far. Granted things are changing and I probably need to change, too, but I've never been very interested in all this inner stuff. Actually, the idea of getting into it makes me a bit nervous."

Jerry, like most of us when we face a problem, would like to "fix the flat tire" and move on. But if he did only that, he'd be just as vulnerable the next time something changed in his work life. To be ready to face whatever the future will bring, Jerry will need to examine his underlying attitudes toward work—his frame of reference. This will help him ensure that he sees clearly what's going on in the overall work environment, and can move beyond his personal biases to make quick, contemporary and effective decisions in response.

The Carrot and the Stick

The molecular marketplace is creating stronger and stronger demands for us to change. To see what's required of us to survive, we have to learn to expand our own frame of reference, to look beyond our windshield to see the coming reality clearly. So why does it seem that so many people— employers and workers alike—are still focusing on the raindrops on their windshields rather than on the reality beyond? The answer is that most of us haven't been exposed to the idea that we even have a frame of reference, let alone to the concept that we need to expand it. It's always easier to blame someone or something outside of yourself as the cause of your problems than it is to decide to change the way you look at things.

We've all heard the complaints, and have probably voiced some of them ourselves: "The immigrants, legal as well as illegal, are taking jobs away from Americans!" "The government is shutting down military bases which have provided secure jobs for years!" "Corporate executives are lining their own pockets with untold wealth at the expense of the worker, who's the victim in this process!" Whether or not there's any truth in the complaint is beside the point. Blaming anyone or anything else is a dead-end proposition; it can become a set of blinders which narrows the available options. How do we get out of this blaming trap, and focus instead on expanding our own frame of reference into a vision that will ensure work success?

The well-known picture of the donkey with a carrot dangling in front of him and a raised stick behind represents the two types of motivation that can cause you to start moving beyond your limited frame of reference to create a new vision for your future. Here's a great example of the stick at work. A man named Francisco lived on the slopes of Mount Pinatubo, a volcano in the Philippines. He had lived in one town his whole life and was determined never to leave. In 1991 the volcano became active and deposited one foot of lava inside Francisco's house, so he raised the house 10 feet on stilts. In 1992 more lava flowed in, so he raised the house another 10 feet. Finally, in 1995, a mammoth onslaught of lava destroyed his home, and Francisco had no choice but to evacuate.

When a situation becomes difficult or intolerable (the stick), you're forced to make the changes required to survive. The volcano, with its slowly moving lava and increasing spouts of steam, is a great metaphor for the steamroller of the changing work environment. And, as with the volcano, when you *truly* perceive the reality there is no choice but to change.

In contrast remember Lucy, pondering the possibilities for a lump of clay? A short time ago she went into a serious slump, sure that she'd never be able to sculpt again. To try to find some inspiration, she decided to take a trip that she had dreamed of her whole life: to see the Rodin Museum and Garden in Paris. There Lucy saw the famous works created by the great sculptor; in particular, she was awed by the original "Thinker" in all its glory. She returned home so inspired that she immediately began work, transforming a lump of clay over a period of days into a wonderful sculpture. For her, the carrot was the experience of being in the presence of a master.

Occasionally life offers a profound experience full of joyous possibility, which can jar you into thinking new and taking positive action, as Lucy did. The 10 Steps in this book may be such a carrot for you, enabling you to think new about your relationship to work and about the process needed to ensure a successful work experience.

The molecular marketplace certainly contains both carrots and sticks for all of us. The carrot is all of the new potential for independence, innovation and meaning, while the stick is jobs (and whole industries) going away. Either way, the situation creates an opportunity for new thinking, and those who can expand their frame of reference to encompass the whole will be able to respond creatively, rather than just reacting with a limited perspective—to be proactive rather than reactive.

Employing Your Frame of Reference

Frame of reference has a profound influence on the way we work. Heather is a good example. A successful professional in England, Heather's a department head in a London university; serves as a keynote speaker at international conferences; established a master's degree program in her field; and functions as the main bread winner for her family of four. Clearly she's an accomplished person.

Anne, an American colleague, told Heather: "I'm really excited about my plans to start a private consulting business."

Heather responded: "I can't imagine! I would never dream of setting off on my own business. I wouldn't know where to start."

As they talked further, some elements of Heather's frame of reference came to light. Heather's family had run a small farm (a private enterprise) and were considered lower-middle class. Also, the British are just beginning to accept the value of privatization, and Heather reflects this in continuing to be much more comfortable with a group, or socialistic, approach than with expressions of individual initiative. Heather quoted a common British expression: "We are a tight little island and we don't like change."

Clearly Heather has deeply ingrained personal and cultural attitudes that bias her against the idea of starting her own business. What experiences might motivate her to change her attitude? If the stick comes into play (for example, if her department at the university was to be closed and she was going to be forced to leave) she might then seriously consider embarking on a private enterprise. Or the carrot could come in the form of a well-known colleague who asks Heather to help in establishing an innovative private consulting business in the United Kingdom with bright financial prospects. If this interested her enough to work through the limitations she (like all of us) has in her frame of reference, she might muster the courage to take the plunge.

Each of us carries a wonderfully rich, personal, but limited frame of reference which constrains us to think about work in specific and narrow ways: "this is the way work *should* be." Unfortunately, the rapidly changing molecular marketplace doesn't fit with our old views. To address this cognitive dissonance, each of us must do two things: first, examine and understand our traditional attitudes about work (some of the raindrops on each of our windshields) to glean from them what is useful in today's work environment; and second, expand our frame of reference to look differently at the changing world of work. Only then can we pull the two types of information together into a new whole view.

What's In A Vision, Anyway?

So how do you expand the horizons of your frame of reference? Marcel Proust said: "The real voyage of discovery lies not in seeking new landscapes, but in having new eyes ..." To paraphrase him, the answer is to develop a personal vision of—and for—the future. Your vision will become a bridge that will help you transcend the limitations of your past and instead focus your strengths and energy to successfully respond to the future.

The bridge—your vision—will enable you to align the BE (what you are) with the DO (what you will accomplish), giving you a vantage point from which to choose the path for your life's journey, including your livelihood. And if you're one of those who feel a strong urge to "get on with it" and move into DO-style action, take heart! You'll begin tackling the DO activities in the following Steps. But action can be disjointed and uncoordinated at best, and at worst counterproductive, if it's not inspired and directed by a positive view of the future through a clear personal vision.

Identifying or finding a vision is as important to an individual as it is to a group or company. A newly forming company, generating its first business plan, will always start by developing a vision statement. A vision statement expresses the highest possible hopes and aspirations of the company, and it can do the same for an you as you begin the process of setting down your own personal business plan. In fact, in *First Things First* author Steven Covey notes that a clear vision is one trait that many highly effective people share.

We all have a vision for ourselves, whether conscious or not. This vision affects the choices we make in our lives and, as a direct result, determines how we spend one valuable commodity—our time. Your vision determines what you can (or can't) become and what you are (or aren't) drawn toward. A clearly understood and expressed vision allows you to identify and formulate your own positive view of yourself and of your future course. It differs from frame of reference, which comes from your past and helps you color and interpret what you experience. Frame of reference is the foundation on which a strong and inspiring vision is built.

The Value of Vision

Author Victor Frankl suggests that we don't invent our vision; rather, we discover it waiting inside each of us. A survivor and student of the Nazi concentration camps, Frankl found, as he studied himself and other camp survivors, that the single greatest factor predicting survival and useful post-war functioning was having a vision that transcended the day-to-day horror. Far from being a luxury, a significant personal vision made the difference between life and death to camp prisoners.

In an example closer to home, developing a positive personal vision made a great difference for one family. Brenda and Fred had two kids: Carrie, a 12-year-old daughter, and Bud, a 10-year-old son. Brenda's own difficult childhood had left her preoccupied with herself: in perpetual doubt about her value to others, with strong feelings of resentment toward her parents, and with an image of her husband as a negative authority. In the unconscious vision she held for herself, Brenda was emotionally responding to life as a twelve year old.

Brenda had been a good mother for the children when they were small, and both were great kids. Carrie was an exceptional child, intelligent and quick to sense what was happening in relationships. She attended gifted classes in school and always excelled. When Carrie turned 12, Brenda realized that if she were going to be able to give Carrie the guidance and love she needed as an astute pre-teen, Brenda herself would have to grow up—quickly. The urgency of this need offered Brenda both carrot and stick motivations: the carrot was Carrie's potential if given support, while the stick was the personal pain and sense of failure that Brenda felt as a mother.

Brenda took an assertiveness class in which she began to develop a new personal vision. She started to face her anger and take responsibility for herself, and then felt she could actually take on the responsibilities and joys of being a caring mother for Carrie and Bud, and a loving wife to Fred.

Creating and holding a clear and meaningful vision enabled Brenda to transcend day-to-day ups and downs, assumptions of personal limitation, and her narrow frame of reference. It gave her a positive basis upon which to make choices, and supplied motivation to achieve her purpose. While she still had times when she struggled with her emotions, over time Brenda's vision became integrated into her life, and pulled her toward the thoughts, emotions, and actions that supported her dreams.

Compare these positive effects to those resulting from what too many people practice unconsciously: envisioning (or dreading) the worst. Every time we create a roadblock in our mind, we set up a negative vision which begins to steer us toward failure. How many people sabotage results by foreseeing a myriad of negative outcomes? And how many individuals never even set out on a possible path, imagining dire consequences before they even take the first step?

The bottom line is, you are what you envision, and what you are totally controls what you do: "what you see is what you be." This is hard for most of us to believe, but it's been proven over and over again; in fact, many experts on success argue that this one trait separates the few most successful people from the rest of the population.

Most of us have read about the cancer victim given little or no chance for recovery who nevertheless finds renewed health. Richard M. Restak, in his book *The Mind*, describes one such patient. Having survived several bouts with breast and lung cancer, she put it this way: "I'm sure I would not be here now if I hadn't developed this absolutely total and utter determination that I personally am going to beat this thing, and I was going to win." She was part of a study done by Dr. Steven Greer of the Royal Marsden Hospital in London, who found that the women with an active "fighting spirit" had the best outcome and were twice as likely to be alive and well ten years later when compared to women who showed helpless or hopeless attitudes.

Likewise, there's the high school sports team who adopted the motto, "The team that *won't* be beaten, *can't* be beaten." Troy, the team's star forward, said: "It wasn't that we never lost again, because sometimes we did, but we came off of the losses with a completely different attitude. Instead of dragging, we got more committed to practice, drills, and teamwork, and we had a great winning season."

These aren't isolated incidents, as experts in self-help, healing, and sports motivation can attest; the results consistently validate the importance of a positive vision. The fact is, the power of a vision is limited only by the belief of the person creating it.

Your Vision Statement

When first introduced to the idea of creating a vision statement, people sometimes express their own unique and personal vision in very general terms, such as "I'd like to help people everywhere" (what might be called the "Miss America" approach to vision). While the sentiment expressed above might be admirable and sincere, as a vision statement it's unfocused. Using that general statement as a foundation, a person then might ask him- or herself, "What about this statement is particularly important to me, and how would I go about reflecting it in my life?" With further probing, a more directed and useful vision begins to take shape: "I want to work with at-risk teenagers to help them develop self-confidence and life skills."

Characteristics of a powerful, inspirational vision statement will include:

- deals with both what you want to BE and what you want to DO in your life;

- draws from the most profound resources of your inner self;

- communicates to and inspires you on the most essential level;

- integrates the four basic areas of your life: physical, mental, emotional, and spiritual;

- applies to and integrates all the significant roles in your life— personal, family, work, leisure, and community;

- is written for you, not to impress anyone else;

- functions as a beacon which continually lights the way for you to travel your own path;

- is part of an evolving process, changing as you grow in age, experience, and wisdom.

If this sounds big, it is—a dynamic and meaningful expression of your vision serves as a foundation for everything else in life. But remember, the key to a fulfilling vision statement isn't how many of the above characteristics are included; the key is whether your vision provides you with a compass to what you want to be, and the motivation to be it.

Creating a Vision

In developing a personal vision statement, the power of the BE side can be an invaluable resource. Using your right brain will allow you access to hidden and unexplored possibilities; as a result, your personal vision will gain dimension and depth. The following inner activity will set the stage for you to gather important information to use in creating your vision statement.

This is the first of three similar imagination exercises in this book. If you find this type of exercise unfamiliar or difficult, keep in mind that there is immense practical value that can come from tapping your inner resources, helping you move beyond intellect and reason into intuition and image. Also keep in mind that using your imagination effectively takes practice, so don't be surprised if visual images don't immediately pop into your mind; keep trying.

There are three alternative ways to proceed with this imagination exercise. The best way is to have another person read the exercise to you while you listen and use your imagination. If that's not feasible, prepare by reading the exercise into a tape recorder in advance, and then when you're ready, play your tape recording while you listen and use your imagination to experience it. The final option is to read the exercise and pause each time when indicated, taking the time to experience it while you are reading. Whether someone else is reading for you or you're doing it for yourself, be sure the exercise is read slowly and thoughtfully, allowing plenty of time at each pause for the visual picture to emerge.

Before starting the exercise, create an environment that's conducive to being inner-focused: remove any distractions, such as bright lights, noises, or telephones.

Exercise:

Allow yourself to relax and to encourage your usually active mind to be at rest. Relax your body. Get comfortable in your chair and put your feet flat on the floor in order to feel grounded; keep your hands relaxed in your lap. When you feel comfortable, take several deep breaths low in your abdomen. As you breathe, be aware of places of tension in your body: neck, shoulders, jaw. Move those areas, trying consciously to relax them. Feel the tension draining out of your body. Still your mind, so that you can truly concentrate on the images your imagination creates.
(PAUSE)
You see yourself walking on a path outdoors, in a place that is peaceful and quiet. As you look around, observe the beauty and tranquillity of the scenery. Experience the colors, the sounds, the smells, and any other sensory impressions. As you walk along the path, you become aware that it leads you toward a lake. What is your sense of the water? Is it still or busy, large or small?
(PAUSE)
Once you have arrived near the water's edge, you see someone sitting, clearly waiting for you. As you come closer and are able to observe more, you see that it is someone you value highly. It might be a historical figure, a person from your past who has passed on, or someone you know now; in any case, the person greets you and knows you well. As you come up to the person, you experience a deep sense of gratitude for the opportunity to see and to speak with him or her. You sit down next to the person.
(PAUSE)
While you feel great joy at this meeting, you also become aware that this is not a time for idle conversation. Rather, you have a chance to ask this person two deep and important questions that will help you clarify your personal vision. After a warm welcome, you tell the person that you have two questions to ask, and that you would appreciate answers because of his or her deep wisdom and the value of your relationship. The first question is: "What is most valuable about me?" You listen to the response.
(PAUSE)
The second question is "What is most important to me?" Again you listen to the response.
(PAUSE)
Take a moment to reflect on your experience. When you feel ready, come back to the present time and place.

This kind of right-brain, contemplative exercise may be unfamiliar, and even uncomfortable, for you. As you work through the 10-step process, you'll become more comfortable with your BE side, and you'll find that it offers insights and possibilities not previously tapped. Bear in mind that self-assessment and self-knowledge are key success traits in the molecular marketplace. In this case, the answers you received to the two questions in the exercise will help you as you create your own vision statement.

Here are some additional ways that you can clarify your vision:

- draw a picture of your vision;

- think about what you love to do when you have a block of time completely to yourself;

- consider your happiest moments;

- reflect on your greatest strengths;

- when you're in your 80's, what would you want to tell your grandchildren were your greatest accomplishments and the ways you contributed most to others;

- spend time considering your vision while in a favorite natural setting;

- listen to a favorite piece of music;

- talk with others to hear their ideas.

Example Vision Statements

Remember Mark, who we met in the opening quote of this Step? Here, as an example, is his vision statement:

> *I love my family, my work, my country and being healthy and active. I have started to reduce the number of hours I spend at work by taking on fewer projects and helping others more. I'll continue to reduce my work time gradually over the next five years and actually retire at age 57, with adequate income from investments and my 401K plan. I will continue to work part-time after retirement to stay professionally current and for extra income for travel, but my first priorities will be family activities, staying personally fit, and doing volunteer work with veterans groups.*

The four people in the case studies have each developed vision statements which can serve as examples for you as well. What they've written in their case studies will provide more insight into what's behind each of their visions.

Using the information in this Step, you have an opportunity to develop your own vision statement. Remember that developing your vision is an on-going process; your vision statement can and will be changed and enhanced as time goes by and as you become more aware of what consistently holds your interest and stimulates your energy. Ideally, you will develop a dynamic relationship with your vision statement, living with it and using it to guide and inspire you. With your vision statement in hand, you're ready to move on to exploring and developing the "product" for **MMI, Inc**—you!

Case Studies

1. *Shannon*

I came into this 10-step process expecting to get some help in finding the right job and/or career. When I first started into the Step 2 information on frame of reference and vision, I admit that I was a little bit surprised. It seemed more like going to a therapist than career help! But I think that the best thing about doing the personal work in Step 2 is realizing that the real solution for job issues or questions doesn't come from someone giving you a list of jobs, companies, or salaries. Instead, it really requires knowing something about yourself—how you work and what you want.

Drawing my frame of reference "windshield" was the first time I'd pulled together pieces of who I am and where I come from, and even using stick figures to represent those aspects of me created a significant picture of where I've come from.

As for vision, I have to admit that creating a vision seemed more important when I realized that businesses all do this process; if I'm going to try to compete as **MMI, Inc**, it gives the vision a lot more importance. When it came time to write my vision, I knew that I needed to create something that would give me a direction as well as a good feeling, so I worked hard to balance the "deep" with the practical:

> *I am an independent, enthusiastic person. I understand the importance of balance in my life: old with new, work with leisure, money with values, and my needs with those of others. I live my life as an adventure, finding new challenges without leaving behind things that continue to be important. In my work, I will explore to find good ways to use both my strong analytical and relationship abilities outside of a traditional "big" company. Socially, I value the friends and relationships I have now, and will build and take care of them as well as*

making new connections. Personally, I continue to discover what's really important to me and to incorporate those things into my life.

I guess part of the power of a good vision statement comes from its uniqueness—in mine, there is so much behind each sentence that only I know and relate to. But I can also see how it will probably change as time goes along, so I've decided to spend some time each birthday to review and update it. I consider it a present to myself!

2. *Brent*

I found this Step of developing my vision to be difficult and time-consuming. I'm not accustomed to deep personal introspection, and, although I *have* a vision, putting it into a simple paragraph wasn't easy. Changing one's life—or at least discovering something new about it— takes some effort. I read the chapter, then re-read it again, stopping at every activity and answering its questions *in writing*.

The first "imagination exercise" sounded almost silly when I first read it, but when I tried it (with my wife reading it to me), the results were surprisingly powerful. Not only did the experience help define who I am, but I found that immediately after the exercise I was very open to seeing connections between feelings, actions, and experiences that I hadn't seen before.

It took nearly a week of working with the activities before I was happy with my first vision statement:

> *I am a creative individual who thrives on the challenge of finding solutions to complex problems and participating in unique projects. I will approach each challenge with eagerness, loyalty, an eye for detail, and respect for my colleagues.*
>
> *Regardless of my role in the workplace, I will act as a responsive 'contractor' by providing my 'clients' with the highest quality product possible, delivered on time and on budget. My advice will be well considered, honest, and in their best interests. My goal is to be such an asset to my colleagues that they will say, "We couldn't have done it without Brent."*
>
> *Although my work life is important, I will not forget the things that are most important to me: my love for my wife and my children. Our time together is precious; I will always make the most of it. Without their love, respect, and support, I would not be a complete person.*

3. *Emily*

Reading about the value of understanding one's frame of reference in helping to build a personal vision was a real eye-opening experience for me. It was interesting to identify where elements of my perspective on life originated and especially interesting to identify where I have a very narrow view. Having grown up in a town with almost no racial diversity, one narrow view I held was my attitude concerning people with different cultural and racial backgrounds than mine. With this gap in mind, during my work at a local community college in association with getting my counseling degree I agreed to work with a program for students who come from diverse cultural and racial backgrounds. Working with these students, I find myself immersed daily in frames of reference and life experiences very different from my own.

The more I experience the wonderful richness of the diversity of people and their cultures, the more I realize we are all basically the same. As I worked with the ideas in this Step I realized how much my frame of reference had to do with how I viewed the world, and how that really created a vision for me. My vision isn't one I "developed," it's more like I discovered it. More accurately, it's like I'm still discovering it as I go. I hope the discovery process never stops.

I will constantly be alert to opportunities to more deeply understand and connect to the four aspects of myself: physical—I will eat healthy foods, exercise, and maintain my weight at a correct level; mental—I will exercise my mind by being open to ideas from others and in sharing my own knowledge; emotional—I will give voice to the depth of both my pain and my joy and, as I am exposed to different frames of reference, will act as a conduit for the expression of feelings of others; spiritual—I will continue regular imagination exercises toward the deepening of my understanding of my purpose in life.

4. *Forrest*

All my life I've had a sense of being part of something else, something bigger. But I'd always taken that feeling for granted, never thinking much about what it meant and never relating it to a vision for myself until I began to work with the 10 Steps.

After 30 years in a big company and three years consulting I was ready to start a different phase of my life, and the ideas started to race around in my head. I realized I was more of an entrepreneur that I'd ever thought; the chance to act like an entrepreneur just hadn't come up before. Now that I'd escaped (or been set free) from the bureaucracy and had consulted a bit, what next? That's when I discovered the ten-step process and first thought about my vision for myself at work.

As a person who usually sought out new and different experiences, I've always felt that expanding my frame of reference to try to see things differently was interesting and rewarding, so I don't recall ever facing a strong threat from the stick to change or be overrun by circumstances.

But after working with this Step I knew a lot more about who I was, and how I viewed the world in ways that were different from other people. Understanding my frame of reference and doing the imagination exercise led me to a clear picture of my vision at this point in my life. Here's how I state it:

> *I make an important difference in the lives of people, starting with my family and friends, moving out to people who will find my services useful enough to pay for them, and extending in some small way to all the world's people. I bring more value than I take, which is satisfying to me and which attracts customers to* **MMI, Inc.** *I am growing in knowledge and finding new things of interest. In five years I will begin a transition from being paid for my work to being a volunteer, in order to better target the opportunities that I enjoy most, both in helping others and in my own leisure.*

Step 3

Define Your Product

Larry, a 29-year old cabinet maker: *Recently, when the owner of the cabinet shop where I worked told us he was going to retire, I knew I was in trouble. After all, I've worked for him since high school and know my job inside out. Now, I suddenly have to decide to get a new job, do something completely different, or even try to buy the shop. I don't know what I want to do, what I might be able to do, or how to begin to figure it all out.*

Maybe you, like Larry, are finding that your job has defined who you are in the work environment, and because of this, you sense that your options are restricted. What can you do to free yourself from these restrictions? How can you take the vision that you've developed for **MMI, Inc** and build it into the right future for you in the molecular marketplace? Part of the answer will be to learn to see yourself as a product.

Larry knows a lot about the product of his work—cabinets. He knows about all the different types of woods that can be made into cabinets, about the most cost effective resources for these materials, about different cabinet styles that will be attractive to potential buyers, about different makes and styles of hardware as well as resources for these materials, about the different ways to put cabinets together, and even the different types of finishes. In short, Larry knows everything he needs to know about cabinets,

44

in order to be competitive in the home building marketplace.

To deliver a high quality, competitive product in the molecular market-place, you will have to know as much about your product as Larry knows about cabinets, but there's a difference—in this case, the product is *you*. In short, you'll have to understand a lot about yourself. In the past, self-examination was often considered interesting but too much on the BE side to be particularly relevant in the DO-oriented "real world." However, now that you can gain an advantage by increasing your product knowledge, the concentrated effort of this Step will pay big dividends. You'll learn the value of diversity, gain knowledge about your personality type and how to use it to your advantage at work, learn more about your current skills and develop a clear view of what you most value. With a clear vision and a well-defined product, you'll be well on your way to making your mark in the molecular marketplace.

Your Past Successes

What does it mean to think of yourself as a product? Let's begin to understand this question by focusing on what you've achieved in the past. This will serve several purposes—including giving you a better sense of where you have come from, a base on which to build **MMI, Inc**, and a way to help clarify your unique skills and values.

Think about your past achievements. Try to identify ten or more accomplishments or projects in which you have demonstrated some degree of skill, achieved a desired goal, or explored a new challenge. These accomplishments can be from any segment of your life, including work, school, leisure, family, and community. Include accomplishments that made you feel good and that you enjoyed, not only ones that won you outside praise or rewards. Something you are proud of need not be of significance to others.

Identifying your past achievements can be hard. Most of us find it difficult to affirm ourselves, and many are taught that it is culturally incorrect to do so. If you had trouble thinking of at least ten specific achievements, try thinking back over a recent day in your life, and remember what you accomplished. Your achievements might look like these:

- I got my three kids ready and off to school on time.

- I finished my report and presented it to my work group.

- I kept the five people on my redesign team productively busy during a slack period.

- I walked three miles in my fastest time ever.

Also, try putting yourself in the shoes of someone who knows you well and imagine what they would say about your achievements.

Noting your achievements is a first step toward looking at yourself objectively, as a product. Once you give yourself permission to see your accomplishments clearly and objectively, you'll be surprised at how many examples you can come up with. You'll refer back to these achievements several more times in the process of completing the 10 Steps.

It Makes A World Of Difference

Your achievements are unique because you're unique. But what difference does that make? A lot, it turns out. Let's explore the differences between people, and in particular how understanding diversity can help you develop and refine your product.

There are many ways to discuss the differences between people, ranging from the in-depth analysis of Carl Jung's study of psychological types to something more superficial like the analysis of which clothing colors best complement a person's skin tone. But there is immense value in any process which helps you understand both who you are and how you can better relate to others who are different.

Clara, Mary and the Seasons

Clara and her teenage daughter Mary personally experienced the value of understanding their differences. They often went shopping for clothes together. This generally was a pleasant experience for both of them and they would often stop in the midst of the hustle and bustle for lunch at a nice restaurant. Only one thing marred the experience. Mary usually chose clothes of a certain style that her mother Clara really disliked, such as patterns of little, repetitive flowers, Peter Pan type collars, pastel colors, and what appeared to Clara to be "fussy" styles. Clara herself would tend to pick out more dramatic styles, perhaps with big bold flowers and more yellows, browns, or reds for color choices.

For a Christmas gift on Mary's fifteenth birthday, Clara gave them both an appointment with a color consultant to "have their colors done." Many of Clara's friends had gone and had found that it was not only fun but also helpful in working with their wardrobe. The first to sit down with the consultant was Mary, who had fabrics from the four different color types—Autumn with its earth tones; Winter and its dramatic, pure tones; Spring with its bright, true colors; and Summer with pastels and little patterns—draped around her shoulders. It was clear from the beginning that she was a Summer type. The soft pastels were dramatically more attractive against her skin than any of the other seasonal colors. As the consultant talked about what summer types like, she listed all of the things Mary preferred: pastel colors, Peter Pan collars, and small floral patterns. While observing Mary's consultation, Clara had an "a-ha!" experience about why the preference differences between them existed and about the fact that both were very legitimate! When Clara had the swatches of fabric draped around her shoulders, it became clear that her season was "Fall" and her preferences were more bold appearing styles and the yellow, brown, and muted red tones that are naturally associated with the fall season.

This seemingly trivial example opened the eyes of both of these women to the reality of diversity, the value of each being unique, and the beauty of being able to accept the individualistic expression of another. These benefits of better understanding diversity can apply to all arenas of your life, from your family environment to your work situation.

The Value of Diversity

The point here is to underscore the fact that people are fundamentally different and that this is okay! And in fact, beyond being okay, this diversity is what brings richness, variety, challenge and dimension to our existence. Imagine always being with others who are exactly like you. At first this might seem ideal, but in the not-so-long term, the sameness would become deadening—always knowing what another would say, why they would say it, and without any of the subtleties that enable our wonderings to be exercised and our imaginations to take flight.

In the molecular marketplace, being part of a diverse population has great advantages. Bringing together people in a strategic alliance who have different personality patterns produces a more creative and competitive result, and provides for a more dynamic process in getting there as well.

It's What's Inside That Counts—Your Personality Type

A critical element in understanding yourself as a product is to know your personality type. The study of your personality type can produce amazing insights into the BE side of you and how much it affects the DO activities of your life. For instance, it can clarify why one person feels great around energetic and outgoing people while another prefers quiet and introspective types; why one person is uncomfortable being out of doors while another doesn't like to be cooped up behind a desk; and why one person might really look forward to a day spent trying to fix the engine of the old lawnmower and another can't stand the thought of having to change a light bulb!

In *Boundaries of the Soul*, author June Singer describes the different personality types defined by psychiatrist Carl Jung. She begins her description with these words: "Ordinarily when we as individuals find ourselves in uncongenial discussions, we are forced to come to terms with people whose typology is quite different from our own. They will see things one way and be quite convinced that they are correct, while we will see things in another way and be just as convinced. There can never be any reconciliation between opposing views unless there is first a recognition that matters may be seen in other terms than that of correctness or error.... For always, there is one set of facts which is regarded by different people in different ways." In other words, people's frames of reference produce personalized views of reality based on personality type and past experience, and these views are neither right nor wrong, just different.

Introvert or Extrovert

Jung describes two fundamentally different ways of interacting with the world around us: introversion and extroversion. An introverted person replenishes energy by being alone while an extrovert becomes energized from being with people. For example, an introvert and an extrovert attended a conference together and the introvert commented at the end of a long day, "I can't wait to get off by myself, take a nice long bath, and pull my thoughts together." To which the extrovert replied, "I feel totally energized; let's go out, get together with our friends and talk about the conference workshops." While the introvert looks for an internal understanding of what is experienced or perceived, the extrovert processes or assimilates personal involvement with life through external communication and discussion. The introvert is territorial, needing private space internally as well as externally, while the extrovert is sociable, needing people around.

Many people feel a bit uncomfortable placing themselves firmly in one category. "Sometimes when I've been reading or thinking I'm more introverted; other times after a meeting or presentation I act like an extrovert." And that's true for everyone. But there's still a fundamental, natural approach for each person. Try asking yourself which set of characteristics feels more like you. Or answer this question: if you had to choose between being stranded on a desert island alone or being permanently stuck at a Mardi Gras celebration, which would you choose? These activities can help you identify your own innate function.

Here's a comparison of attributes of introverts (I) and extroverts (E); check which attribute in each pair fits you best.

✓ Introverts (I)	✓ Extroverts (E)
___ inner focused	___ outer-focused
___ energized by having time on own	___ energized by interacting with others
___ prefer a deliberate approach	___ prefer spontaneity
___ think before acting	___ act before thinking
___ there has to be a reason to communicate	___ communication comes naturally
___ in a group, prefer interacting with one other person	___ in a group, prefer to mingle
___ resolve problems by reflecting internally	___ resolve problems by interacting with others
___ tend to let others plan activities	___ tend to be the social director
___ probably have one or two close friends	___ probably have a wide circle of friends and acquaintances
___ **Total ✓ for I**	___ **Total ✓ for E**

Based on the number of attributes you checked in each category, where do you fit on the scale of introversion (I) and extroversion (E)?

Number of E ✓	Number of I ✓	Where You Fit
9-7	0-2	Strongly Extroverted (E)
6-5	3-4	Extroverted (E)
4-3	5-6	Introverted (I)
2-0	7-9	Strongly Introverted (I)

The Next Dimension

In addition to introversion and extroversion, Jung's typology includes a further set of characteristics that add dimension to personality typing. He classifies these four characteristics as thinking (T), feeling (F), sensation (S) and intuition (N). Each of these four types is also associated with either introversion or extroversion, so that there are eight potential types, shown in the diagram below.

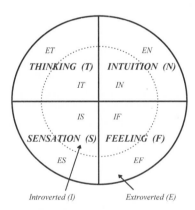

Jung also discovered that every person, extrovert or introvert, is most strongly identified with only one of these four types. Read through the following descriptions of these four types to get a sense of what feels most familiar to you.

Thinking

A person who has the primary characteristic of *thinking* finds great value in holding to principles and upholding what is right according to rules or the law. Analysis feels like the most accurate way of interpreting a situation, since a thinking type of person wants to break things down into their various parts rather than looking at the whole picture. Wrestling with a problem or a puzzle in the mind is more interesting than reaching a specific conclusion. Thinking types of people feel very comfortable using the scientific process to prove or to disprove something; on the other hand, they are uncomfortable with feelings unless they can be logically explained. Achievement is held to be extremely important. To others, a thinking person may seem to be a great problem solver, while at the same time may also seem cold and calculating.

Here's a list of attributes of a thinking (T) personality type:

- Has lots of ideas.

- Enjoys analyzing problems using cause and effect relationships.

- Plans and organizes effectively.

- Is accomplished at theorizing.

- Tries to align life with logically thought-out conclusions.

- Is uncomfortable with expressions of feeling.

- Enjoys communicating about ideas.

Feeling

A person who has the primary characteristic of *feeling* places a high value in the arena of the subjective. Faced with a decision, a feeling person will quickly reach a conclusion based on an absolute internal preference between clear opposites. For this type of person, expressing feelings is important, and is a positive way to communicate deeply with others. How a situation will impact other people is the basis upon which to make decisions. A feeling person is highly concerned with doing things for the good of society, and looking for harmony in all things. A feeling person may be thought by others to be caring and nurturing, but may at times seem to be overly emotional or illogical.

Here's a list of attributes of a feeling (F) personality type:

- Reaches value-based conclusions.

- Gives objects or ideas values such as "good/bad" or "beautiful/ugly."

- Sees the world through the perception of opposites.

- Forms opinions based on internal sense of right and wrong.

- Desires a rich inner life, with a deep sense of spiritual connectedness.

- Feels comfortable with expressions of sentiment.

- Connections with people take priority over principles or ideas.

Sensation

A person who has the primary characteristic of *sensation* wants facts, and strongly relies on his or her own personal experience. When faced with doing a project like baking a cake, a sensing person will follow the recipe precisely. A sensing person will focus on what actually happened in a situation, and can recite the specifics such as colors, images, and sounds with clarity. To a sensing person, if an item or an experience provides a practical application to life it has value; otherwise, it's irrelevant. He or she is oriented to the present, and feels that the future will take care of itself. A sensing person may be seen by others as perceptive and detail-oriented, but possibly also lacking in imagination.

Here's a list of attributes of a sensation (S) personality type:

- Places high value on sensory things, appreciating aesthetics, colors, smells, tastes.

- Perceives and describes a situation by giving only facts.

- Is aware of and interacts with the immediate environment.

- Analysis is seen as simply someone else's opinion and not of much consequence.

- Values practical applications of ideas over abstractions.

- Focuses on details.

- Is aware of what's going on in the present.

Intuition

A person who has the primary characteristic of *intuition* gives high value to imagery and day dreams, and the future holds the greatest attraction. An intuitive person has the ability to see the whole picture when presented with elements of a situation. He or she may be less interested in day-to-day reality. An intuitive person will excel at the start-up phase of planning and will bring unending suggestions and ideas to any brainstorming situation, but often won't enjoy the long haul. He or she will like to learn new skills and explore new horizons. To others, an intuitive person may be seen as bringing energy and generating new ideas, but may also be seen as overwhelming and not fully considering the reality of the situation.

Here's a list of attributes of an intuition (N) personality type:

- Sees the big picture.

- Values being ingenious and unconventional.

- Sees possibilities in every situation.

- Longs for exciting new possibilities.

- Is uncomfortable with a set routine or schedule.

- Is good at brainstorming.

- Focuses on what's going to happen in the future.

Your Personality Type

Now that you've had a look at each of the four characteristic types, look again at the list of attributes of each type and check those that seem to fit you best.

✓   **Thinking (T)**

___ Has lots of ideas.
___ Enjoys analyzing problems using cause and effect relationships.
___ Plans and organizes effectively.
___ Is accomplished at theorizing.
___ Tries to align life with logically thought-out conclusions.
___ Is uncomfortable with expressions of feeling.
___ Enjoys communicating about ideas.

___ **Total ✓ for T**

Feeling (F)

___ Reaches value-based conclusions.
___ Gives objects or ideas values such as "good/bad" or "beautiful/ugly."
___ Sees the world through the perception of opposites.
___ Forms opinions based on internal sense of right and wrong.
___ Desires a rich inner life, with a deep sense of spiritual connectedness.
___ Feels comfortable with expressions of sentiment.
___ Connections with people take priority over principles or ideas.

___ **Total ✓ for F**

Sensation (S)

___ Places high value on sensory things, appreciating aesthetics, colors, smells, tastes.
___ Perceives and describes a situation by giving only facts.
___ Is aware of and interacts with the immediate environment.
___ Analysis is seen as simply someone else's opinion and not of much consequence.

____   Values practical applications of ideas over abstractions.
____   Focuses on details.
____   Is aware of what's going on in the present.

____   **Total ✓ for S**

Intuition (N)

____   Sees the big picture.
____   Values being ingenious and unconventional.
____   Sees possibilities in every situation.
____   Longs for exciting new possibilities.
____   Is uncomfortable with a set routine or schedule.
____   Is good at brainstorming.
____   Focuses on what's going to happen in the future.

____   **Total ✓ for N**

Based on the number of attributes that you checked and how closely each of the above descriptions seems to match you, which is your primary characteristic type: thinking (T), feeling (F), sensation (S) or intuition (N)? Your overall personality type is made up of I for introverted or E or extroverted, and the letter that represents your primary characteristic type. For example, you may find that your type is "ES" (extroverted sensation) or "IN" (introverted intuition). While everyone has a dominant characteristic type, you may find that you also scored high (5 or more) on a secondary type. If you have a strong secondary characteristic type, which many people do, you can add that letter to your type as well, for example "ESF" (extroverted sensation feeling) or "INT" (introverted intuition thinking).

Making Differences Work For You

One of the most valuable things about understanding your personality type is the benefit you can experience in improving relationships, in both personal and work situations. Claude and Pete, who were partners in a startup software venture, provide a negative example. They had not known each other for very long but both had similar high-tech backgrounds, had mutual friends, and had decided to start a business together. The first several months went well, with both men contributing their skill and time toward the development of the company. Claude was particularly good at thinking of new, innovative approaches to product development and Pete was an expert at getting down to the nitty-gritty part, including setting up financial programs and thinking through marketing scenarios. But after a few months, Claude began to make comments about being dissatisfied and wanting to get out, to look for broader horizons, and to find more challenge and meet new people. Pete, who was feeling good about the work, was surprised and thought Claude was developing a very irresponsible attitude toward the business. Other differences surfaced and the two men eventually sold the business, parting company with negative feelings towards each other.

If the two men had had the opportunity to evaluate themselves using the personality types discussed above, Claude might have learned he was an Extroverted Intuitive type, while Pete was Introverted Sensing type. What propels Claude forward is his insatiable curiosity and interest in everything new while the "same old, same old" quickly becomes boring and of little appeal. At the same time, Pete thrives on doing routine, hands-on work and has little interest in always pursuing new and different things.

Imagine how different types might function together (or not!) in a strategic alliance within a work environment. Suppose there are several Introverted Feeling types who make snap judgments knowing without a doubt that their opinion is the right one and there are also a few Extroverted Thinking folks who take a long time coming to decisions based solely on the facts of a particular situation. It is most likely that these two groups of people will clash strongly unless they come to the level of understanding which we have been discussing and learn to value and incorporate the differences. People who know about their own and others' personality types, and therefore know what to expect, can avoid becoming deadlocked or reacting angrily to others. This knowledge can be a tremendous competitive advantage in the molecular marketplace.

Try to identify the personality type of someone close to you. How have the differences in your personality types influenced your relationship? What difficulties and what benefits have each of you experienced as a result of the interaction of your personality types? In your present work environment, can you identify the personality type of the person that most gets on your nerves? Can you see how a difference in your personality types may be contributing to what bothers you about the person?

The subject of personality type is very large and complex. Each of us has one particular personality type which is most representative and dictates the way we most typically respond. But each of us also has elements of each type within our personality, and research has shown that we also have superior, auxiliary and inferior functions. Many people find the subject of their personalities to be of great interest, and we've just scratched the surface. If you want to know more, you might want to start with *Please Understand Me* by David Keirsey and Marilyn Bates, or *Do What You Are* by Paul D. Tieger and Barbara Barron-Tieger. Even more detail about your personality type can be gained by using the Myers-Briggs Type Indicator (MBTI), available from career resource centers or professional career counselors.

Another interesting conceptual framework for looking at your personality type is the Enneagram system. A good resource to learn more about this system is *The Enneagram: Understanding Yourself and the Others in Your Life*, by Helen Palmer.

You're Full Of Skills

You've begun to identify the product for **MMI, Inc** by noting your past achievements and your personality type. The third major element in your product definition is skill identification. Chances are you have more skills than you think. For example, Marvin had sold shoes in a mall store for several years and, while he was good at it, he felt it was time to try something else. He made an appointment to see Eleanor, a professional career counselor, to get some ideas on how to proceed. Eleanor said, "It will help us explore what you might want to do if we know more about your existing skills. Tell me what your skills are." Marvin replied: "Well, I can sell shoes and I know how to manage the shop when the boss is gone." Eleanor said: "Good. And what others?" Marvin thought hard, since Eleanor obviously wanted more, but he couldn't think of any others. He said: "I think that's it, to tell the truth."

Marvin's response is common. Like all of us, he has a lot more skills than he could quickly bring to mind. The purpose of discussing skills at this point in the 10 Steps is not to encourage you to get new skills, but to become conscious of all the skills that you already have. As you proceed, you'll be surprised and gratified as you uncover these hidden treasures.

According to the Oxford Dictionary, a skill is "practiced ability or expertness." This definition acknowledges two important elements that make up a skill: a person's innate ability, and doing some work to actually develop it. There are three basic types of skills: self-knowledge, work-specific, and transferable skills.

Self-Knowledge Skills

The first type of skills, self-knowledge skills, are the most BE of the skill types and are an integral part of your frame of reference. They have to do with your attitude—how you relate to the people around you, how you relate to your environment, and how you relate to different types of work. For instance Alicia, who at 45 was planning to return to work after twenty years of parenting, developed the following list of self-knowledge skills: I enjoy working out of doors; I work well with outgoing, energetic people; in stressful situations, I clearly see the differing points of view; I am keenly aware of when someone is trying to take advantage of me; and I have a great sense of humor.

With awareness of self-knowledge skills, you can choose to emphasize your own natural strengths as well as consciously develop weak areas for **MMI, Inc**, allowing you to become a good self-manager. For example, Alicia was aware that her skill at seeing differing points of view sometimes made her appear to be "wishy-washy." But by learning to consistently communicate the different points of view she saw, she was able to effectively help other people resolve conflicts. We don't traditionally think of self-knowledge as relating to skills, yet self-knowledge skills can make or break you in the new work environment. In fact, attitude plays such an important role in **MMI, Inc's** success that we'll come back to it in much more detail later in the book.

Work-Specific Skills

Work-specific skills are a second, DO-based type of skills. These traditional skills come in two varieties. The first is on-the-job skills which are learned quickly and through experience. Skills of this variety include, for example, working on a computer, knowledge of software programs, using a particular filing system, understanding the ins and outs of high quality telephone customer service and operating a backhoe.

The second variety of work-specific skills is acquired through formal education or training, and is often subject to a licensing requirement. Skills of this variety include, for example, computer design of aircraft, doing private counseling involving psychodrama, providing medical expertise as a specialist in the field of geriatrics, installing electrical wiring and selling securities. Work-specific skills used to be the only ones that mattered, but now you'll be changing projects, tasks, and positions often so you'll be re-learning or acquiring work-specific skills over and over again. This is often described as the trend toward "continuous learning" in the work environment.

Transferable Skills

In the molecular marketplace, the third type, transferable skills, has become much more important. These are skills which can be carried from one work situation to the next. In this migratory work environment, knowledge of your unique set of transferable skills will be critical to understanding and defining your product.

The strongest transferable skills show up early and are usually a theme in your life. They can feel so natural that you take them for granted and don't even consider them to be skills at all. As you read the following list, notice which transferable skills have been most prominent in your life.

Transferable skills are divided into three categories. The first is **data skills**:

- **logical intelligence**—thinking, planning, evaluation, organization

- **intuitive intelligence**—imagination, whole seeing, creativity, brain-storming

- **verbal ability**—reading, writing, listening, discussing

- **numerical ability**—number use, analysis, budgeting

- **precise detail**—following directions, attending to and caring about small details

- **multidimensional awareness**—understanding, visualizing, 3-dimensional awareness

- **computer literacy**—basic computer use and software knowledge

The second category is **people skills**:

- **business-like contact with people**—management, negotiation, cooperation

- **influencing people**—inspiration, teaching, sales

- **helping people**—counseling, caring for others, offering services

The third category is **thing skills:**

- **finger/hand agility**—repair, tool operation, playing musical instruments

- **whole body ability**—handling, carrying, coordination, sports

- **work outdoors**—animals, plants, the environment

Theresa and Emma, roommates in their mid-twenties, provide a great example. Emma was envious of Theresa's skill in "whole body ability;" in other words, she was well-coordinated. As a result, Theresa is a natural at most sports where her whole body is put into play, such as tennis, swimming, and skiing. For her, coordinated physical activity seems as natural as breathing itself, but in fact it represents a powerful asset in the world of work. For instance, her first several jobs involved life guarding and she is thinking of developing a career as a high school physical education teacher.

Theresa asked Emma, who had a university degree in English, to help her prepare a resume for a short term contract job. Emma had a way with words, but she had never felt very confident about her employment prospects because throughout her college years, people would often ask "What will you *do* with your degree? Isn't it too general to be of much use in the real world? Shouldn't you look at a more practical degree, like one in nursing or teaching?" With Emma's help, Theresa got the job she wanted, and her gratitude made Emma aware that her analytical and writing skills were great assets and had been fundamental to her many successes at school, in internships and at work.

The bottom line is that in the past, when people tended to stay in one job for a long time, work-specific skills were most valuable, while transferable skills were secondary. In the molecular marketplace, skills that can be put to use in more than one arena are becoming more important as workers move more often into new work environments. The more conscious you become of your transferable skills—these natural ways of relating to life—the more you can put them to use in developing a successful product. Your transferable skills represent one constant factor you can rely upon to make you marketable no matter what changes you need or want to make in your work.

Your Transferable Skills

Now you'll have an opportunity to identify your own strongest transferable skills. The worksheet on pages 59-61contains a list of skills, divided into seven broad categories: Technical/Mechanical, Analytical, Creative, Service, Physical, Manage/Persuade and Detail/Organize. Use the worksheet below to identify those skills you perform well or have ability in, and also those skills that you are motivated to use, or enjoy using.

Worksheet directions: For each skill listed, check in the "Ability" column the level of ability you feel that you have: *Can't Do This Skill, Do This Skill OK,* or *Do This Skill Well.* Then think about how much you enjoy using that skill, and in the "Level of Motivation" column rate it from 1 to 4: *1 = Dislike Doing This Skill, 2 = Neutral About This Skill, 3 = Like Doing This Skill, 4 = Really Enjoy Doing This Skill.* After you complete the ability and motivation information for each skill, go back through the list and put a check in the box in the "Best Skills" column if that skill is one that you both do well and really enjoy.

In the "Best Skills" column on page 60, circle the 10 to 15 skills you would most like to use at work. Then check (✓) the two or three skill categories below in which most of your Best Skills fall:

☐ Technical/Mechanical   ☐ Creative   ☐ Physical
☐ Analytical   ☐ Service   ☐ Manage/Persuade
☐ Detail/Organize

On the Skills Identification worksheet, you can see those skills you do well and those you really enjoy using. Your greatest job satisfaction will come from using skills that energize you and bring you enjoyment. As you'll discover in Step 4, you'll want to identify and target work situations that allow you to use your most-enjoyed skills the majority of the time.

If you're working now, you might find that you too often have to use your "ball-and-chain" skills—the skills you can do well but that you dislike using. Using your ball-and-chain skills can result in thoughts like: "I am really good at sales but I feel my energy being drained and it upsets me every time I have to actually knock on a potential customer's door." You probably can't avoid using your ball-and-chain skills altogether, but you can try to rearrange your work to create a better balance with skills you really enjoy using.

This skill activity will have helped create or bolster self-confidence about your many useful skills. Knowledge of your transferable skills is another important milestone toward developing a dynamite product definition statement for **MMI, Inc**.

Skills Identification Worksheets

SKILLS	ABILITY (✓ one)			LEVEL OF MOTIVA- TION (1 = Dislike, 4 = Enjoy)	BEST SKILLS (✓)
	None	Do OK	Do Well		
TECHNICAL/ MECHANICAL					
Transport					❑
Operate mech. equip.					❑
Operate computers					❑
Construct/build					❑
Install/repair					❑
Use mech. abilities					❑
Program computers					❑
ANALYTICAL					
Forecast					❑
Estimate					❑
Evaluate					❑
Analyze					❑
Problem solve					❑
Observe					❑
Calculate/compute					❑
Synthesize					❑
Explain					❑
Program computers					❑
CREATIVE					
Use intuition					❑
Write					❑
Speak					❑
Design					❑
Music ability					❑
Entertain/perform					❑
Make arts and crafts					❑
Edit					❑
Visualize					❑
Draw					❑
3-D ability					❑
Invent					❑

SKILLS	ABILITY (✓ one)			LEVEL OF MOTIVA- TION	BEST SKILLS
	None	Do OK	Do Well	(1 = Dislike, 4 = Enjoy)	(✓)
SERVICE					
Counsel					❏
Teach/train					❏
Care for others					❏
Mediate					❏
Listen					❏
Coach					❏
Advise					❏
Liaison					❏
Provide hospitality					❏
Advocacy					❏
Take risks/act in emergency					❏
PHYSICAL					
Use physical co-ord.					❏
Use hand dexterity					❏
Work outdoors					❏
Work with animals					❏
Work with plants					❏
MANAGE/ PERSUADE					
Influence					❏
Motivate					❏
Sell/promote					❏
Supervise/manage					❏
Represent/be agent					❏
Negotiate					❏
Mediate					❏
Initiate					❏
Delegate					❏
Make decisions					❏

SKILLS	ABILITY (✓ one)			LEVEL OF MOTIVA-TION	BEST SKILLS
	None	Do OK	Do Well	(1 = Dislike, 4 = Enjoy)	(✓)
DETAIL/ ORGANIZE					
Organize					❑
Make arrangements					❑
Attend to details					❑
Budget					❑
Categorize					❑
Maintain records					❑
Implement					❑
Data entry					❑
Research					❑
Collect					❑
Administer					❑

What's Important To You? Your Values

Now that you've identified some past achievements, your personality type and your transferable skills, you may be getting a sense of how the ideal product for **MMI, Inc** will emerge from all this information and introspection.

This section will add information about your values, which form a foundation upon which to build your product definition. The final section of this Step focuses on your ideal working day, which will bring in your hopes and dreams to help you complete the picture in a way that's perfect for you.

So what are values anyway? They are deeply held beliefs which guide your behavior—in short, what's important to you. Are you consciously aware of what's important to you? Is it simply doing what you like? What feels right? What works in the moment? What others are doing? What your parents or teachers told you was right? What your boss wants you to do? What people close to you want of you? What comes from your own inner sense of right and wrong? Can you decide what's important, or does it have to come from somewhere else?

Most people have trouble answering these questions, because they've never really figured out what's important to them, and why. They may often feel pulled in different directions at the same time. The directions can be conflicting, and the conflict can be harmful to emotional health, productivity, and to relationships with others.

In contrast, when you know what's really important to you, your values will guide your actions, forming a bridge between the BE and DO aspects of your life. Values spring from deep in the BE side of an individual, and move into the DO side as they are expressed in action and direction. Values have little impact if they're vaguely-held beliefs; they become extremely relevant when they guide what you do with your life. In other words, what you actually do, not what you say you believe in, reflects your values. For example, justice is an abstraction for many people, but helping people and assuring fairness are true values for an attorney who donates some of her time to help needy people through a poverty law center. Or think about New Year's resolutions: Do you make them? Do you keep them? They are only based on true values if you keep them over the long term.

Use the following values worksheet to clarify your values.

Worksheet directions: Read through each of the three lists below, evaluating the level of importance each value has for you—*unimportant, not very important, important, or critical*. Do not think too long about any one item.

Action Values "I would like to:"			

	Un-Important	Not Very Important	Important	Critical
Create Ideas	❏	❏	❏	❏
Make Things	❏	❏	❏	❏
Fix Things	❏	❏	❏	❏
Help People	❏	❏	❏	❏
Design Systems	❏	❏	❏	❏
Perform Physical Tasks	❏	❏	❏	❏
Organize Things	❏	❏	❏	❏
Create Beauty	❏	❏	❏	❏
Explore Ideas	❏	❏	❏	❏
Follow Directions	❏	❏	❏	❏
Take Responsibility	❏	❏	❏	❏
Experience Variety	❏	❏	❏	❏
Improve Society	❏	❏	❏	❏
Take Risks	❏	❏	❏	❏
Be In Nature	❏	❏	❏	❏
Manage People	❏	❏	❏	❏

Result Values "I would like to have"			

	Un-Important	Not Very Important	Important	Critical
Achievement	❏	❏	❏	❏
Beauty Around Me	❏	❏	❏	❏
Knowledge	❏	❏	❏	❏
Pleasure	❏	❏	❏	❏
Power	❏	❏	❏	❏
Recognition	❏	❏	❏	❏
Wealth	❏	❏	❏	❏
Adventure	❏	❏	❏	❏
Comfort	❏	❏	❏	❏
Independence	❏	❏	❏	❏
Leisure Time	❏	❏	❏	❏
Possessions	❏	❏	❏	❏
Security	❏	❏	❏	❏
Structure/Order	❏	❏	❏	❏
Stability	❏	❏	❏	❏
Wisdom	❏	❏	❏	❏
Family Harmony	❏	❏	❏	❏
Friendship	❏	❏	❏	❏

	Un-Important	Not Very Important	Important	Critical
Self-respect	❑	❑	❑	❑
Inner Harmony	❑	❑	❑	❑
Integrity	❑	❑	❑	❑
Equality	❑	❑	❑	❑

> **Personal Qualities**
> **"It's important to me to be:"**

	Un-Important	Not Very Important	Important	Critical
Altruistic	❑	❑	❑	❑
Autonomous	❑	❑	❑	❑
Healthy	❑	❑	❑	❑
Moral	❑	❑	❑	❑
Physically Attractive	❑	❑	❑	❑
Spiritual	❑	❑	❑	❑
Ambitious	❑	❑	❑	❑
Caring	❑	❑	❑	❑
Cooperative	❑	❑	❑	❑
Disciplined	❑	❑	❑	❑
Positive	❑	❑	❑	❑
Needed	❑	❑	❑	❑
Efficient	❑	❑	❑	❑
Open-minded	❑	❑	❑	❑
Competent	❑	❑	❑	❑
Logical	❑	❑	❑	❑
Sensitive	❑	❑	❑	❑
Creative	❑	❑	❑	❑
Fair	❑	❑	❑	❑
Environmentally Aware	❑	❑	❑	❑
Honest	❑	❑	❑	❑

Select and make a note of the five values that are most important to you ("Top 5 Values") and the five that are least important ("Bottom 5 Values"). Are the top 5 values reflected in the achievements you identified earlier in this Step?

To help clarify your values further, you may want to have someone you trust—your significant other or a close friend—use the values worksheet above to independently note what they think are your most important values. You can then discuss with the other person the similarities and differences between your two views of your values. You can also ask yourself this question: " If someone followed me around on a typical day, what would they say my values are?"

Clarification of your values forms the foundation upon which you build the other pieces of your product definition. The more clearly you understand your values and how they're reflected in your life, the more effective and useful your product definition for **MMI, Inc** will be as you prepare to market your product in the molecular marketplace.

There's a Balloon In Your Future

You've now gathered information about your past achievements, personality type, skills and values. The final act of preparation, before you complete the definition of your product for **MMI, Inc**, will bring in the BE side, allowing access to your inner resources to express and include your hopes and dreams. The following exercise, called the "Ideal Working Day," will help bring the abstract skills and values you've assembled into a concrete picture of you in your ideal working environment.

The Ideal Working Day is similar to the imagination exercise used to develop your personal vision statement in Step 2. As before, if you find this type of exercise unfamiliar or difficult, keep in mind that there is immense practical value that can come from tapping your inner resources, helping you move beyond intellect and reason. Also keep in mind that using your imagination effectively takes practice, so don't be surprised if visual images don't immediately pop into your mind; keep trying.

There are three alternative ways to proceed with this imagination exercise. The best way is to have another person read the exercise to you while you listen and use your imagination. If that's not feasible, prepare by reading the exercise into a tape recorder in advance, and then when you're ready, play your tape recording while you listen and use your imagination to experience it. The final option is to read the exercise and pause each time when indicated, taking the time to experience it while you are reading. Whether someone else is reading for you or you're doing it for yourself, be sure the exercise is read slowly and thoughtfully, allowing plenty of time at each pause for the visual picture to emerge.

Before starting the exercise, create an environment that's conducive to being inner-focused: remove any distractions, such as bright lights, noises, or telephones.

Exercise:

Allow yourself to relax and to encourage your usually active mind to be at rest. Relax your body. Get comfortable in your chair and put your feet flat on the floor in order to feel grounded; keep your hands relaxed in your lap. When you feel comfortable, take several deep breaths low in your abdomen. As you breathe, be aware of places of tension in your body: neck, shoulders, jaw. Move those areas, trying consciously to relax them. Feel the tension draining out of your body. Still your mind, so that you can truly concentrate on the images your imagination creates.
(PAUSE)

In your mind's eye, see yourself in a grassy field. It is a pleasant sunny day, and a gentle breeze is moving the grass. As you look around you, take in the beauty and tranquillity of the scene.
(PAUSE)
As you continue to look around, you notice a hot air balloon nearby. Its many colors are beautiful against the bright blue sky. You see someone nearby and realize that the person, who is the pilot, is waiting for you. You walk over to the person and ask any questions you need to in order to feel confident and safe during the trip.
(PAUSE)
You find that the person is fully qualified and you give full consent to the adventure of riding in the balloon. You also discover that you will be traveling through time as well as space. You climb in and settle into a comfortable and safe place for the flight. The person fires up the balloon and it gently ascends into the blue of the sky for a brief flight. As you drift along, you realize that time is passing in an accelerated way.
(PAUSE)
After a few minutes, the person flying the balloon gently brings it down to land on the earth. You climb out of the balloon and thank the person for the flight. As you begin to look around, you realize that you have traveled five years into the future and arrived at your ideal working situation. With a growing sense of excitement, you walk toward the working place, which may be outside, in an office, or whatever is ideal for you. You become aware that it is morning and that the day is just beginning.
(PAUSE)
You look around with delight. Notice the working space. What is the environment around you? Is it exotic or familiar feeling? What items and colors do you see? What are you wearing? Who are you working with, or are you alone? See yourself doing the work. What are you doing?
(PAUSE)
Observe yourself as lunch time arrives. Where and what do you eat? With whom do you eat?
(PAUSE)
Continue through the rest of the day. What do you do, and with whom? Is there variety to your activities? Spend as much time as you need to get a very real sense of this ideal working time and place.
(PAUSE)
When you are ready, you walk back to the balloon and the pilot again invites you inside. You settle comfortably and safely for the return flight. Once you have landed, you realize that you have returned to your beginning time and place. You thank the pilot and exit the balloon.
Take a moment to reflect on your experience. When you feel ready, come back to the present time and place.

Your imagination of your "Ideal Working Day" contained many elements, including the setting, the people, the work you're doing and your activities. Which of these elements are essential to you—things that are critical for you to have in your work life—and which are optional—nice to have but not critically important? For example, in her ideal working day, Marion saw herself in a glass-front building in Carmel, California, with a view of the ocean. She was the food and fashion editor of the local newspaper and thoroughly enjoyed both the research and the writing involved with the position. For Marion, the glass-front building with the view is optional while the research and writing are essential. Both are at the heart of what would make for an ideal work environment.

Can you see how your personality type is reflected in your "Ideal Working Day"? How about your transferable skills? Your top 5 values?

You've just experienced a vision of your ideal working day, and analyzed it to discover what is most important about it. You've looked at some things vital to you and some things which are nice to have, but which you can do without. Now you can use this information, along with the other personal data you've assembled, to complete your product definition statement for **MMI, Inc.**

Your Product Definition Statement

You now have all the pieces of information you'll need to define what you will offer to the work world as **MMI, Inc.** So, exactly how are you going to transform these separate pieces of information into a coherent whole? You'll build a Product Definition Statement, which is a brief paragraph bringing personal aspects together in a statement that is *positive* and *active*. Preparing this statement will take some time and effort to think and rethink what goes into it, but the result will be a valuable statement of identity for **MMI, Inc.** It will also be very useful as you develop your marketing strategy. As examples, here's how two of the people we met earlier in Step 3 transformed their personal information into product definition statements.

Larry, our cabinet maker, discovered these things about himself:

- **Personality Type:** Introverted Sensing; quiet, values aesthetics and high quality, has a few friends that are a close-knit group, often skeptical and needs to be convinced.

- **Skills:** Good at and is motivated to use: construct/build, use hand dexterity, design, estimate, attend to details.

- **Values:** Make things, independence, disciplined, friendship, be in nature.

- **Ideal Working Day Essential Elements:** Working with my hands, creating something tangible with high quality craftsmanship that's appreciated by others, working independently and running my own show.

Larry's Product Definition Statement

I build and restore woodwork, including cabinets and furniture, for people who value quality. I enjoy renewing old wood pieces of high quality, and also designing and building something new to meet a customer's need. I work independently, but can also work well with craftspeople in other trades so long as they do quality work. My work expresses my belief that quality is important in a chaotic world.

Emma, who helped her roommate write a successful resume, discovered the following personal information about herself:

- **Personality Type:** Extroverted Sensing; practical and realistic; has a natural head for business and mechanics, not interested in abstract subjects; likes to organize.

- **Skills:** Good at and is motivated to use: plan/organize, classify, make arrangements, budget.

- **Values:** Loyalty, physical beauty around me, take responsibility, honesty.

- **Ideal Working Day Essential Elements:** Working with individuals with whom I have a good relationship, not cooped up behind a desk but being close to the beauty of the out-of-doors, and being given full responsibility for the various tasks involved in the work.

Emma's Product Definition Statement

I take initiative in planning, organizing and arranging things. I keep projects, plans and budgets on track. I see changes and make adjustments accordingly, and honestly communicate those changes with my team or partners. I enjoy working with and around things of beauty. I value the respect and loyalty of others, and treat others the same way.

Using your past achievements, personality type, top 5 skills, top 5 values and the essential elements of your Ideal Working Day, you can now create your own Product Definition Statement. This statement will represent what you, as **MMI, Inc**, will bring to the molecular marketplace. As you develop your statement, use these three questions as a guide to be sure it's focused and relevant:

- Is your statement directly applicable to your work?

- Is your statement positive, and stated in the present ("I do," rather than "I will")?

- Do you use action-oriented words whenever possible ("I do...," "I create...," "I initiate...," "I lead...," "I bring...," "I excel...," etc.)?

Case Studies

1. *Shannon*

The idea of thinking of myself as a product first struck me as a bit demeaning. It seems so impersonal, like I'm one of lots of similar items out there that needs a good ad campaign to make me "seem" valuable. But as I went through all of the activities, I began to see that the point wasn't that I was interchangeable; rather, it was to define exactly why I *wasn't* the same as everyone and everything else out there.

I enjoyed finding out something about my own personality type, but I think the most helpful part of that section for me was the information about working well (or not working well) with people of other types. In one recent work situation, I regularly described one of my colleagues as being from outer space! With knowledge of different personality types, maybe I could learn to get along with him better.

As far as skills, I sympathized with the guy who could only come up with a few. I'm pretty young and haven't really settled into a work pattern, so my list of "work-specific" skills always leaves something to be desired. But the number of transferable skills I had surprised me, as did their significance in the Molecular Marketplace.

The most surprising things for me in doing Step 3 were values and Ideal Working Day. Of course I realized that values are important for life, relationships, etc., but work seemed like another thing entirely. Taking the time to associate values and dreams with work still feels a bit threatening; am I setting myself up for a disappointment when I take this product out into the real world? But on the other hand, trying to incorporate values into work and do the "right" work for me makes good sense; if I have to spend so much time working, it might as well have some meaning for me.

The important information that came out of Step 3 for me was:

- Personality Type—ETN
- Primary Skills—synthesize; write; teach/train; make decisions; implement

- Top 5 Values—explore ideas; experience variety; independence; caring; competent
- Essential elements of Ideal Working Day—high level of responsibility; enough income to support my chosen lifestyle; professional but not stuffy; lots of variety in work and interaction with people; travel; working with words.

The Product Definition Statement that I came up with out of these pieces is:

I get things done in a timely and effective way, while maintaining good team relationships. I take responsibility and feel comfortable with leadership, working well both independently and with others. I thrive on variety and new challenges, meeting or surpassing expectations. My expertise in working with words gives me great communication and writing skills.

2. *Brent*

After the week I spent working on my vision statement, creating a Product Definition Statement in Step 3 seemed much easier—it certainly took less time. I think one important reason for this is that I was able to use my vision statement as a tool to honestly evaluate my Product Definition Statement. I can't imagine satisfactorily finishing Step 3 without doing Step 2 first!

I learned a lot about myself from the skills and values worksheets, but I found the skills worksheet a bit overwhelming at first. Trying to complete it by working horizontally—assessing my ability to do a skill, judging my level of motivation for it, and deciding whether it was one of my "best skills"—was too complicated. Working vertically—first finishing my ability assessments, then assigning all the levels of motivation, then picking my best skills—made the task much easier for me.

While finishing this Step, I came up with the following information about myself. Although none of it came as a shock to me, it was amazing to see so many core truths about myself written on one piece of paper.

- Personality Type—INT.
- Top 5 Skills—designing, visualizing, inventing, problem solving, and computer operating skills; mostly from the analytical and creative skill groups.
- Values—making things (which I broadened to include creating and designing), experiencing variety, recognition (to which I added being needed), family harmony, and leisure time.
- Ideal Working Day Essential Elements—variety, creativity, working on many small projects, using a wide range of creative and analytic skills, and staying out of stifling corporate environments.

My product definition statement practically wrote itself:

I develop solutions to a wide variety of technical problems using my unique blend of analytic, creative, and artistic skills. I enjoy using computers both as an invaluable organizational and analytic tool and as a canvas on which to explore my artistic interests. My endeavors, while fulfilling in themselves, also support and enhance my strongest loves—my wife and children.

I believe that this statement will be of great value to me. Before, when I chose jobs based on pay or benefits or some other lure, I was surprised when I lost interest with them in a couple of months or years. Now I have a tool that will help me make decisions based on what I fundamentally want out of a job, which makes my career direction much clearer and more satisfying.

3. *Emily*

I've spent a lot of time in the past identifying my skills, values and personality type. The part that I found to be exciting and new was putting all of these pieces together into a Product Definition Statement, which draws the separate ideas into one cohesive whole focused on **MMI, Inc.**

Since I interact with the world as an Introvert, I found that I very much identified with the woman who wanted to take a hot bath after a conference to try to make sense of the experiences of the day rather than going out to discuss the ideas with others. I observe the world mainly through my senses and also have a strong Feeling side, making decisions based on what is clearly right and wrong (at least to me!) So I am an ISF personality type.

The transferable skills that are most important to me are: teaching; counseling; organizational skills; using physical co-ordination; and listening —with the clear category winner being in the area of Service.

Deciding on what I most value was not difficult for me: I would like to *help diverse people* as one of my top values. I would also like to be in an environment where I can spend time *doing research. Integrity* and *recognition* are important. Finally, it is important to me to be *spiritual*—or to constantly be growing in my awareness in this area.

So my Product Definition Statement is as follows:

Because I am a strong Introvert Sensing Feeling personality type, I am interested in working in an environment which enables me to focus on a one-to-one counseling situation. I would also do better working in a physical environment with attractive surroundings, preferably with windows that have inspiring views. I am excellent in teaching and counseling environments—especially with diverse populations where interesting points of view, life experiences, and needs capture my interest in helping people and also my desire for variety in a work setting. I am also good at doing independent research and enjoy spending time on this type of project.

4. *Forrest*

So here I was, thinking about another career change quite late in life by most people's standards. At least it was a positive step for me, not something I had to do in a crisis, so I felt very lucky. Now I knew a lot more about the work environment and had a vision for myself, but how exactly did it all fit into what I was going to do for a living while I got financially ready to retire?

I'm familiar with the basics of personality typing; my type is ENT. What was a new idea for me was how I might have worked differently with others in the past if I'd thought about their type and how it mixed with mine.

I felt sure about some of my skills, particularly those dealing with the specific and technical aspects of my work in telecommunications. From the transferable skills worksheet my top five are: problem solve, listen, influence, organize and advise. I knew I could do these things, but I'd never thought about them as marketable skills before—like selling or designing.

Picking my values was harder—I liked them all. But by agonizing over some tough choices, my top five values are: create things, organize things, wisdom, integrity and caring.

From the ideal working day imagination exercise the essential elements for me are: working with people; influencing how others see things; sharing ideas and developing new ideas with others; and finding ways to improve things in others' lives and in my own as well.

My product definition statement is:

> *I provide ideas, advice and/or assistance to companies that are building or changing telecommunications customer service centers. My work brings more value than it costs my customers. I work with multiple customers to keep learning fresh ideas and to see what works best, in order to share the best practices with my customers. My proposals support the best interests of three stakeholder groups: my customer, my customer's customer, and my customer's employees or contractors.*

Step 4

Develop Your Livelihood

Mohammed, a 22-year-old graduating college senior:
I studied marketing with the idea of working for a small business and eventually owning my own company. I learned a lot about myself in college, and after six years in fast foods I know I don't want to keep flipping burgers. But now it's crunch time—I have to get a job, and the best offer for work I've had so far was to be a management trainee for a fast food chain. I'm really confused about what to do now, to get where I want to go.

From your work with Step 3, you now have a pretty good idea of who you are and what product you want to take into the molecular marketplace. Like Mohammed, you may now face this critical question: "Just how will my product—**MMI, Inc**—fit into the molecular marketplace?"

It used to be so simple. People were part of the work force, they were in a trade or occupation where they held a job or maybe even had a career, and most of them worked until they retired on a pension with health care benefits. Life was good (well, less complicated, anyway.) Now the whole thing is being turned upside down. Jobs often come and go and never seem to last very long. Careers don't seem to stay on a single track, and benefits are reduced if they're offered at all.

We now know that each worker in the US will hold an average of eight different jobs during his or her working life, and the number is climbing. The average term of a single job is about three years. As a worker today,

73

you have to develop a new mindset. You'll need to approach each job as though it were a temporary position, and plan for how each position fits into your work future.

Creating this new mindset and approach to your work will involve making some new decisions, or at least reassessing old decisions you've made in the light of new information. In this Step and Step 5 you'll make three critical decisions: field of endeavor, livelihood (traditionally called occupation or profession), and a new category that's become very important in the molecular marketplace—your niche.

Field Of Endeavor And Livelihood

Field of endeavor is the broadest category for work. Each field of endeavor encompasses a number of livelihoods. Normally, when you've settled on a field of endeavor, it's a long-term decision that won't often change in your working life. The selection of a field of endeavor tends to be permanent because you often have to qualify or be trained to enter it in the first place, and it isn't always easy to requalify for another field later.

The list below includes some examples of fields of endeavor and some typical livelihoods associated with each.

Field of Endeavor	Livelihood
Health Care	Physician, Nurse, Administrator, Dentist, Assistant, Veterinarian
Construction	Carpenter, Plumber, Architect, Equipment operator, Electrician
Religion	Minister, Priest, Rabbi, Teacher, Nun, Monk
Computer Science	Systems designer, Systems analyst, Software engineer, Operator
Education	Math professor, Drama coach, Administrator, Tutor, Librarian
Manufacturing	Assembler, Line maintainer, Engineer, Manager, Machinist
Social Work	Family counselor, Caseworker, Recreation director, Nurse, Clerk
Marketing	Salesperson, Marketing rep, Market research director
Management	CEO, Director, Manager, Supervisor, Union agent, Consultant
Financial services	Stock broker, Insurance agent, Accountant, Banker, Bookkeeper
Arts	Musician, Fine artist, Movie director, Actor
Design	Architect, Graphics designer, Landscape designer, Web site designer

In the molecular marketplace, the lines that used to define fields of endeavor and livelihoods are becoming blurred for two reasons. First, the way we work today creates livelihoods that often don't fit the old occupational definitions. Second, even existing livelihoods are being restructured in ways that make the concept of occupation less useful.

For example, Julia was hired thirteen years ago at a snack food plant to put packages of potato chips into cardboard cartons. It was boring but steady work. The plant completely reorganized three years ago, and now Julia works as a leader of a team that does everything in the plant—slicing and processing potatoes, maintaining processing equipment, packaging and shipping, quality control, analyzing reports to improve financial performance, and interviewing new team members. Julia knows that making potato chips is her livelihood, but what's her occupation? It's hard to say.

Like Julia's, many new livelihoods have been created in the last few years. Here are some more examples:

Personal shopper	Telecommuting advisor
Internet trainer	Agricultural geneticist
Multimedia journalist	Computer network specialist
Cloning geneticist	Web page developer
Consultant on aging	Nanotechnologist
High speed transport developer	Gene researcher
Mobile auto detailer	Multimedia designer
Ready-to-eat home food	Video conference arranger
deliverer	Temporary/consultant CEO
Virtual reality developer	Women's studies instructor
Personal fitness trainer	Buddy broker (friend-finding
Satellite data specialist	service)

What'll It Be For You?

Even though fields of endeavor and livelihoods are becoming less precisely defined, the fact remains that while you are working for a living, at any given time you'll have one of each. Together, they are a description of how you're going to bring your vision and product definition of **MMI, Inc** to market.

Perhaps you're already certain of your future livelihood—because you're working there now and know you want to continue, or because you've already figured out that your skills and values clearly point you in one direction, like equipment operator, teacher or architect. On the other hand, maybe you haven't yet decided on the field and livelihood you want to work in. Perhaps you're just starting out into the world of work, like Mohammed in our opening example. Or maybe you're planning to make a complete change in what you do for a living: you're bored, you're retiring from one job but want to continue working, the physical demands of your work dictate a change, you want to gain new skills, you want to make more money, or you can see downsizing in your future.

If you already have your livelihood in mind, here are some things you can do to help you feel certain that you're headed in the right direction. If you haven't yet picked a field of endeavor and livelihood for **MMI, Inc**, these ideas will help guide you toward a decision that's right for you.

- Share your Product Definition Statement with a friend, partner, and/or a co-worker, and ask the other person to help in brainstorming suggestions about your livelihood.

- Look back at the achievements you identified in Step 3. Do any patterns or preferences emerge that suggest a livelihood for you?

- Think back to what you really wanted to be when you were a child. These early dreams may have expressed a deeply-felt pull toward a fulfilling livelihood for you.

- Your field of endeavor and livelihood can have a significant impact on your lifestyle. Issues that can affect your lifestyle include geographical location, relocation requirements, child care, workplace flexibility, flex time, telecommuting, dress or uniform requirements, requirements to work indoors or outdoors, and travel. Can you foresee lifestyle issues that rule out certain livelihoods for your consideration, or that suggest a livelihood would be right for you?

- Look back at your Best Skills from page 59 in Step 3, and review the following list of typical examples of livelihoods associated with each of the skill categories.

Skill Category	Example Livelihoods
Technical/Mechanical	Equipment operator, Mechanic, Electronics technician, Computer operator, Engineer, Appliance repair person, Electrician, Draftsperson, Driver, Systems analyst, Building inspector, Printer, Gemologist
Analytical	Financial analyst, Information manager, Administrative assistant, Appraiser, Programmer, Mathematician, Quality controller, Engineer, Purchasing agent, Architect, Paleontologist, Geneticist, Statistician
Creative	Performing artist, Visual artist, Craftmaker, Sound designer, Performance director, Musician, Composer, Chef, Editor, Fashion designer, Architect, Writer, Graphic designer, Web site designer, Event planner
Service	Social worker, Educator, Health professional, Psychologist, Counselor, Religious director, Customer service representative, Librarian, Dietitian, Pharmacist, Diplomat, Mediator, Spiritualist, Athletic director, Emergency medical technician, Law enforcement officer, Food service worker
Physical	Athlete, Mason, Carpenter, House painter, Forest

	berjack, Laborer, Agricultural worker, Veterinary assistant, Gardener, Landscaper, Animal breeder, Building maintenance worker, Military enlisted person, Assembler
Manage/ Persuade	Retail salesperson, Advertising manager, Motivational speaker, Supervisor, Real estate salesperson, Lawyer, Lobbyist, Manager, Stock broker, Negotiator, Contract administrator, Talent agent, Manufacturer's representative, Collections agent, Military officer
Detail/ Organize	Project manager, Funeral director, Programmer, Researcher, Records manager, Accountant, Data entry worker, Budget analyst, Antiques collector, Event coordinator, Administrator, Lab technician, Transcriptionist, Print shop assistant

If you haven't yet made a decision about your field of endeavor or your livelihood, you've reached the point where it's time to do so. If you've already made an earlier decision, use this opportunity to rethink and reaffirm your decision based on any new information or insights from the above ideas. Either way, this is an important decision with a lot at stake. How can you be sure your decision is the best one for you?

The Skill Of Making A Decision

Like any other skill, decision-making can be mastered and done well, or it can be done haphazardly. Why do we say that decision-making is a skill? Isn't making a decision just a rapid, almost unconscious response that happens many times every day, in the natural course of living your life? The answer is "Yes—and no."

People make surprisingly few decisions based on conscious consideration of the relevant issues, especially when faced with a decision they'd rather not make. When you face a tough decision, you may find yourself procrastinating, postponing, hiding from the facts, or denying the need to make a decision. There are a lot of ways to avoid a decision by not taking action.

For example, if a family member asks you to come and help with a project while you're engrossed in a TV show, you can decide to go help or to stay with your program. If you make a decision, you'll act accordingly: going to help, or replying that you won't. But you can also do nothing, ignore the request, and take no action at all. Maybe that's all you ever hear of it, or maybe the other person gets angry, or asks again. The result is out of your hands, rather than being influenced by your conscious decision and action. If you exclude the situations where you don't consciously act to resolve an issue, you probably don't make as many decisions as you might think.

But if you avoid making a decision, the situation will still be resolved some other way. Things will progress along the path of least resistance, whatever happens will occur without your conscious involvement, and you've lost the initiative. The problem is that the resolution may not be in your best interests. In the example above, if you make no decision and ignore the request for help, you could find later that your lack of response has caused friction in your relationship with the other person. Assuring that the important decisions in your life are made consciously, and that the outcome is in your best interests, requires a degree of attention be paid to decision-making—and this is why it's a skill.

Gregory Vlastos, a noted philosopher, put an interesting twist on the subject of making a decision in 1934, when he said: "To compromise...is to decide; to postpone or evade is to decide; to hide the matter is to decide...there are a thousand ways of saying NO; one way of saying YES; and no way of saying anything else."

So how can you build your skill in making decisions, assuring that important issues are resolved in your best interests? Here's a straight-forward process that will help you understand how to make decisions consciously, and be sure that you're not letting opportunities slip by. Although the examples used to illustrate the process are work-related, improving your skill in making decisions will be helpful in every area of your life.

The Decision-Making Process

Phase 1: Perceive Reality

Making a decision starts with being open to and clearly understand-ing the issue to be resolved. This understanding occurs at two levels, the inner (BE) and the outer (DO). For your decision about your field and livelihood, at the outer level you'll need to be aware of what trends are impacting the employment market, which livelihoods are hot and which are not, and where workers today are and are not finding job satisfaction. At the inner level, you'll need to keep in mind your own vision and product definition statement for **MMI, Inc** as standards against which to weigh your thinking as you go through the process.

Meet Sally, whose experience we'll follow as an example of how the process works. Sally has worked for the same company as a sales representative for a number of years, and is no longer feeling challenged. She's a person who enjoys taking care of details and keeping on the move. Sally is outgoing, has a lot of friends, and entertains often in her home. She's also a fastidious housekeeper, one of the rare people who actually enjoys the work involved in keeping her home clean and neat.

Phase 2: Understand Motivation

The decision-making process continues as you become fully aware of what is motivating you to make a decision. Why does it matter to you that this issue is resolved? Do you want to change something that's wrong, or to move toward something that's more attractive? Are you confident that you have your priorities straight, including those from your BE side? For the decision you face on your field and livelihood, you now have a lot of information that will help you identify what you're motivated to move toward—including your vision, product definition and ideal working day—and what you're motivated to move away from.

Sally recognized that she had two primary motivations to make a decision. She had a strong need to move away from work that didn't challenge her, and a deep desire to work at something she loved, found challenging, and which allowed her to be her own boss, if possible.

Phase 3: Brainstorm Ideas

This is the point where you'll unleash your creativity, drawing from your BE side to develop ideas. Based on your perception of the issue and a clear picture of what's motivating you, what kind of new alternatives might resolve the issue? Develop as many alternatives as you can, including your wildest and craziest ideas. For the decision you face on your field and livelihood, create lots of ideas for work situations that would allow you to avoid what you haven't enjoyed in past jobs, while fitting well with your vision, product definition and ideal working day.

Sally brainstormed some interesting ideas, but felt she hadn't fully explored the possibilities. She decided to get several friends and relatives involved and to also include their ideas. Working with other people helped her generate a lot of new alternatives, which fell into four general categories:

- do the same work in another corporate setting;

- learn a new area of her present employer's business;

- start her own business using her present work skills;

- do something new, based on her other interests.

Phase 4: Narrow Options

Start by eliminating all of those alternatives that are "non-starters." These will include ideas that violate a basic value (for example, something illegal or unethical) or ones that put an excessive burden on you or others you care about (for example, something requiring long absences from loved ones). Brainstorming will produce some wild ideas and some great new alternatives; the unworkable ideas can be eliminated, reducing the viable ideas to a manageable number. When you have a reasonable number of viable alternatives, continue the process of elimination by considering how well each alternative matches what is motivating you to make the decision. One way to do this is to set up a chart to help you objectively compare alternatives—a pro and con matrix. For the decision you face on your field and livelihood, look back at what's motivating you from Phase 2 to identify what you value most about your work, and then compare how well each alternative helps you reach those values.

Sally eliminated a lot of her brainstorm ideas as non-starters, especially some of her new business ideas, which would have required lots of money or training. The two new business ideas that remained were starting her own marketing business and starting a maid service business. Here's the pro and con matrix that Sally used to weigh her serious alternatives. There are many ways this can be done, but Sally simply rated each of the alternatives against what was important to her: P for "pro," C for "con" and blank for neutral. She added up the P's for each alternative, subtracted the C's, and the resulting score gave her a priority ranking of her alternatives.

Alternatives: ➡ Values: ⬇	Change comp- anies	New posi- tion, same company	Start own marketing business	Start own maid business
Work at what I love			P	P
Find a new challenge		P		P
Be my own boss	C	C	P	P
Increase my income		C		
See new places and meet new people	P	C	P	P
Total P (pro)	1	1	3	4
Minus total C (con)	-1	-3	-0	-0
Score (higher is better)	0	-2	3	4

When starting her own maid business emerged as the top alternative, Sally realized she didn't yet know enough about such an enterprise to make a decision. She continued her narrowing process by doing some additional research to assure herself that the result of her comparison of alternatives was valid. She headed to her local library to read up on industry trends, statistics and demographics. In the process, she discovered that 80% of American women will work outside the home and that 80% of two-income households will have household help by the year 2000. Her business idea was looking more and more attractive!

Phase 5: Decide

You've now prepared yourself to make a conscious, informed decision to pursue one of your alternatives. The decision may not necessarily be painless, because often no alternative satisfies all aspects of what's motivating you. But having laid out all of your needs and preferences for review, you'll know that your decision will be based on considering all the relevant information, and will be in your best interests.

Sally's decision was to start her own maid service business. It was an emotional moment for her when she concluded that she was going to leave her familiar work environment and her friends there. However, once she made up her mind she felt a great sense of relief and a rush of excitement about where this decision was going to lead her.

Phase 6: Clarify Approach

Before you act, it's important to design the action you'll take. Taking time to carefully consider your action will help you implement the decision in a way that will actually produce the outcome you intend. This phase may be unimportant for small decisions, but it can be crucial to the right outcome for the biggies—those that impact your life. For your decision about your field and livelihood, use whatever internal and external resources you need to determine how to implement your decision to achieve a successful outcome. Your resources include your vision and product definition statement, and information you can gather from additional research about your livelihood. If you've decided to keep working in your present livelihood, you already know a great deal about it. If you'll be entering a new field or livelihood, the research you'll do in Step 5 will help you complete the clarification phase.

Sally clarified her approach to action in several ways. She ordered an informational binder from the Small Business Administration about how to set up and operate this type of business. By joining her local chamber of commerce, she expanded her list of network contacts to include more people who run their own businesses. She did field research, contacting other people running maid services to learn about day-to-day operations and their level of job satisfaction. Sally worried that the other business owners would see her as an unwelcome competitor, but found that they treated her warmly. In fact, when they realized she had a marketing background, they sought her advice on how they could build a cooperative marketing plan for their "cottage industry."

Phase 7: Act

Your decision will require action. If no action is required, then it's not really a decision but simply a situation being resolved by the path of least resistance. Even if your decision is to stay with the status quo, you'll take action by stopping your search for a change. Whether you've decided to remain in your present livelihood or to embark on a new one, you'll have plenty of action ahead as you develop and live out your vision for **MMI, Inc.**

Sally began acting on her decision by resigning from her job and starting to set up her own business. The details seemed endless— getting licenses, insurance, equipment, financial backing, a lawyer and an accountant; developing marketing plans with a catchy logo, a unique cleaning system and a potential customer base; and hiring and training employees. She was thrilled to find she enjoyed learning about the details of a business, and loved not having to keep someone else's schedule. A few weeks later at a party with her former co-workers she told them: "This is the best thing I've ever done. I know it will be interesting and fulfilling for a few years. By then, I bet I'll be ready to re-examine my work situation again, and who knows? Maybe I'll decide to take yet another route."

Final Thoughts on Making A Decision

Notice how much your BE side is involved in the first four phases of the decision-making process. Involving the BE aspect is necessary in order to DO appropriately. People often try to short-circuit the decision-making process by jumping too quickly to decision and action without doing the preparation. The result is often a bad decision—one which does not lead toward the intended goal.

Even if your decision is a good one, made skillfully, you still can't see around corners to know with certainty how future circumstances may change the outcome of a decision. Reflect on a life-impacting decision you've made in the past—for example, going off to school, getting married or having a child—and you'll probably observe that the outcome was very different from anything you had originally visualized.

But whether or not you accurately predict the outcome, and whether or not your decisions are always right, both you as a person and you as **MMI, Inc** will fare better if your decisions are based on this seven-phase process—conscious, informed and well thought-through. The alternative is to be a victim of circumstances that are just flowing along the path of least resistance. Will Rogers said it well: "Even if you're on the right track, you'll get run over if you just sit there."

Making Your Livelihood Decision

Choosing your livelihood is one of the most important decisions you'll ever make. Using the decision-making process can help to assure that you make the best choice, based on the information you have to work with at the time. Before you make your own livelihood decision let's see how Mohammed, our graduating college senior who didn't want to flip any more burgers, used the phases of the decision-making process to select his livelihood:

1. Perceive reality: Mohammed felt that on his way to becoming an entrepreneur, he should first get some marketing experience in a small business. But he quickly found that it was impossible for him to find a marketing position armed only with a college degree and no experience. As he interviewed prospective employers, the only marketing positions he was offered were in fast foods. He didn't abandon his vision for the future, but decided to explore a number of options that he hadn't considered earlier. He talked with many people he met in the fast-food restaurant where he worked part-time and got lots of suggestions, opinions and advice—some good and some not so good.

2. Understand motivation: As he was preparing to graduate from college, Mohammed faced strong financial and family pressures to begin working full-time, and to represent his family's pride in his education. In addition, he personally wanted to start paying off his student loans and begin moving toward the vision he developed in Step 2, starting with owning a nice car and having a home of his own. Later, he wanted to marry and have a family, but he thought it would be wonderful if he could work and live abroad for awhile before he settled down. He wanted to gain a broad set of marketing skills and selling experience that would help him with his own business in the future, and to begin studies for an MBA degree fairly soon.

3. Brainstorm ideas: Mohammed listed the ideas for work that he'd heard from others and added some of his own. The suggestions were mostly to begin by going into retail selling. One particularly interesting idea came from the route sales/delivery woman for the soft-drink company that served the fast-food restaurant where he worked. In her company, all new marketing management trainees start with a sales/delivery route where they generate sales, manage accounts and deliver products to learn the business from the ground up. If successful, they quickly progress to corporate marketing positions. Mohammed wanted to consider some bolder ideas as well, so he drew on his memory of childhood "dream jobs" such as being a firefighter and inventing a computer game. He also spent two afternoons at the career center at his university and added several more ideas from the research he did there.

4. Narrow options: After Mohammed felt he had a thorough list of ideas, he tested each against his long-term vision of owning a business, which eliminated a lot of possibilities. What remained on his list for serious consideration were three possible positions: management trainee with the fast-food chain where he now worked; retail sales in an upscale men's clothing store with a promise to move into an assistant manager position in one year if all went well; and the route sales/delivery position with a soft-drink company which could lead to a great marketing position. He used a pro and con matrix to compare how well each alternative met his work values. For his matrix, shown below, he used one or more pluses (+) for positives, zeroes (0) for neutrals, and minuses (-) for negatives.

Alternatives: Values:	Fast Food Manage- ment Trainee	Clothing Retail Sales	Soft Drink Sales/ Delivery
Maximum income	0	0	+
Prestige	-	+	0
Gain broad-based marketing skills	+	-	+
Possibility of international opportunity	+	-	++
Preparation for business ownership	0	+	-
Assistance for MBA degree	+	0	+
Total + (pro)	3	2	5
Minus total - (con)	- 1	-2	- 1
Score (higher is better)	2	0	4

5. Decide: Based on his matrix, Mohammed saw that the highest score was associated with working for the soft-drink company. He reviewed again the advantages and disadvantages of the decision to be sure he'd considered all the important factors. He knew he'd have to drive a route and work hard physically for at least a year which didn't sound very attractive, but on reflection he decided a route would give him real hands-on experience in consumer marketing. And some of the other advantages were indisputable—good pay, an opportunity to get good experience in a premier marketing company, and possibly even an opportunity to work overseas after he'd worked for the company for a couple of years. He decided it was the right choice.

6. Clarify approach: Even though the soft-drink company had sent recruiters to his campus a few months earlier, Mohammed hadn't talked with them because at the time he thought he wasn't interested in a position with their company. Now that he'd learned more about their marketing trainee positions and had decided to try for one, he remembered that the route salesperson had assured him that she could easily arrange for an interview with the company if he was interested. Mohammed decided to ask her how to proceed when he saw her the next day. He then returned to the career center and visited his library to read everything he could find on the company.

7. Act: The next day, Mohammed told the route salesperson he'd like an interview with the company, and she gave him the name of the person to call. Using her as a reference, Mohammed was able to schedule an interview for the following week. He used his time before the interview to do further research on the company, creating and refining a list of questions he would ask at the interview.

The decision-making process and examples have provided you with enough information to now make—or to reconfirm—your livelihood decision. If you still aren't able to reach a decision at this point, you may need additional help. For more self-help information on reaching a livelihood decision, a good resource is *Wishcraft*, by Barbara Sher. Alternatively, you may want to obtain the guidance of a certified career counselor. Through discussions and tests, a career counselor will help you understand your aptitudes, skills and preferences which will suggest possible fields for you to research and choose from. You can find a career counselor in the yellow pages of your phone book, or you can be referred to a counselor in your area by telephoning the National Board for Certified Counselors at 1-910-547-0607. In addition, schools, colleges and many larger employers often have career centers, with resources available which can help you decide.

Finding Your Best Work

Choosing the right field and livelihood is important in matching your work to your own needs and preferences. But it's seldom possible to find a perfect match between **MMI, Inc** and your livelihood. It may be that the perfect position—one which exactly matches your vision and product definition—doesn't exist, or that the perfect position *does* exist, but it just doesn't pay enough to support your family! This collision with reality may be a strong source of cognitive dissonance, leading to feelings of anger and resentment.

For example, in selecting a livelihood, you may have had to compromise some of your income expectations in order to meet your strong preference for working outdoors. Perhaps you selected a design engineering livelihood for practical reasons. The design work will allow some self-expression, but doesn't involve enough creativity to fully satisfy your artistic talents. Or, like Mohammed, maybe you'll start with an entry-level position which isn't your ideal and use it as a stepping stone to something better. Because you're a human, not an automaton, you'll have complicated and sometimes conflicting goals and preferences, and by definition these will create some areas where **MMI, Inc** and your livelihood don't fit perfectly together.

How good a fit is good enough? Different people will have different needs and tolerances; only you will know. But looking at the situation as a picture can help. In the diagrams below, one oval represents **MMI, Inc** based on your vision and product definition, and the other your livelihood. The area of overlap represents where they match up: if a 100% fit would be perfect but is unlikely, what level of fit is good enough? These diagrams show two different levels of fit: 40%, which is probably unacceptable, and 80%, which may be within an acceptable range.

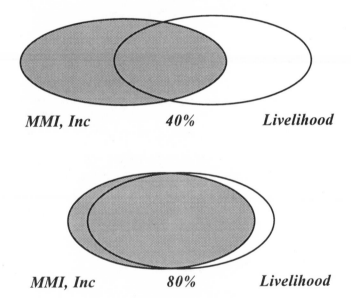

MMI, Inc   *40%*   *Livelihood*

MMI, Inc   *80%*   *Livelihood*

How well do you feel that **MMI, Inc** and your livelihood decision fit together? If you find that the fit is not good enough, how can you modify your decision on field of endeavor and livelihood—or your vision and product definition statements—to improve the fit?

Your work experiences will provide lots of varied, first-hand information about where to find work that fits you best. One of the great advantages of being a portfolio worker in the molecular marketplace is that you will probably experience numerous work assignments, niches and even livelihoods. So if you're in a situation with a poor product fit, it's likely that before long you'll move on to another assignment where you may be able to create a better fit from the outset. If you choose to remain in an assignment for a longer term, your experiences will help you "bloom where you're planted," improving the fit of whatever you're doing by creating the right niche.

Creating the right niche for **MMI, Inc** is a critical part of assuring that you enjoy what you do, and that you do it well enough to be successful in a competitive environment. You'll learn how to create the right niche for **MMI, Inc** in Step 5.

Case Studies

1. *Shannon*

I knew as soon as I started reading Step 4 that this was where I really needed to work. The short opening example about Mohammed—young, had some skills, didn't want to be stuck doing something dead-end—had me saying "I can relate." At first I wondered why someone like me couldn't just start here on Step 4, but I had to keep reminding myself that there's more to this than getting "a good job."

At the same time, the idea of actually making a commitment to one path felt uncomfortably restricting to me. Do I really have to know what I'll do for the rest of my life by the end of Step 4? What if I'm wrong, or don't like it when I get there? I realized I was scared to dive into this section of the process because it felt like there would be no turning back. What convinced me to keep going was the knowledge that I want to move ahead in my work, and the scattered way I've worked up until now wasn't getting me anywhere.

I found that the list of "cutting-edge" livelihoods was a fun way to think more widely about what I could do. I actually went and found out what a "video conference arranger" does (by talking to one). I also found the question about livelihood and lifestyle helpful. I'm very aware of what I want my lifestyle to be like: flexible, creative, and involving travel, for starters. Since lifestyle is clearer to me than what I want to do for work, using my lifestyle requirements to help choose a livelihood makes sense.

I chose four possible directions for **MMI, Inc**: information or systems manager, educator/trainer, health professional, and mediator/negotiator. The last possibility on the list sounded interesting to me, but I had hardly any idea what it meant! Still more things to explore ...

The idea that making good decisions is a skill, and that making bad decisions has serious consequences, made sense to me, but my first impression was the process itself seemed very involved. When I completed the process I realized it was important to be this thorough for big decisions, although I was still firmly stuck between two livelihood alternatives: educator/trainer and mediator/negotiator. I knew a lot more about training than about mediating, but with what I did know they both came up about even. While mediators make more money, people in training are in a supportive environment; mediators have to deal a lot with hostility, while training is seen as optional or even counter-productive in many companies right now. I made an appointment with a career counselor at the community college where I've taken some classes. As I talked to her, she was glad to hear I'd done some thinking already, and suggested that I could both learn more about myself and about my career alternatives at the career center on campus.

At the career appointment I took some aptitude and other tests, which supported both my choices as making sense for me. With the counselor's help, I also got some more information about both livelihoods, including job projections and other job market information. She also pointed out that the two choices don't have to be mutually exclusive; a trainer could go into mediation, and a negotiator could teach or train. However, I still needed to decide. Even though I'm career decision-challenged, I could tell after the appointment that the option I was most interested in was education and training. In the long run it fits me better, though it's less glamorous. And with what I now know about the field, I think that the fit between **MMI, Inc** and training could be 80% or better, especially if I can customize my approach to the livelihood.

2. Brent

At this point in the process, I began to feel like I was jumping off the cliff into the unknown with an untested parachute. It made me realize that I rely on my livelihood—even if it's not my ideal livelihood—for security. This step forced me to look at my livelihood with a critical eye and a bold mandate: "If it doesn't fit, change it!" Even *considering* letting go of my last bit of security was frightening.

Then, just as I started brainstorming a new livelihood, I learned that due to a recent merger and resulting downsizing, my company was dismantling my entire organization! Shutting down that project was like losing a loved one, with all the shock, loss, and mourning that accompany it. Now that I'd been pushed off the cliff I'd dreaded jumping from, I suddenly had a powerful motivation to complete the 10-Step process!

I started brainstorming like crazy! I talked to my wife, my friends, and my co-workers—and explored the Internet sites of a number of companies (mostly my company's competitors, but also a few places I've always been interested in). I also added my company's current job openings in other groups to the mix. At the end of three days, I had a list of 54 possible livelihoods.

I narrowed the list down to the three most likely possibilities: continue working with the same technology but at a different company, move to a project management position within my present company, or become an animator at a leading computer graphics company. I used a decision matrix with values taken directly from my vision and product definition statements, and "animator" came out the clear winner. It had everything I wanted: complex and unique projects, a blend of technical and artistic skills, and heavy computer use. Its only drawback was the occasional overtime requirements that would take me from my family.

Delighted at this new prospect, I contacted an animator at one of the companies and arranged an informational interview. He told me that the computer modeling work I had done in the aerospace industry made me an excellent candidate, but a prospective employer would need to see a portfolio of completely rendered images before anyone would consider hiring me.

That's when reality kicked in. My company had given me 60 days to find a new job, and in order to build a decent portfolio, submit it to a number of animation houses, and wait for offers would take far longer than that. I had mouths to feed, a mortgage, car payments, and no cash reserves to speak of—in short, I couldn't afford to be without a job.

I was heartbroken, and I blamed this book. I felt the book had done me a disservice by describing a simplistic process that doesn't work in the "real" world, and I resented it. But then I re-read Steps 2 and 3, trying to find out where the book had misled me, and I realized that I had instead misinterpreted the information. MMI, Inc is not a goal but a process. Like any business, I would sometimes have to do things that didn't exactly match my values and product definition while I worked toward things that would.

I rebuilt my decision matrix, adding "real world" values like "good transferable skills" and "can start right away without training or preparation." This time, with a better definition of my values, taking a project management position at my present company came up the winner. I talked to my company's director of project management; who said my previous work experience would certainly qualify me for an entry-level position, with a likely promotion in four to six months once I proved my skills.

So I'm going for a project management job, and my view of MMI, Inc has changed. My vision and product definition statements now include words about consistent income and financial security. But I'm also now committed to building my computer graphics portfolio with a few impressive images to try for that animation job in a year or two.

3. *Emily*

I had to laugh when I first read the section in this chapter about the importance of making a considered and conscious decision when thinking about a livelihood. Two years ago, with our children out of the house, at least temporarily, I was ready and eager to go to work "in the real world".

This would enable me to contribute in a new way both to my own personal development and to the family finances which were in need of an infusion.

I already had a Bachelor's degree in Psychology and knew I wanted to continue in this arena. After that given, the sole consideration when it came to making a decision about which graduate program to pursue was which one would take the shortest amount of time, allowing me to jump quickly into the world of work. I read the catalogue of the state university near my home and, when I found a graduate program that would take only one year to complete, that was it for me! So after going through all of the testing and registration processes, I found myself in an Educational Psychology graduate program. Being a person who's more verbal than mathematical, imagine my surprise when I realized, after starting the very first class, that this course of study focused on learning about and performing statistical analyses, explored different kinds of psychological testing, and culminated in a thesis based on these statistics and measurements. I am OK at math but really don't enjoy spending time sitting in front of a computer working with numbers.

While working on the Ed. Psych. required courses, I branched out with elective classes and quickly realized that the field of counseling was of great interest to me. It was at that point that the ideas in this book were introduced to me and I began to take a more considered approach to this next step of livelihood decision making.

Since I enjoy doing research I spent a good deal of time looking into the various fields of counseling—from Marriage, Family and Child Counseling to Career Counseling. I also discussed the options with my family and friends in the counseling field to try to discover what was just right for me. Since I was already committed to and working towards my Ed. Psych. degree, I was particularly interested in seeing how the skills I was now learning could be connected to my real love, working with people. I was narrowing my options and felt sure the right one would soon emerge.

4. *Forrest*

I thought there was no question about my livelihood. I was going to continue working as a telecommunications consultant, but spend the last few years of my working life operating my own small consulting business; perhaps with a few employees, or maybe just by myself. The general direction for my livelihood didn't change as I read through the material in this Step, but it did help me put a sharper focus on my niche.

My skills and background made it natural for me to continue consulting, since I knew many people in the field, was already working as a consultant, and had enough of a reputation that I could get in some doors to make proposals. But as I thought about the work I'd actually be doing, I realized that it was pretty old hat to me, and I was interested in doing some fresh new things. How could I use my skills and experience and still introduce some elements that were new and exciting, and might help me feel like I was doing more good for a wider audience in the process?

I used the decision-making process to evaluate several ideas: contracting back to my previous employer to do work similar to what I'd been doing (a safe path), branching out on my own to consult in the same field with other companies (which would be more exciting and involve some travel), and becoming a consultant in the area of organizational development (riskiest idea but most interesting to me personally.) Through the decision-making process I decided to take the middle path and consult with other companies, starting with the field where I had the most technical expertise: customer service centers.

I knew from my internal reaction to the decision that it was the right one for me. I was moving away from being an employee and out on my own, which felt good. I'd work with new companies and meet new people, which could lead to opportunities to do more organizational development work, which I loved to do. It was another movement toward career independence, but I'd still have my experience, skills and network contacts to give me a base of security through a time of transition.

My livelihood decision meant that I resigned from my consulting company employer, and started to set up my own consulting company. I found that to keep my options open to work with a variety of companies, I'd need to set up my business as a corporation. The cost of incorporating was about $1500, so I decided to go ahead and do it. Incorporating gave me flexibility and made it easier to hire others to work with me, if necessary.

The fit of this livelihood to me was good, I estimated it to be 70%. As I moved into my new livelihood and gained my sea legs, I planned to be alert to ways I could gradually move more into the area of consulting on organizational problems like employee satisfaction, which was the area I was most excited about.

Step 5

Create Your Niche

Charisse, a 38-year-old supermarket assistant manager: *My husband and I live in a small farm community, where I've worked at the local supermarket since we were married. When I became assistant manager I thought it would be great, but I've found it's more work and responsibility, and the pay's still not very good. I'd like more money and more interesting work, but there's no way I'll ever manage the store, which is owned and run by a family. An auto plant in the next county has just expanded, and I've been told they're hiring people now for supervisory positions. I grew up fixing cars, and I like being physically active, so working in the plant sounds like the right livelihood for me. I don't know anything about the company or the working conditions. How can I find out?*

Malcolm, her husband, a 40-year-old farm machinery sales rep: *My work is a drudge; I'd like to quit my job and make my living teaching music. I've always played in a band and loved it, but I've never found a way to make any real money at it. If Charisse can get a better-paying job, it will give us the financial elbow room for me to take the plunge. I haven't decided between teaching music at the high school and opening my own studio for private lessons. I have a college degree in music which gives me a head start, but how do I get the information I need to make a choice?*

92

What You Need To Know About
The Playing Field—The Livelihood Cycle

Traditionally people begin to explore the world of work because they're looking for a job. In the molecular marketplace, it's too late to wait until you're looking for work to explore the potential work environments for your livelihood. Long before you hit the streets on your job search, you'll need to know about the competitive environment you'll face as **MMI, Inc.** This will enable you to make the right decisions about choosing employers you'll do business with and creating your own unique niche. Specifically, you'll need to discover the following things about the field of endeavor and livelihood you chose in Step 4: current market demands, trends and prospects for the future, pay and benefit expectations, entry requirements, and the attributes needed for success. This information is essential for you to be aware of how the world of work is changing, and in particular how these changes impact your livelihood.

How do you get this kind of information about your livelihood and potential employers? By doing research, both in the library (or on the Internet) and in the field, to gather data. These research activities are the first two phases of a larger process called the *Livelihood Cycle*, which lays out the processes involved in getting employment, starting with research and culminating with negotiating your deal.

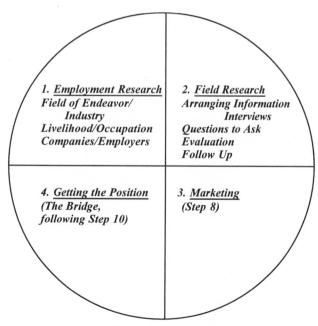

1. Employment Research
Field of Endeavor/
Industry
Livelihood/Occupation
Companies/Employers

2. Field Research
Arranging Information
Interviews
Questions to Ask
Evaluation
Follow Up

4. Getting the Position
(The Bridge,
following Step 10)

3. Marketing
(Step 8)

The Livelihood Cycle

In Step 8, we'll discuss phase 3 of the Livelihood Cycle, Marketing. In The Bridge, following Step 10, we'll revisit the Livelihood Cycle one last time to discuss your actual employment search in phase 4, Getting the Position.

Phase 1: Employment Research

Your investigation into the competitive environment of your livelihood can begin at a nearby library or on the Internet. Use the following references, most of which can be accessed using a search engine on the Internet, as a place to start your research in each of the categories listed.

Field of Endeavor/Industry

Documents in this category will help identify current market demands and trends for the future within various industries, which will be useful in deciding which industry is the best place for your livelihood.

- *U. S. Industrial Outlook.* Department of Commerce, Washington DC. Government Printing Office. Provides the trends and outlooks for 350 manufacturing and service industries. Updated annually.

- *Standard and Poor's Industry Surveys.* An introduction to most industries, with history and a good overview.

- *The Encyclopedia of Careers and Vocational Guidance.* Hopke, William E. Chicago: Doubleday. Volume I provides a general survey of many fields of endeavor. Volumes II and III focus on general occupational categories.

Livelihood/Occupation

Documents in this category yield up-to-date information about what your livelihood actually entails and what pay and benefits to expect.

- *The American Almanac of Jobs and Salaries.* Wright, John. New York. Avon Books. Published biennially in June, lists job descriptions and annual earning information.

- *The Dictionary of Occupational Titles.* Government Printing Office, Washington DC. Tells you what the livelihood actually entails, what the people doing the work actually do.

- *Occupational Outlook Handbook.* Department of Labor, NTC Publishing Group, 225 W. Touhy Avenue, Lincolnwood IL

60646. Provides an introduction to your livelihood by providing general information about what people do, what they earn, and the likely future trends for employment.

- *The Jobs Rated Almanac.* Krantz, Les. New York: World Almanac, Pharos Books. Jobs are rated by environment, income, outlook, physical demands, stress, security, and benefits.

Companies/Employers

Documents in this category will be helpful in targeting specific employers.

- *The Almanac of American Employers.* Plunkett Research, Ltd. P. O. Drawer 8270, Galveston TX 77553. Covers the 500 largest, fastest-growing and most successful corporate employers with over 2500 employees.

- *Dun and Bradstreet's Million Dollar Directory. (Abridged: Dun and Bradstreet's Million Dollar Directory—Top 50,000 Companies).*

- *Hoover's Handbook of Emerging Companies.* Edited by Spain, Patrick J., and James R. Talbot. Covers 250 smaller, emerging, fast-growing companies.

- *The Adams Jobs Almanac.* Bob Adams, Inc., 260 Center Street, Holbrook MA 02343. Samples major companies in 31 industries, with state-by-state index of major employers. The same company publishes a *National JobBank*, as well as a *JobBank Series* for many individual urban areas.

- *The 100 Best Companies To Work For In America Revised Edition.* Levering, Robert and Milton Moskowitz: The Penguin Group, 375 Hudson Street, New York, NY 10014. Lists the best companies to work for based on pay/benefits, opportunities, job security, pride in work, openness/fairness and camaraderie/friendliness.

In addition, there are other resources that will provide information about the particular field of endeavor and livelihood you've selected. A reference librarian will be able to direct you to additional resources which cover specialized livelihoods or focus on your geographical area. If you have access to a career center at a community college, university or your place of employment, you should also find many of these resources available there.

The Internet can also provide a lot of additional current information. For example, you can access up-to-the-minute trends and statistics about livelihoods from the US Bureau of Labor Statistics (*stats.bls.gov/bls home.html*). To discover employers you may want to check out further, browse one or more of the big six "job boards:" America's Job Bank (*www.ajb.dni.us*); Career Mosaic (*www.careermosaic.com*); Career Path (*www.careerpath.com*); E-Span (*www.espan.com*); Monster Board (*www.monster.com*); and On Line Career Center (*www.occ.com*). Many employers have their own web sites with detailed information about their organization, what it's like to work there, and positions they are currently trying to fill. You can learn a lot at an employer's web site about its goals and plans, and whether or not it's a good fit for **MMI, Inc**. If you aren't on-line, there are Internet access locations at universities, community colleges, state employment offices and public libraries.

As you do your employment research, keep in mind that you want to learn the following things about your livelihood: current market demands, market trends, livelihood specifics, pay and benefit expectations, and potential target employers.

Phase 2: Field Research

In the field research phase, you'll be looking for very specific information about your future work environment from people actually doing the work. Even if you're already working in a livelihood in which you expect to continue, this research will help you gain insights into creating a better niche for yourself and a competitive advantage in the long run.

Field research involves conducting information interviews, which are the best way to get current, first-hand information. Doing field research will help you discover both the good and bad aspects of what people in your livelihood do, day in and day out. You'll learn what skills are needed. It's likely that you'll learn details and nuances of working in your livelihood that will help you determine a niche for yourself. You may also learn about other related positions or livelihoods you hadn't known about. Expect to gain some idea of the future prospects of the field, the livelihood and the employer of the people you interview. Finally, you'll add to your self-confidence in an interview situation and—very importantly—you'll add to your list of network contacts.

Your first activity in field research is to arrange enough information interviews to get the data you need. How will you find people with whom you can hold an information interview? Scan written materials such as newspapers, magazines, directories of employers, alumni publications and career resource books to determine good prospects for an interview. Talk casually with people whenever and wherever you meet them to help generate ideas. Try asking people in these categories:

- friends, relatives, and acquaintances

- people in your community working in your livelihood

- staff at your local Chamber of Commerce

- professional associations, including people you meet at conferences and gatherings

- your alumni club or network

- your local reference librarian

Once you know whom you'd like to contact, how will you arrange the information interview? Depending on what's most comfortable for you and appropriate to the other person, you can:

- send a letter stating your request and make a follow-up telephone call to arrange an appointment;

- telephone directly, using a prepared statement of your request;

- go in person on a drop-in basis, usually to establish a future appointment.

When you've contacted the person you will interview, always begin by stating that you're asking only for information (you're not on an employment search at this point) and that you'll need only 20 to 30 minutes, at his or her convenience.

Here is a list of possible questions for your information interview, which you should tailor to your specific needs and interests and to the time available.

General livelihood/occupation

- What led you to this livelihood/occupation?

- What do you like and what do you not like about your work?

- What is the general tone of the work environment in this livelihood (for example, creative, exciting, monotonous, driving, even-paced, etc.)?

Changes in field of endeavor

- Are there outdated elements in this field, such as too many middle managers or outmoded techniques? If so, what are they?

- What do you think will be the important developments in this field over the next few months or years?

- How is technology being used in this field, and how will it change the field in the future?

- What competitive pressures exist in this field?

Unique opportunities

- What is your specialized niche in your livelihood?

- Is there an aspect or niche in this field that is not being met? If so, what might it be?

- Is there a support system that you need that isn't readily available, either within or outside of the system? What would that be?

Employer specifics

- What is the salary range? (beginning and advanced)

- Is travel required?

- Is relocation required? If so, how frequently?

- Is overtime required? If so, how often?

- What benefits are available?

- Is assistance provided for child care?

- Are there opportunities to learn new skills?

- Are there opportunities to work in cross-functional teams?

- In your organization, how much autonomy do workers have?

- Is your employer open to new technology?

- What is the general tone of the work environment in your organization?

- Are there opportunities to express new or creative ideas?

- Is there room for flexibility, such as telecommuting from home or flexible work hours?

- How well is your employer dealing with competition?

What do you do?

- What are the different elements of your day-to-day work life?

- How much time do you spend doing the different aspects of your work?

- Is there room for individual creativity and if so, in what ways?

- Do you work mostly alone or in a team environment?

- What do you like best about your work? What do you like least?

- If you could change anything about your work, what would it be? Why?

What preparation is required?

- Do you recommend any specific training or education to be successful?

- Where is the best place to get this training or education?

- What would you suggest I do to prepare to enter this line of work?

- Who else do you know who might be a good source of information for me?

Immediately after an information interview, evaluate the experience. Write down the name and address of the person you interviewed, and the answers to the following questions:

- What positive and what negative information did I learn?

- How does what I learned fit my vision and product definition?

- What else do I need to know and with whom do I need to talk?

- What is my next research activity?

Last but not least, follow up on your interview. Something that's critically important and often overlooked is to write a thank-you note expressing your appreciation within 48 hours. Once you've sent your thank-you note, organize the information you've gathered into a file or computer database, and if you haven't completed your research, promptly set up your next information interview.

Field Research Examples

Charisse, who we met at the beginning of Step 5, didn't need help in targeting an industry or employer. When she selected her new livelihood, there was only one choice—the automotive plant nearby. But she had a lot of questions about the work that was done in the plant, and about the stability of the industry and the company that operated the plant. She thought about what she needed to know, and wrote down her questions:

About the industry

- What are the long term trends for the American automotive manufacturing industry?

- Will technology change the way work is done in the future? Will this mean downsizing or layoffs in supervisory positions?

- What is the competitive outlook globally, nationally and for the company that owns the plant?

About the company

- How long is this plant expected to operate?

- Is the plant based on the latest technology, so that it won't quickly become obsolete?

- Does the company promote a positive working environment?

- What is the company's attitude toward women in non-traditional positions? In management positions?

- Is the company's senior management hierarchical in approach, or more team-oriented?

About the position

- What's the current demand for shop floor supervisors?

- Are supervisors hired from outside, or only promoted from within?

- What exactly does a supervisor do in the course of a day? Is there any latitude for individual creativity?

- Will working in the plant develop transferable skills that could be used elsewhere, if necessary?

- What are the training requirements? Is training provided by the company? If so, how and when?

- How much would someone have to know about cars to get a supervisor's position?

- How satisfied are other supervisors with their work?

- What organization(s) do the supervisors belong to? Are they optional?

- What is the level of pay and benefits, at entry, mid-range and top? How long does it take to get to top pay?

- Is progression to higher pay and/or a better job based on performance? Seniority? Both?

- What's the commute like from my home to the plant?

- Is a flexible work schedule possible?

- What are the expected overtime requirements?

Charisse visited the local library, and found most of the information she needed about the industry and the company. The plant was being expanded and modernized, and the librarian had a lot of good information about it, including whom to talk to about working there. Armed with this, Charisse contacted her friends who knew people at the plant, and asked them to help her arrange interviews with several people. From her interviews, she got answers to all her important questions and thought that this looked like a good livelihood choice for her. She and Malcolm decided she should apply for a position.

In the meantime, Malcolm was starting his own research. He was quite excited about the idea of being able to teach music if Charisse got a position at the plant, and he wanted to be ready to make the change as soon as possible. Malcolm's research goals were very different from Charisse's. He didn't need to select an industry, but only to decide between two different possibilities: teaching in the public school, and starting his own music studio business. He drew up his own list of research questions:

About teaching in school

- What is the demand for high school music teachers? Are there any positions available now? If not, when is one expected?

- What are the requirements for a credential to teach music?

- Is there a nearby college or university that offers a music teaching credential program?

- Can someone start teaching before completing credential requirements?

- What's the pay and benefit package for a teacher?

- How much out-of-hours work is required? Is there more pay for extra-curricular activities?

- What are the working conditions for teachers at the local high school?

- What is the school administration like, from a teacher's perspective? Do the administrators promote teamwork and a good environment for teachers?

About opening a music studio

- How are the other music studios and private teachers in town doing financially?

- What is the expected annual gross income for the first and later years?

- What is the expected level of expenses for the first and later years?

- Is a license or bonding required?

- Is it possible to teach at home until the business can afford to open a studio?

- Are any permits or special permissions required?

- What are the insurance requirements?

- Is it best to incorporate as a business?

- What's the best way to advertise or market music lessons?

- Will another piano be required? How much will it cost? Are professional quality used pianos available?

- Is it best to use a proprietary teaching system, such as the Suzuki method? Why?

- What is the level of job satisfaction for private music teachers who have been teaching for many years?

- Are other teachers available to work part-time or full time if the business is successful?

Malcolm had only a few questions for his employment research, including the issues to consider when starting a business, and the credential requirements for teaching. He found he could qualify for a credential with a one-year course of study at a nearby state college, and could possibly teach with a temporary credential during that year if there was a shortage of fully qualified teachers.

For his field research, Malcolm knew several teachers and administrators at the high school, as well as everyone who was active in the music scene in town. It was easy for him to contact the right people, and he got straight answers to his research questions—along with a lot of free advice. He found there was an immediate need for a long-term substitute teacher at the school, and that he could teach on a provisional basis as long as he was enrolled in a course leading to a credential. He would have to take a cut in pay, but he would also be able to do some private teaching on the side. He and Charisse decided he should make the move even though she hadn't heard about her new position, because it fit so well with his goals and because it was likely to lead to a relatively secure position in the future.

As you conduct, evaluate and follow up on information interviews, keep in mind that the overall goal of this field research is to identify the key characteristics that make someone successful in your field and livelihood, including those attributes that will be most certain to create success in the future. As examples, these might include education, specific training, attitude, personality traits or experience.

Based on what you've learned when you've finished your research, ask yourself if there are attributes that you could develop that would set **MMI, Inc** apart from others who are working in the same livelihood. That's a great way to start identifying a successful niche.

A Niche Is More Than A Little Hole

You've now done the research required to know a great deal more about the field of endeavor and livelihood you selected in Step 4. In particular, you've explored what makes someone successful in your field, at least by today's standards. The work you've done gives you a big head start into the molecular marketplace; the next phase—creating a niche for **MMI, Inc**—is how you customize your work, to become "fireproof" in the future.

The concepts of field of endeavor and livelihood are useful, but dated; they're rooted in the work environment of the past, which was permanent and stable, and which no longer exists for most people. Like the concepts of job and career, they stem from a world of work in which the employer defines exactly how the job will be done. In the old world of work, a job was a box, sized and shaped by the employer, and carefully defined by the job description. The worker had to be—or become—the same size and shape as the box, and his or her individual capabilities, skills and preferences were useful only if and when they fit within the confines of that box.

A niche, in contrast to the job box, is a custom-fit solution to an employer's need. It benefits the employer because the worker brings added value to the task by contributing his or her own experience, creativity and unique perspective. It benefits the worker, who is no longer stuffed into a one-size-fits-all box. Instead, the worker helps adapt the position to his or her own personal shape; a shape which, like an amoeba, continues to change and grow all the time, as new circumstances develop and creative ways are found to improve the match between the person and the task.

The concept of a niche fits right in with seeing the workplace as a marketplace. Picture a busy public market, where buyers and sellers of goods and services are all crowded together in a space that's alive with negotiations and transactions. Most sellers have a booth or space from which they operate; your niche is like your booth in the molecular marketplace. It displays the quality and features of the product or service you're selling. It's also a platform from which to tell buyers about the advantages of your product, answer questions and negotiate deals. If you were selling baked goods in a public market, you'd probably locate your booth near other bakers, but you'd try to differentiate it to make it look more attractive. If the marketplace changed and you found the foot traffic around your booth had diminished, you'd be flexible enough to pack up and relocate to a place that was more lively. As **MMI, Inc**, your booth (niche) expresses your workplace identity in the current environment, functions as your home base, and differentiates you from the rest of the crowd.

To be successful, every worker today will need to develop a niche. Whether you're a long-term shop-floor employee, a temporary office worker, an executive, a professional or an entrepreneur, your niche will put you in charge of your own destiny—self-reliant, self-managing, and able to act at your own discretion. Creating a niche requires that you first understand and meet your employer's needs, and then exceed those needs by bringing added value through contributions only you can offer. Your niche will create a unique place for **MMI, Inc**, and your uniqueness will make you indispensable, too valuable to let go in a crunch.

In contrast to your field of endeavor and livelihood, which will tend to change slowly if at all, your niche will be much more dynamic. You're likely to modify your niche or develop a new one often during your working life, as a result of unforeseen shifts in the marketplace. You may also plan ahead to expand your niche as your contributions and value to employers increase. In addition, you may decide to change your niche as you gain experience and find that another would be more satisfying or challenging.

Developing Your Niche

So how do you create the right niche for **MMI, Inc**? Let's look at current examples of how other workers have found personalized, fulfilling niches.

Anne: Since her children had reached school age, Anne was beginning to feel restless at home, and also wanted some extra money. She took a job as a food-stand manager at her local farmer's market, where she noticed that the fastest selling items were hand-rolled pretzels. The pretzels sold for 55 cents, but she checked out the cost of the ingredients which came to only about 7 cents. Anne went home to her kitchen and worked out a better recipe for the pretzels by varying the ingredients, texture and size. Then she opened her own stand at the market, selling her new, improved product and getting feedback from customers. She used the feedback to continue to improve the product and learn how best to sell it. You may have tasted her product—she now has hundreds of "Auntie Anne's Pretzels" franchise shops across the country.

Tony: As a marketing manager in a large firm, Tony had already gone through two waves of downsizing. His work was good and his department was seen as vital to the company's future, so Tony survived both downsizing cycles. He was happy to keep his job, which he liked, but he saw how the downsizing had made him feel negative toward the company, and lowered the morale of those around him. Everyone feared another round of layoffs, and worried that they'd be the next to go. Some dusted off their resumes and left for other companies, but most developed a sort of bunker mentality, keeping out of sight and complaining at every opportunity. Tony, concerned about the low morale, asked his director if there could be a team meeting to involve the employees in helping to reorganize and revitalize their department. Tony's boss agreed, and asked Tony to facilitate the meeting. After the meeting, which brought an immediate improvement in the morale of the department, Tony realized that he enjoyed helping people deal with change. The department's success attracted company-wide attention, and Tony was appointed to a permanent committee to design ways to involve employees in planning for change.

Jody: As a specialist doing facials and make-up at a local beauty parlor, Jody was an expert. She enjoyed her work, but felt as though she'd like it to have more significance in order to make more of a difference in the world. Jody heard about a new reconstructive plastic surgery procedure, and saw that her expertise could be helpful for the patients. She discussed her idea with plastic surgeons, who encouraged her to work with them. With the doctors, she developed a process to assist people in presenting themselves attractively after major facial plastic surgery.

Jason: A successful accountant with several years experience, Jason's hobby and passion was long-distance bicycling. With his full-time work commitments he couldn't ride long distances very often, and felt a time conflict between work, bicycling and family. He was offered a supervisor's job, but knew he didn't want to be a manager. The job offer acted as a spur for Jason to clarify his goals and, as a result, he decided to become an accounting consultant, doing more or less the same work but as a contractor. This enabled him to work for twelve to eighteen months, then take six months off. During the time off he spends a lot of time cycling, and still has time for his family. He says: "Why wait until I'm 55 or 60 to retire? I'm including my retirement as part of my life now!"

Chet: As a part-time customer service representative at a telephone company, Chet didn't receive any benefits with the position. He wanted to work as a technician, had applied for the job, and had even gone through the necessary training. However, the company was using temporaries from outside the company for technician positions instead of hiring permanent employees. Chet decided to quit his part-time job with the company and go to work for a temporary agency to get the position as well as some of the benefits he wanted.

Meg &
Florence: Both Meg and Florence were in their thirties, and each had young children. They worked as professional colleagues in the employee development division of a large utility company. They were responsible for developing programs to help employees address conflicts between their work and their lives. As the two women worked together they shared their personal circumstances, and found a similar theme: they both wanted more time at home and were willing to have less income, but also wanted to remain professionally active in their field. They developed a plan to share one position, and proposed it to their employer. Their plan was accepted because both had solid reputations and did good work, and the proposal was in line with the company's goals of improving work/life balance. Now they each work two and a half days per week, and fill in for each other for vacations. The arrangement has worked so well over the past five years that many other job-sharing teams have been created in their company.

As you think about the niche you'll create for **MMI, Inc**, here are some key points about successful niche development drawn from the examples above:

- The best niches are very specific to both the worker and the work environment. Knowing your vision and product definition in advance are crucial to creating the right niche.

- Most successful niches are created by someone already in a particular work environment who sees how to do something better, differently, or with more pizzazz. If you're not now in your ideal work environment, the research you've completed in this Step will provide enough information for you to develop an initial niche idea.

- A successful niche is often the result of identifying and filling a need the employer didn't realize existed.

- Once a successful niche is established, it not only serves the employer's needs but also supports the worker's personal needs and preferences.

- Great niches aren't created by people with an attitude of victimization, who focus on blaming someone or something else for what's wrong. Instead, great niches are created by people with responsive attitudes who are able to see clearly what's happening in the work environment and create positive solutions. You'll explore the broader implications of attitude at work further in Step 6.

- A niche is the product of the worker's unique qualities in a particular environment at a specific time; all of these conditions will change, and the niche will need to adapt and change also.

Let's catch up with Charisse and Malcolm, who were both planning livelihood changes, and see how their plans worked out six months later. Malcolm started teaching, and at the same time started back to school at night to get his permanent teaching credential. He found he enjoyed teaching music, as he knew he would, and that the high school was a great place for him. Even though he was a long-term substitute teacher, he quickly developed a niche to increase his value to the school and highlight his best skills. Malcolm started two new ensembles at the school, a jazz instrumental group and a vocal chorale. His own experience with public performance gave him a natural ability to coach in the art of performing, and he was becoming a popular teacher with music students and their parents. His niche as a musical performance coach was developing nicely, as he had planned.

Charisse had a different experience. At the auto plant, she was accepted into a supervisor's training program, which didn't go very well. After a few days discussing leadership techniques and role-playing how to be a good performance coach, Charisse asked to meet with the trainer. She confessed that she didn't see any point to the philosophical stuff, she wasn't enjoying the class and she was afraid that she wasn't suited to be a supervisor in this environment. The trainer appreciated Charisse's candor, and said she herself was having some doubts about whether Charisse would succeed as a supervisor in the plant. Together, they agreed to have her try a hands-on, shop floor position. Charisse was interviewed by a team of four other workers whose task was to assemble gearboxes, and when the team unanimously agreed, she was assigned to work with them. The other people on the team were great to work with, and quickly taught her all aspects of their task, helping her to become useful and productive from the first day. Charisse loved the work and the people, and the team was one of the most productive in the company, which added significantly to her income through healthy productivity bonuses. Charisse's niche turned out to be something unexpected—a member of a high performance team, rather than a supervisor—and she was happy that she'd persisted long enough to find it.

Using what you've learned about your field of endeavor and livelihood, the decision-making process, what makes someone successful in your livelihood, and what makes a successful niche, here's an opportunity for you to consider what your initial niche for **MMI, Inc** might be. If you've recently decided on a field of endeavor and livelihood, you may not yet have a lot of information available to develop a precise picture of your future niche. Use the employment and field research you've just completed to identify your best idea so far, keeping in mind that you'll be able to modify your niche decision when you have more experience in your livelihood.

Can you see how your niche can help to improve the fit of **MMI, Inc** with your livelihood? It probably makes a big difference, but remember that you're unlikely to find a 100% fit. If the fit is good enough to be acceptable to you, there may still be parts of **MMI, Inc** that don't fit with your livelihood. These can be addressed through other aspects of your life outside of work, which you'll consider in Step 9, dealing with integrating your work and the rest of your life.

Unfortunately, most people make career choices by grabbing a convenient job at an opportune time in their life, sticking with it as long as possible, and reluctantly changing to another job only if necessary. It's very common for someone to spend more time planning a vacation than planning his or her ideal work life. In contrast, you've made your livelihood and niche decisions—or rethought and reaffirmed decisions made earlier—based on a carefully-developed vision and product definition statement for **MMI, Inc**. Your conscious effort to develop the right niche will give you a great advantage over others in getting where you want to go.

Case Studies

1. *Shannon*

As soon as I saw the word "research" in the early part of Step 5, I hesitated. Doing research has never been my favorite activity; I'm the kind of person who likes to do or make what others have researched. Fortunately, there were two factors that got me through the research section. First, I'd done some research while working with the career counselor during Step 4, and second, the book suggested doing some of the research on the Internet. Surfing for information is a lot more interesting to me than using a reference system at a library.

In trying to find more specific information about my chosen livelihood of education and training, I quickly realized just how broad that category is. It was obvious that I needed to narrow down my livelihood selections, and I began to get some ideas of more specific directions to go. Both technical/computer training and teaching English as a Second Language (ESL) looked interesting. Since I grew up with grandparents who spoke another language and one of my top work values is traveling, ESL looked especially good.

The problem was, I was back in Step 4 again! I knew I wasn't ready to look into specific companies or salary and benefit information yet, so I (frustratedly) returned to Step 4 and the livelihood decision process. This time I got information on three more specific education options: technical training, ESL, and in-house corporate training. Going back through the decision process clarified that teaching ESL made the most sense for me, which also fit with my gut feeling that it was the most exciting option.

NOW I was ready to do Step 5 (guess I'm not the quick study I always thought I was). I gathered information on trends and the future of ESL teaching, salary and benefits, education and training required (I'll need a bachelor's degree), and began to find companies and institutions that do this kind of work.

The best part of this Step for me was doing field research. Since I knew so little about ESL teaching, talking to people who'd done it or knew about it was fantastic. I generated a long list of questions I could ask, which worked out fine because I tailored my questions to each person and situation. I'd never done interviews like this before, and wondered if people would be responsive; to my surprise, almost everyone was willing to help with suggestions and referrals. I ended up doing three interviews: a family friend who'd taught English in Japan for a year, an elementary teacher with ESL experience and a special certificate, and an ESL teacher at the local community college. I was even invited to sit in on an adult-education class at the college.

In thinking about the best niche for me in this livelihood, I am most drawn to the idea of traveling and teaching ESL abroad. It's hard to get much more specific than that, since I've never done any ESL teaching and right now don't even have the degree needed. If the best niches are created by people already in the field, I've got a ways to go. But I did learn that there are volunteer and aide positions available to begin working with young ESL students, so I can get a taste of the work. For me, this niche isn't going to be "decide and do"; it's going to take time, commitment and money to get there. But for the first time in my working life I have a direction I really feel good about, which gives me the right attitude to eventually make a great niche in my livelihood.

2. *Brent*

I quickly found that books in general are not good sources of information for new and emerging career opportunities in the high tech arena, because their coverage of those fields is weak and outdated. But I found good sources of information for my possible livelihoods on the Internet, after finding the right Web sites.

I went to the local library to find trade journals and magazines associated with my field of interest. I looked through them and jotted down the names and Web sites, if provided, of the companies that advertise in them. If no Web site was given, I'd find the company's site using an Internet search engine. Looking at these Web sites provided news releases, product reviews, and lists of similar companies—a veritable wealth of information!

Of course, there is no better source of information then straight from the horse's mouth. I've learned more from a thirty-minute information interview than from a week's worth of library or Internet research. When I researched the computer animation livelihood, for example, I began with a long list of questions to answer. Many of them were basic ("Where are most of the companies located?", "What is the anticipated demand for animators in the next five years?"), but some were more in depth ("What is the work environment like?", "How much overtime is involved?"). As I did my research, I found the answers to many of the questions, but some I couldn't answer completely—these became the core questions for an information interview. I called the largest and most established of the animation companies and asked for a telephone interview with an experienced animator. They agreed, and the person I interviewed was wonderfully helpful, answering almost all of my questions (he wouldn't comment on any salary or cash incentive questions, as is common for most people). By the end of that call, I had nearly everything I needed to decide on animation as a possible livelihood.

Building a niche (or several niches) is critical for survival in today's job market, but building one before starting a livelihood is tough. I find it hard to know what's needed until I get into the working environment. It's much easier to find my niche after I take the job.

Building niches has always come naturally to me. In fact, I think most companies expect it—isn't that what the "extra duties as required" clause in every job description is all about? I always start by taking on filing projects; it familiarizes me with what's going on in the office and soon makes me the expert in knowing where everything is. I try to learn new software early on and then act as a trainer to bring the rest of the office up to speed. I'm also a pretty good writer, so I volunteer for any documentation duties. My strategy is to build a collection of niche activities and make myself as valuable to my department as possible—job security today, I feel, is a measure of how irreplaceable you as **MMI,** Inc make yourself to your "clients."

I've also found occasionally that some companies (or work groups, at least) discourage niche building. One large aerospace company I worked for preferred "pigeonholing"—assigning small projects until the manager found a useful talent, then assigning only that type of work. Any broader niche work that was needed was assigned either to the overworked staff associate or to another department. Individual talents beyond the job description were not appreciated. Needless to say, I did not stay long at that company.

3. *Emily*

Developing a unique niche holds great interest for me. Since I am coming into the working world without a lot of previous work experience, and since I am not exactly a "spring chicken" in terms of my age, I am sure I will need to offer something unique and interesting to a potential employer. So really focusing my further educational efforts as well as possible internships towards something that will evolve into a niche will be important. I also want this direction to fit my own personal needs and interests, especially in being helpful to people in some way.

Another source of my interest in this subject comes from within my own family. My niece, who has recently become a teenager, has always had learning difficulties—not able to concentrate for any length of time as well as being slow at both reading and spelling. She is showing signs of being less and less interested in school and could easily turn to harmful directions. I am sure it is some type of learning difficulty that, if diagnosed early on, could help turn around her negative attitude toward education.

I have already done some research into this subject with the professors in my Ed. Psych. program. They suggested I look into educational resource counseling as a possible direction to meet both my interests and needs as well as learning how to be of help to my niece. Also, with awareness of learning disabilities and Attention Deficit Disorder (ADD) growing, it appears that there will be a quite a demand for this type of test-interpretation and follow-up counseling in the future so the prospects look good.

Being a portfolio worker has always appealed to me, so if possible I would want to do several things at one time: teaching at a local community college, working with colleagues or in a private practice, working for a large employer such as a school district on a contractual basis, and perhaps doing speaking engagements in this area of expertise.

My first step will be to get on the Internet to do research, and then to go to my local library to continue doing general research into just what people do in this field. I want to learn how these professionals actually help people that come to them; for instance, what might be offered to my niece to better understand her situation. I am also interested in the options for actually going to work, such as setting up a private practice, working with a team, or working for an employer.

I plan to write letters to educational resource centers in my area for further general information as well as to set up information interviews. In this way, I also hope to find a congenial environment where the professionals are open to helping me get an internship.

4. *Forrest*

The niche I want to fill in my new consulting venture has two phases to it. First, drawing on my strengths and network contacts, I'll continue pretty much what I've been doing as an employee: helping to set up and manage large customer service center operations. Then, when my business is independently established, I'll try to move gradually into the area I'm really interested in: improving the jobs of the people in those centers so that the organizations are more efficient and the people more satisfied.

My field research consisted of talking with all my network contacts over a two-week period, telling my contacts of my plans and asking for ideas for initial clients. I generated six good leads and from those picked two for follow up, with one of them has become my first independent consulting customer. I'll be able to do ongoing field research on the longer term niche in the normal course of my consulting work.

Using the attributes of a successful niche from Step 5, I can see clearly how to develop a niche in the direction I prefer:

- Working with organization development in service centers will be very specific to both my skills and the customer's particular problems in the work environment.

- I'm already working in that environment, which gives me a detailed, personal insight into the problems that develop, along with ideas about their causes and cures.

- I can easily identify needs that employers don't realize they have. I've "seen it all" in other environments, and know what benefits can come from working on the "soft side" issues of improving jobs and communication in the workplace.

- Working on organizational issues will be fulfilling to me because I love doing it, and I can actually demonstrate to employers how much could be saved by the improvements I suggest.

- I've learned to have a positive attitude in most situations, and know I can use positive enthusiasm to sell my ideas and demonstrate their tangible value.

- I see this niche not as static, but shifting and developing in the way I want it to go. I also know that constant change in the field will keep things changing for as long as I work—which is just the way I like it.

My initial niche has been a pretty good fit for me, but beginning to develop the longer term niche progressively over time is really exciting because I see that it will improve the match between me and my livelihood to nearly 100%. If I can make the grade by establishing this niche, it will be so much fun that I may never want to stop working!

Step 6

Create Your Competitive Advantage

Keiko, a 43-year-old executive secretary who was recently down-sized: *When our branch office closed, they offered us all some outplacement counseling. In the process, I learned quite a bit about myself and what I want. I went back to school to become a court reporter. I like the work and I'm really good at it, but it's hard to compete with others who have been court reporters for a long time. I'd really like to know how to get more work and better assignments.*

Standing Out In The Crowd

The research you performed in Step 5 has given you a basic understanding of what the molecular marketplace demands from a successful worker in your niche. But, like Keiko, your next question probably is: "How can I assure that my product, **MMI, Inc**, will find success in the complex, faceless, sometimes ruthless environment of a busy employment market-place? How can I be sure that **MMI, Inc** will stand out in the crowd?"

The first and most important answer has to be that **MMI, Inc** is a "class act," which means that your product performs well, is of high quality, is known and respected. The quality of your product must always be foremost. But that's not the end of the story.

For example Keiko, in her previous job, was an excellent secretary and a real whiz at shorthand, with speed and accuracy that far exceeded anyone else around. But after she was laid off she found that there was virtually no need for stenographic skills in the new world of work. When she considered

114

her product definition, she realized she needed to replace her shorthand skills with something more contemporary. She took a court reporter training course, and with her practiced ear for listening and her excellent eye-hand coordination from years of typing, she graduated at the top of her class. In Keiko's case, the additional edge that **MMI, Inc** needed *beyond* high quality was updated skills.

The competitive pressures of the molecular marketplace are strong and growing stronger, whether we like it or not. And there is more to selling a product in a competitive environment than simply the quality of the product itself. What other things in addition to the quality of the product are needed to assure success for **MMI, Inc**? We call them *success factors*, and they're the subject of this Step.

Remember the past achievements that you identified in Step 3? What about those events or accomplishments made them feel like achievements to you? In other words, what made them feel successful? The elements that made your achievements feel successful to you will have a great deal in common with the qualities that will enable **MMI, Inc** to achieve competitive success in the molecular marketplace. But hold on a minute; there's that word "competitive" again, which makes many of us pretty uncomfortable. Let's spend some time looking at why you might feel an emotional charge about competition, and how to respond to it in a new and creative way.

The Case For Redefining Competition

Emotions run high when the word competition is spoken. Some people feel the adrenaline start to pump; they're ready to get something stirred up and see who wins. Others have a feeling of distaste, sensing that the word suggests hostility or warfare. And some people just don't want to stand out in the crowd. What's your first response?

Clarence, a sanitation worker, had this to say about what was happening to him: "Hey, I understand the company has to compete for customers, but that's as far as competition ought to go. I can't do my best work if I feel pressure from somebody else trying to take my job away. After all, I signed up for a job for life, and even though the work's changed a lot and gotten more demanding, I've been loyal. So why should I have to deal with the added stress of competing for my job?"

In the new world of the molecular marketplace, competition at the level of *me* is very much a reality. If you've been through downsizing or re-engineering, you've been personally touched by competition. If you haven't yet had to compete to get or hold onto a job, stand by—it's almost certainly going to be part of your working future.

When competition for your livelihood does come, it can be really frightening if you view it from a conventional frame of reference: the law of the jungle, where you eat the other guy or get eaten. Of course, now that we're much more "civilized," we talk instead about "eating the other guy's lunch!" But it's really the same thing: a fight where someone wins and someone loses, spawning a "kill-or-be-killed" attitude.

That kind of attitude can bring a lot of negative baggage along with it. In the search for a more positive approach, a new model of competition has emerged from developments in fields like Systems Thinking and Total Quality. These two major trends in organization theory suggest that competition to win at any cost becomes a destructive game because the win/lose scenario doesn't add to the value of the whole. On the other hand, when competition becomes the search for a better way, or for *continuous improvement*, then the whole is improved. Even those who don't "win" the competition can learn from the pioneer who develops something better, so the whole group or system moves to a higher level.

In this model of competition, the most successful competitor is the one who contributes the most toward the good of the whole. Since your work, whatever it may be, is always done in or for a group—whether family, organization, company, industry or all humanity—this model will work better for you in the long run than a model based on win or lose, live or die.

In all models of competition, the most successful competitor is rewarded for doing well. But the difference in this new model is that other competitors aren't eaten; in fact, they may also do better, right alongside the "winner," because the system is improved as a result of the higher standards set by the top performer.

Of course, we still hear a lot about the old model of win/lose competition; it's fashionable in some circles to behave as if there were still dragons out there to be slain, or enemies to be annihilated. But there are also a lot of examples of the new competitive model around, often brought about by economic necessity. For example, AT&T, Lucent Technologies, DuPont, Johnson & Johnson, and other companies formed the Talent Alliance, which aims for sweeping collaboration among these giant companies to match their employees to jobs in the other companies. On a more global level, the European Union nations are inching their way toward a single currency, despite centuries of tradition behind the mark, franc, pound, etc.

The new model for competition doesn't eliminate failure. People, businesses, nations all can and *do* fail from time to time. But when the focus is on overall improvement rather than on win/lose, the "loser" doesn't carry such a stigma and can use the experience of the failure to gain knowledge and to begin again from a higher starting place.

One of the lessons for a worker in the molecular marketplace is that sometimes each of us *will* fail; in fact, we should *plan* and *prepare* for it, which is one main purpose of the 10 Steps. Planning will allow for periods of failure by preparing a cushion and charting the recovery that you'll need to make in order to re-establish your own personal competitive advantage. Of course, you'll also plan for success and understand its value in carrying you through the low points and transitions.

So competitive advantage, based on the new model of competition, isn't about surviving at someone else's expense. Rather, it's about being the best you can be and expecting to contribute to and participate in the resulting rewards.

Let's look at an example of competition in an office setting. Picture two supervisors: one is an "empire-builder," jealously guarding her turf and even withholding information from other groups if she feels that her power base is threatened. Another manager in the same division concentrates on building coalitions, doing her best to keep her employees involved in decision making and to keep others around her posted as changes occur or new information becomes available. While the first manager is competing in the old sense of the word, the second manager is using a win-win approach to keep herself, as well as her employees and the company, competitive. Which of these two managers would you prefer to work for or with? And, perhaps more critically, which manager is more likely to be successful in the long run?

All of which is interesting, but how does it apply to you? Like the two managers above, your own style of competition will likely influence your long-term success. Working with a team and seeing the bigger picture aren't just nice ideas; they're indispensable success factors. By exploring these and other success factors that will help you compete effectively in today's molecular marketplace, you will be assuring the success of your product, **MMI, Inc**.

Doing Business In The Molecular Marketplace Versus Holding A Job

What's the difference between this new notion of the marketplace and the "job" model of employment with which we've lived for a couple of hundred years? Here are some key differences.

Different Forms Of Work

One difference is that the molecular marketplace encompasses several forms of work, all of which are just as valid as any "job." In fact, most workers will participate in all of these, at some time—maybe even simultaneously—in the future.

Wage

This is the traditional job model: you have a long-term employment commitment to one employer, who in turn provides you with compensation and benefits.

Fee

Project-based or contract work. The work is contracted in advance, with a set fee generally paid upon completion.

Temporary

Work that is understood to be short-term in nature, sometimes (though less often than in the past) for the purpose of replacing a missing employee; generally paid on an hourly basis.

Home-based

Any work done primarily from home, including some new employment alternatives like telecommuting.

Volunteer

Work that is unpaid, though it can result in valuable skills, networking, and experience.

Think about which of these types of work you've done throughout your working life. For example, did you mow lawns as a teen? That's fee work. Have you done emergency baby-sitting for a sick friend? Probably home-based volunteer work. When the boss is away and you've been asked to step in as interim decision-maker, that's temporary work. Most of us have already experienced most, if not all, of these work forms; the difference now is that they're moving into the workplace mainstream. Notice, also, that a position can include more than one of these descriptive categories: you might have done temporary work that moved into wage, or home-based fee work. The point is, in the molecular marketplace all of these are viable ways to work; jobs are simply one of many possibilities, no better nor worse than the rest.

Independence

Another difference in the molecular marketplace is that you'll need to be far more independent. In fact, unlike in most jobs, where loyalty and doing what you're told are usually highly valued, independent thought and action are key to survival in the new world of work. For example, a woman was going shopping and was looking for a parking space in a full lot. She saw a man in a van parked in a prime space, so she waited, assuming he would leave soon. After a long wait, she parked elsewhere and came back to ask if the man was OK. Surprised, he answered "Yes, of course. I'm actually at work. This is my mobile office." He was surrounded in the van by his computer, cellular phone with fax connection, and files, comfortably working and making telephone calls. Physical independence from an office is becoming common enough that it now has a name: the "virtual office."

Another type of independence is freedom from reliance on a "womb-to-tomb" work position. For example, Kevin, a contract personnel consultant with a mid-sized radio broadcasting company, was interviewing Stephen, an employee, who was a candidate for a higher-rated position.

Kevin: *"Tell me a bit about your background."*

Stephen: *"Well, I worked for a broadcasting company for a few years in my mid-twenties. At that time, I resigned so that my partner and I could start a distribution logistics and trucking business.*

Kevin: *"What happened to your company? What brought you back to working in radio?"*

Stephen: *"The company is still going strong. My partner likes the detail work it involves, and I found it was beginning to wear on me. We talked about selling the business, but that wasn't something he wanted to do. So we agreed he'd run it, while I kept a financial interest and served as an advisor, but that I'd also work somewhere where I felt more challenged. And I really love the radio business—right now, it's really a hot place to work."*

Kevin: *"I'm impressed! Didn't you come back to us as a contractor in an entry level job? Wasn't that a cut in pay for you?"*

Stephen: *"You bet. But it was worth it. A few months ago I was hired back as a full-time employee and got back to my former salary. But the money is less important to me now that I have some income from my own business. Now I'd like this promotion to get into the advertising part of the business, which is something I haven't done before."*

Kevin: *"What do you think you'll be doing five years from now?"*

Stephen: *"I don't really know, but I know it will be something interesting. Right now, the most interesting thing I can think of is to get some experience in this new advertising position."*

Kevin agreed that neither of them knew what Stephen would be doing in five years, and that it wasn't very important. What did matter was that Stephen was ensuring his own success by staying independent, regardless of the role he was playing at the moment: business owner, consultant, or employee.

As you, like Stephen, find yourself relying less on employer guidance, you'll move toward being self-guided. Employers, out of economic necessity or callousness or both, are stepping away from taking responsibility for careers. For example, outplacement, which offers transition support when jobs are eliminated, has mushroomed in popularity. Outplacement services are nice to have if you lose your job, but the bad news is that it's also a way for an employer to step away from responsibility for an ex-employee's future and perhaps avoid guilt feelings. And for continuing employees, many companies have introduced career centers. These sound like a forward-looking aid for employees, and they can be, but again they signal the end of employer responsibility for the career: the message is "take care of yourself." More and more traditional career "ladders" within large businesses are closed, re-routed, or at least much less secure. All of these factors contribute to the need for a change in belief from "career management" to "career independence."

Downsizing and job losses are in the news constantly, regardless of the momentary state of the economy. In many cases, the jobs are *not* lost because of the performance of the individual employee, but for strategic business reasons. But whatever the reason, many of us are being left to fend for ourselves, whether we're up to it or not. The emerging molecular marketplace requires your *own* hand to be firmly on the tiller guiding you in your niche.

Be Valuable to be Valued

In the past, employers usually saw value in an employee because of what or who he/she was: trained, available, loyal, maybe even "part of the family." Seniority was often rewarded as the highest value. Now, the value of a worker has to be clear, current and relevant to today's needs—which are changing rapidly for most employers. Workers have to be measurably valuable, and they have to remain so.

In a not-uncommon example, a man at a large electric utility company was laid off after a twenty-five year career because his performance was *good*! The problem was that his performance was less than outstanding, and only those with outstanding performance made the cut when the work group was downsized. What examples have you personally seen where "good enough" is no longer good enough? The value equation is changing, and workers in the future are going to have to be ready to quickly answer the dreaded question: "What have you done for me lately?"

Differences From a "Career" Perspective

The table below is an interesting summary of some of the differences between a career in a "job" environment and a niche in the molecular marketplace.

Holding A Job	Molecular Marketplace Niche
Career planning is a one-time decision.	Portfolio development planning is a flexible ongoing process.
Progress means moving up.	Progress can mean moving up, down, across or out.
Employees have limited information about opportunities.	Position information/work opportunities are available or are created as needed.
Single, long-term goals are set with a narrow focus.	Multiple, short-term goals are set with a broader focus.
Career plans are created based on me and my company.	Plans take into account societal and organizational changes.
Education, training, and development are chosen from a set menu of options.	Education, training and development are driven by development gaps.
Career planning was a supplemental benefit.	Planning is a business necessity.
Raises based on tenure.	Compensation based on contribution.
The work environment is us vs. them (secrecy, distrust).	The work environment is team-oriented (work together).

Career success equates with promotions and titles.	Success equates with personal satisfaction.
A stable, linear career plan is created.	A multidemensional plan grouped around several objectives is developed.
The organization charts career direction.	The individual determines his/her own portfolio development direction.

Comparing some of the differences side by side, two underlying themes show up pretty clearly: first, a lot that was linear is now more random or cyclical (advancement, salaries, career planning); and second, individual decisions and performance have a lot more influence. The focus has shifted to present and future effectiveness, what's working and how to make things better, rather than blindly following an existing path or an established way of doing business.

Fulfillment

This final difference is especially interesting, partly because in the past it was rarely associated with the traditional employer-employee relationship. Fulfillment simply wasn't the employer's business; most jobs were the kind of activity that you had to *endure* in order to have the means to pursue personal fulfillment in other ways, often through family or non-economic activities. Today, we're much more aware that fulfillment is possible and desirable. As a result, workers are finding it more and more difficult to devote a third of their waking hours to drudgery while they defer the need for fulfillment.

You can get a sense for how much the possibility of fulfillment at work has increased in recent times by contrasting your own expectations with those held by your parents or grandparents. Most people find that their parents had little or no expectation of expressing or satisfying themselves through work—it just didn't cross their minds.

When Cal Ripken Jr. broke baseball's record for consecutive games played in 1996, he gave us a great example of the power of fulfillment at work. Watching him on TV was impressive, especially because he seemed sincere and genuinely humble. He didn't seem particularly interested in the record; what he was interested in was playing baseball as well he possibly could. You could really sense that this was a guy who was doing what he loved, playing ball, and because he honestly cared about his niche he was able to fill it well, and longer than any of his competitors.

Everywhere from sports to pop psychology we hear that satisfaction and fulfillment are required for peak performance. And certainly employers are ever-more interested in peak performance as they struggle to keep up with their customers' expectations and competitors' actions. If peak performance requires fulfillment, and if competitive advantage demands peak performance, then you'd better make sure you're fulfilled in your economic endeavors. The important point, and the big difference from the past, is that it's not optional anymore; it's required.

Success Factors

Having looked at some general differences between the old job model and the molecular marketplace, let's explore in more detail what traits an individual will need to be successful in the new environment. The following list contains specific success factors that have been identified by workers as important to their future. Check those which apply to you as **MMI, Inc**, and add any others you come up with in the spaces provided. Be sure to consider both the BE and DO aspects of your future as **MMI, Inc**.

___ Empathy	___ Creativity
___ Initiative	___ Listening skills
___ Writing skills	___ Speaking skills
___ Presentation skills	___ Multiple languages
___ Cultural awareness	___ Sense of humor
___ Multi-tasking ability	___ Attention to detail
___ Adaptability/Flexibility	___ Openness to new ideas
___ Be organized	___ Planning ability
___ Be energetic	___ Marketing skills
___ Take 100% responsibility	___ Work well in teams
___ Computer literacy	___ Continuous learning
___ Deal well with people	___ Support network
___ Analytical skills	___ Self-knowledge
___ Manage people	___ Be well informed
___ Manage money	___ Work/Life balance
___ Dress appropriately	___ Able to relocate
___ Able to prioritize	___ Decision making skills
___ Know workplace trends	___ Strong sense of values
___ Know where going	___ Networking skills
___ Clear goals	___ Work with numbers
___ Self-directed	___ Financially stable
_____	_____
_____	_____

The Big Six Success Factors

Six success factors from the above list are especially important because they apply to almost every worker, in every situation.

1. Taking 100% Responsibility

How can one person be 100% responsible? At work, shouldn't employee and employer each have 50% responsibility? In the molecular marketplace, the employment social contract is changing to eliminate employer responsibility for workers' futures. For self-preservation, the worker has to take up the slack. In addition, workers who take 100% responsibility will stand out in the crowd by finding new ways to contribute to their own and their employers' success.

2. Adaptability/Flexibility

The world around you is changing faster than ever before. To prosper amid this change, you'll need to stay aware of what's going on in your field, think through how you fit in, and then make your own changes to keep up as often as necessary. Creating **MMI, Inc** by mastering the 10 Steps will keep you on the cutting edge.

3. Self-knowledge

You are the best source of information about what's right for you. Identifying your vision in Step 2 and your product definition statement in Step 3 have helped you build a strong base of self-knowledge about **MMI, Inc**. Being aware in every work situation of the knowledge, skills and abilities you're using and gaining new capabilities from each experience will keep your product state-of-the-art.

4. Continuous Learning

In the past, learning was separated from work, taking place in school or training situations. Today, as **MMI, Inc**, you'll need to take advantage of opportunities to learn all the time, wherever and whenever possible. Getting and continuously improving the skills needed for a competitive edge is the subject of this Step, while Steps 7 and 8 deal with the specifics of managing personal finances and marketing.

5. Marketing Skills

Getting the word out about **MMI, Inc** may be hard, but it's essential to success. Why and how to market your services is the subject of Step 8.

6. Working In Teams

"No one is an island" has never been more true, as information, relationships and communication dominate the way we work. Enhancing this vital skill for success is discussed later in Step 6.

Here's an example of how the big six success factors will increase in importance as livelihoods change in the molecular marketplace. Today, the skill requirements for a retail clerk selling women's clothing are fairly well-defined. They consist mainly of knowing where in the store specific items are located, and knowing something about the inventory, pricing and the product being sold. In more upscale stores, the clerk will have had some training in customer service, and may walk the customer through the selection process, direct her to the dressing room and bring alternative selections if needed.

In twenty years, the situation will be quite different. The customer will be invited to the store by a personal invitation announcing a special sale on items she prefers. The salesperson will be an independent consultant to the clothing manufacturer, assigned to work at this store. She'll quickly scan her hand-held computer terminal to learn the customer's past purchases, preferences and size from the manufacturer's data base. Prompted by the computer, the salesperson will then make a suggestion about the next appropriate wardrobe addition, check or measure for any change in the customer's size, and help choose style and fabric. The order will be instantly sent via the computer directly to the salesperson's work team member at the factory, with whom she communicates regularly. The customer's purchase will arrive in the store the next day, fitting exactly as ordered.

Our successful salesperson of the future will be very *sales-oriented*, while still being quite *flexible* in catering to the specific customer's needs and working in a variety of stores. She will be completely *responsible* for the customer's satisfaction as a productive member of the *team*, which includes the store and its suppliers. She will constantly have to be *learning* about new products, styles, fabrics and sales techniques. And to do all of this successfully, she'll have to be secure in the *self-knowledge* that she is doing something she loves, and is rewarded and appreciated for it.

The Gap

We've discussed what it will take, in general, for **MMI, Inc** to be successful and you've created your own personal list of success factors. Now, it's time to get "up close and personal" by objectively taking stock of yourself in the light of your aspirations. How do the two pieces of your future, you and your chosen niche, fit together? The answer to this critical question will help you build the bridge across the "gap" between the portfolio of skills, abilities and knowledge that you bring to the workplace today, and what will be needed to ensure the success of **MMI, Inc**.

The term gap implies a shortfall or lack of something, but it's also simple and direct. It's used a lot in business, where a "gap analysis" is often performed to understand what's needed in a given situation. In this Step, the term gap describes the result of comparing your present knowledge, skills and abilities (as determined in Step 3) to the attributes of a successful competitor in your chosen niche (from your field research). The point is not to feel bad because of something you lack; on the contrary, the goal is to look at this gap objectively, and then to find the ways to bridge it by developing the additional attributes required for success.

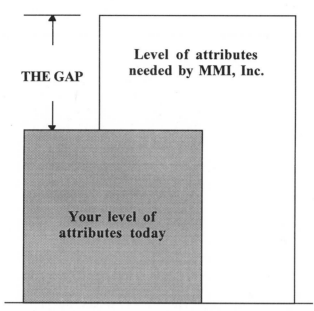

(Attributes include skills, knowledge and abilities.)

Keep in mind that identifying a gap *doesn't mean something is wrong or lacking in you.* The gap is created by lots of factors, including changes in the environment which are outside of your control, and the development of new goals that naturally occurs as we go through life. The task is to use the gap to figure out how to make the playing field more level, and, once that's done, figure out how to stand out in the crowd.

Sometimes—and more often than you might think—closing the gap can be as simple as repackaging what you already know or have. Bill, the exterminator from Step 1, successfully repackaged himself from a traditional exterminator—killing termites, mice and fleas—into "Animal Gidders" by creating a specialized, profitable niche for humanely capturing raccoons and skunks in affluent suburban areas. Closing the gap may also mean acquiring new skills, continuing an education, or developing a new attitude. But it's certainly better to have the gap clearly identified and laid out, and to be working on how to bridge it with a series of planned actions, than it is to suffer on without ever knowing what the gap consists of, or identifying what to do about it.

There are a lot of ideas and suggestions for closing the gap in the rest of Step 6 and throughout the book; some will be especially useful to you. It would be impossible and counterproductive to try to reshape yourself in each area discussed. Your best approach will be to start by focusing on a few key changes that will make the biggest difference.

So don't try to tackle too much at once. On the other hand, don't give up! Yes, there are a lot of ideas to think about. And maybe you feel like the gap you find between yourself and the "ideal" is too big. But experience working with others shows that buried somewhere among these issues are the keys to your future, so it's definitely worth the effort to keep looking for them. And the rest of this Step will help you find a few "gems" to start with that will absolutely make a difference for your future success. With that in mind, let's tackle the gap.

Look at yourself objectively today, as a product, and compare your current level of knowledge, skills and abilities with those which **MMI, Inc** will need to be successful in your niche. (Knowledge includes education, experience and work-specific information; skills include self-management, transferable and work-specific skills; abilities include areas of accomplishment using your knowledge and skills.) When you make this comparison, what gaps do you see?

Closing the Gap

The good news about having carefully looked at the competitive situation, and then objectively at yourself, is that you can now be specific about *how* to make **MMI, Inc** stand out in the crowd. Perhaps the gap analysis you've just done will make it clear there's an area where you need to focus the development efforts for **MMI, Inc**. And maybe it's clear just what you need to do about it—for example, take a course of study, learn a new skill, or work for a year as a temporary in an industry to gain some needed experience or money.

Or maybe it's not yet clear what your next actions should be. If not, you'll get a lot more information as you continue through this Step and through the book. In either case, the rest of this Step on creating competitive advantage will focus on four topics that belong on everyone's list of "gap closers": attitude, networking, strategic alliances and teamwork, and customer service. Finally, you'll have the opportunity to set specific goals to start the process of closing the gap.

Gap Closer 1: Attitude

In a Wall Street Journal article, Thomas Petzinger, Jr. cited this operating principle at a major Lucent Technologies plant: "Hire attitude over aptitude." Nothing influences success more than one's attitude in a new or changing environment. Change is a hallmark of the molecular marketplace, and as the waves of change sweep over us it's easy to feel victimized by someone or some circumstance impacting us negatively. The precise problem with feeling victimized is that it *always* feels justified, and at the same time it *always* results in a defensive, negative attitude. And, like all attitudes, it tends to be self-fulfilling—if you believe it, it's true.

Cecilia was an administrative assistant in a small moving company for fifteen years. When the owner died, his family took over and in a few months mismanaged the business into bankruptcy. Cecilia was one of the five who survived the first layoff, when sixteen people were fired. The survivors were kept on to help the court-appointed administrator wind down the company, but they knew their jobs would end as soon as the affairs of the company were concluded.

Cecilia couldn't believe it! She'd been loyal to the owner and knew almost everything about the company. How could the owner's family be so stupid as to let the business fail, and not listen to her warnings and suggestions about how to run it? The more she thought about it, the more outspoken she became, complaining to anyone who would listen. Before the company was liquidated, a larger moving company bought the assets and re-started the business. They re-hired some of the laid-off employees, but didn't select Cecilia because, while she knew a lot about the business, they had heard she had a bad attitude. Her attitude may have been fully "justified" from her frame of reference, but in the end it cost her dearly.

As Cecilia's example shows, one of the problems with a bad attitude is that you may be the last one to know its effect. You may feel you can get away with having any attitude you want; as long as you do good work, it's nobody else's business. But from the frame of reference of those on the receiving end of your behavior, your attitude may be poisoning that relationship and perhaps even the larger environment. You may never know until it's too late. But then, of course, when you lose an opportunity because of your attitude, you'll have another reason to feel victimized, to blame others for not treating you right, and the cycle goes on and on.

Another problem with a bad attitude is that it can be very difficult to change, especially when you feel justified in being defensive or angry, like Cecilia did. So why should you even try? The simple answer is that attitude is vital to your economic (as well as personal) success. In the rest of this section we'll explore how attitude can be positive or negative, what causes an attitude that results in feeling victimized and blaming others, how to create a positive attitude, and some techniques for changing your attitude when necessary.

The Opposite Attitudes—Responsive and Defensive

There is always a choice regarding attitude. You can choose to be *responsive* in the face of changes, seeing new alternatives both in the work environment and in your own behavior, and being positive, initiating, and open to future possibilities. Yes, it can be a very hard decision at times, but you can choose to be responsive if you want to. Or, you can allow yourself to be *defensive,* lashing out, feeling victimized, and thereby failing to perceive the opportunities as they arise. Just reading the words used to describe these two contrasting attitudes can give you a sense of how much more appeal and opportunity **MMI, Inc** will generate in the molecular marketplace with a responsive attitude.

To better understand the difference between a responsive and a defensive attitude, consider half a glass of water. If you view the glass as half empty, then your inclination is to *save* what you can so that you can at least have something. You might put it in the freezer to preserve it, put it in an airtight container, or put it on a high shelf so nothing can get at it. The basis of these actions is how to conserve what you have, holding on to it to keep it safe.

If, on the other hand, you view the glass as half-full, then your inclination is to figure out how to fill it up all the way. You might go to a pristine mountain lake, purchase a bottle of water, go to a kitchen faucet, or find a way to mix hydrogen and oxygen to add H_2O to the glass. If you were thirsty, you'd even drink the water, knowing you could replace it with more when you needed to. The basis of these actions is creativity, looking at new possibilities to move forward.

The water and the glass themselves are exactly the same in these two alternative scenarios; the difference is in the way they're viewed, depending on your attitude. It's critical to understand how your attitude influences the way you perceive reality, and to see how much more potential exists in a situation when you have a responsive attitude.

Think about your own attitude, and how it influences what goes on around you. What happens when you have a defensive attitude? What happens when you have a responsive attitude? How does your attitude affect others around you?

Generally, we're all pretty familiar with responsive and defensive attitudes; you've observed them in others and, if you're objective about it, in yourself. Since everyone struggles at some time or other with a defensive attitude, let's explore further what may cause an attitude problem.

What Causes A Defensive Attitude?

A defensive attitude is often the result of *unmet expectations*. When something happens, it's just a fact that's true. But what you *expect* to happen, from your frame of reference, and whether or not that's consistent with what does happen, determines your attitude. If your expectations are met or exceeded, great; if not, you feel bad, angry or perhaps betrayed.

For example, George felt like he'd slaved for years in a boring office to earn his way into the job of his dreams: working on the outside antenna crew for a microwave radio company. He and his three partners covered a large territory, worked on their own far from the boss, traveled through beautiful countryside, spent every working day on remote mountaintops, and were pretty well paid to boot. As he told his family: "I think I've died and gone to heaven!" Before long, though, George's enthusiasm started to fade. Unfortunately, Al, the senior crew member, was becoming a problem. He was twenty years older than George, somewhat lazy, and enjoyed pushing the new guy to the limit. George ended up doing all the hard work without being told how, and was derided by Al whenever he made a mistake. George began to develop a bad attitude, and he was hardly able to talk with Al because he was so angry, afraid that Al was putting his whole future in jeopardy. George's other partners were sympathetic, but told him they were concerned that his anger at Al had begun to affect his work.

Expectations can work the other way, too—you can develop a defensive attitude if you expect something negative to happen, and in fact it doesn't. Sonia's husband Corey had to fly to work in another city for several weeks in a row. He flew home each Friday night, but every week he invariably arrived home later than planned. For Sonia, each Friday was the same. When the expected arrival time came and went, she started imagining the worst—Corey's plane had crashed. Sonia would work hard to control her thoughts, but as time wore on she'd get more and more upset. Finally, when Corey arrived late after flight and traffic delays, Sonia could hardly even welcome him home, because she was so caught up in the negative expectation, and so angry that "he'd put her through all of that." It took most of each weekend for Sonia to get over her defensive attitude and begin to have a loving relationship with Corey, and by then it was time for him to leave for another week.

Creating A Responsive Attitude

The problem for all of us is that we can't live without expectations. Yet when our expectations aren't met, we experience the pain of a negative attitude. This pain can be minor and momentary, like irritation when a bus is running late, or significant enough to strain a relationship with a loved one. Eventually, we all reach the point where the pain is strong enough to get our attention, and we know we need to make a change in our attitude to get our life or relationships back on a productive track. When you reach that point, what can you do?

Here is a process you can use to identify and change a negative attitude. The process isn't one that you can go through one time to fix your attitude once and for all. It's more like a cycle, and you can use it again and again, whenever the need arises.

Phase 1: See the reality clearly

When you find yourself holding onto an expectation—either positive or negative—that may not be fulfilled, practice the technique of developing scenarios. Imagine several possible outcomes for the situation, and think through how you would respond to each possible outcome. This technique is currently very popular in management training and behavior counseling. Past responses are habitual and very powerful, so that even though you've chosen to focus on a different outcome, it's easy to revert back into a defensive attitude. The goal is to become conscious of what's going on inside yourself, to become aware of what is likely to happen, and to plan for how you will deal with what occurs. This will also help you to see how destructive the bad attitude will be to you and your relationships with others, if you don't change it.

Phase 2: Motivation

All of the suggestions and good ideas in the world won't help change an attitude until you personally decide that it's time to do it. What is it that's important enough to you to help you make the tough decision? Is it having a good standard of living? Improving your relationships? Feeling better about yourself? Expressing care or love to others who need your support? Being inspired by a role model?

Your motivation will be unique to you, stemming from your own life experience, personality and needs at this moment. You'll know when the motivation is right, because it will help carry you through the process of making a decision and changing your attitude. The more clearly you can identify what's motivating you to change your attitude, the more often you will be able to succeed.

Phase 3: Decision

A decision is something that's permanent and effective, as discussed in Step 4. It doesn't mean you never backslide. It does mean that when you slip, you catch yourself and go right back to the course you've decided on, without spending energy blaming yourself or anyone else, and without indulging in a bad attitude about messing up.

You may think you've decided on something, but find that in the end nothing has changed. For many people, New Year's resolutions or decisions to lose weight are great disappointments when nothing changes despite their best intentions. If you find yourself wanting to change your attitude but still not able to, go back and look at the decision process discussed in Step 4, and also look to see if you've really connected with your true motivation in the phase above. Keep working at the process until you succeed, because...

Phase 4: In the end, you benefit

The great thing about changing your attitude is that, regardless of who else benefits, you do too. Whatever the reason behind the pain that gets your attention, and whatever or whoever provides you with the motivation to change, when you decide and make a change in your attitude it's a win-win proposition. Once you've consciously changed your attitude and experienced the personal rewards, you know forever after that the process will work to your benefit. Knowing this will help make the decision to tackle your next attitude problem easier.

Let's come back to George and Sonia to see how the process of creating a responsive attitude works. George began the process of changing his attitude about Al by trying to see the possibilities clearly. He imagined different conclusions to the abuse he was getting from Al. He thought about talking with the boss about the situation, having a talk with Al himself, leaving the job to escape the hostility, or living with the situation until he learned the job well enough that Al had nothing to ride him about. In thinking through the scenarios, George clearly *saw the reality* that even if Al never changed, his own *motivation* to continue learning and doing the work he loved was very strong. He knew he'd probably have to continue to take some abuse while he was still learning the job, but he realized he needed to make a *decision* to put his own negativity aside in order to continue doing what he loved. There was no question in his mind that *he would benefit* more than anyone from improving his attitude. He could continue to learn the job, so that in the future his boss would see the competitive advantage he brought to the team—both his job skills and his positive attitude.

Sonia, in the second example, was already pretty good at imagining the scenario of Corey's plane crashing—after all, the image crossed her mind many times every Friday evening. But each time it came up she tried to put it out of her mind instantly, feeling that if she thought about a crash, it would somehow make it come true. Sonia solved her problem of a defensive attitude when Corey arrived home by thinking through two more likely scenarios. First, she imagined the heavy Friday commute traffic around the airport, and the frustration Corey would be feeling while waiting in the car in stop and go traffic, anxious to be home. Second, she thought about the heavy business air travel on Fridays that almost always delayed the afternoon and evening flights. From these, she *saw the reality* that both of these scenarios were quite likely, while a plane crash was extremely unlikely, and that took the power out of her fear. She also realized she had a very strong *motivation* to change her attitude in order to have a good time with Corey during their short weekends together. She *decided* to keep her attitude positive by focusing her thoughts on their reunion and helping him to wind down from his week away and his long trip home. As a result, Sonia saw how much *she benefited* from the warmth and affection of their time together. And she was amazed when Corey noticed the difference in her attitude, and thanked her for supporting him when things were tough.

Creating a positive attitude can be critically important in the workplace. For example, the concept of self-management is popular in some work environments today. Self-management sounds appealing to most workers, and where self-management is practiced, it creates conditions which are beneficial to both employer and employee. But self-management is a double-edged sword, requiring not only a trusting and open approach from the employer to give responsibility and authority to the worker, but also a parallel response from the worker in maturity, responsibility, and willingness to maintain a positive attitude. In other words, self-management is not just a way for workers to get management off their backs. It also requires the worker to take 100% responsibility (one of the big six success factors) to be successful.

What is your attitude about work? Do you see your work environment as a half-empty glass of water, to be conserved or defended? Or do you feel it's a place of possibility and opportunity? Do you think your attitude has any relationship to the level of freedom and self-management you have been given in your work?

Think about how you could use the process described above to identify when your attitude about work is negative, and to change your attitude to one that's responsive.

- What are your expectations about your work environment? Are they positive or negative? What alternative scenarios have you thought through to *see the reality clearly*?

- What is your *motivation* when you need to change your attitude about your work?

- Is there a *decision* you need to make about your attitude with respect to work?

- Can you see how *you would benefit* from a change in your attitude to work?

Changing Your Attitude

Listed below are some common symptoms of a negative attitude. If you find yourself doing or feeling these things, it's time to examine your attitude and find a way to change it. After each symptom are some techniques that have worked for other people in dealing with that symptom and changing the underlying attitude.

Symptom	Possible Ways to Change Attitude
You're angry or fearful because your expectations aren't met—something happens you didn't expect, or something you hoped for didn't happen.	Practice developing scenarios of several possible outcomes to prepare for whatever happens; write about your feelings; keep a journal.
You find yourself talking too much, especially going on about reasons why not to do something, or why something won't work.	Invite silence, using meditation or right-brain activities; focus on making a decision.
You feel confused, even after things have been clearly explained; you've retreated, and no amount of information can help.	Write things down clearly and step-by-step; focus on what you do know and are sure of.
You become obsessive about little rituals or routines, acting like a creature of habit to keep from facing anything new.	Do one altered "risky" behavior each day, no matter how small.

You're easily distracted by digressions and diversions, like procrastination, excessive sleeping, sickness, or watching TV, putting other things off until tomorrow.

Using the "cue" words:
I can't; I shouldn't; I'm not sufficiently _____ (fill in blank with bright, talented, outgoing, etc.); Yes, but...; It feels wrong to just do what I want; I may lose more than I gain; What would people think?; It isn't realistic; I've never done this before; What if I do it wrong?; But I've *always* done it this way; This will never work; This is just a waste of time/energy; Oh, I've tried that before; You'll have to convince me; It's too hard; See, I knew it wouldn't work (after trying and failing); My present job/situation isn't so bad after all.

Get regular physical exercise, which helps you define yourself by action rather than inaction.

Make a list of the opposites to each of these cue words you find yourself using, stating the situation in the positive. Memorize the positive statements and repeat them to yourself, or write and post them where you see them regularly.

Adapted from *The Newsletter about life/work planning,"* Richard N. Bolles, Editor (author of *What Color Is Your Parachute?) Used by permission.*

Closing The Attitude Gap

Think about a situation in which you changed your attitude in the past few days. It doesn't have to be something profound; it can be one of the many small occasions in day-to-day life when we adjust our attitude because it's getting in our way. The point is to better understand the process of making a decision and changing your attitude. This will help you build the important skill of changing your attitude whenever it starts getting in the way of your plans for **MMI, Inc.**

- What was the situation?

- What was your original attitude?

- What was your changed attitude?

- What difference did your change of attitude make in the situation?

- Do you think that learning to change your attitude is a gap closer for **MMI, Inc**? If so, what is it that can and will motivate you to change your attitude?

Managing your attitude is a key survival skill, or success factor, in the molecular marketplace. A defensive or victimized attitude can destroy competitive advantage in a heartbeat; a positive attitude can help you stand head and shoulders above the crowd. Attitude is a very big subject, and we've only scratched the surface. If you want to learn more about how to work with your attitude, an excellent resource is *Emotional Resilience*, by David S. Viscott, MD.

Gap Closer 2: Networking

It's often said that we're in the information age. It must be true, because we have increasing amounts of information coming at us constantly from all directions. For example, Gina's father recently had a bout of sciatica; since she didn't know much about sciatica, Gina went to the Internet to see what she could learn. The response she got back to her query was that there were 13,200 references to sciatica on the Net, so she should narrow down her question by providing more detail. That's a lot of data about sciatica!

For most of us, there's far more information around than we can absorb, let alone understand and utilize to make decisions. Despite this, or maybe because of it, communication has arisen as one of the most essential human activities. Networking is the modern, professional term, but it's really the same basic activity as the conversation, story-telling, and idea sharing that's taken place for eons around camp fires, at family gatherings, or around the water cooler. Networking is essential for people to learn to know and trust each other, to help each other out, and to exchange information.

One of the most important activities you will ever do to make **MMI, Inc** successful is to connect with other people. Through networking you'll learn important things about yourself, the competition, what's happening or about to happen, potential work opportunities, and things to do and pitfalls to avoid in your niche.

You might find the idea of networking unpleasant or threatening, especially if your personality type is introverted. The bad news is that networking is nonetheless a critically important activity. The good news is that you have a lot of choices in how you go about it, and you'll be able to find some ways to network effectively that you'll actually enjoy. It also helps to find that most people with whom you network actually appreciate the contact. You're certain to discover that some, if not most, of your contacts will become friends, who appreciate the help you give them as a network contact as much as you appreciate the help they give you.

For example, Karin made a networking contact several months ago with Wendy, another professional woman in her field. At first, Wendy was standoff-ish, feeling that Karin was just looking for competitive informa-tion. After their first lukewarm conversation, Karin sent Wendy some of her professional materials; Wendy realized that the material was good, and that there might be ways for them to work together. During a cordial lunch at which Karin told Wendy she was writing a book, Wendy really opened up. She told Karin she also wanted to write a book, but didn't know how to get started. From that point on, the relationship became collaborative and the women kept in regular contact.

So who will make up your network? To begin with, it's everyone you now know. Your list will change and grow as networking becomes part of your ongoing professional activity in support of your goals for **MMI, Inc.** Here's a list of potential contacts to get you started.

- Family
- Friends
- Neighbors
- Members of your church, club or association
- Union and professional associates
- Holiday greeting list
- Friends from school
- People you work with now, or worked with in the past
- People you met while working on competitive analysis in Step 5
- People who you respect or admire who share your niche
- Current and past employers, and prospective employers you've been in touch with
- People on the Internet with similar interests
- Anyone else who is in a position to help you with advice, information, or feedback

How do you go about networking? The list below includes ideas that others have found to work.

- A networking relationship can be a long-lasting, close contact, but it can also be based on an occasional, brief contact;

- If you hear something about someone you know, get in touch to congratulate or sympathize or just let them know you're there;

- If you hear or read something and think of someone to whom it relates, or who could benefit by knowing about it, get in touch with the person;

- Pick up the telephone and call;

- Send an e-mail;

- Send a voice mail message;

- Send a brief note or letter about what you're up to, asking the other person a question about your niche or theirs;

- Use the Internet to read current items about your niche, or participate in news groups or chat rooms;

- Add a bit about your work and niche to your holiday greeting;

- Join a group composed of people with similar interests;

- Talk with people in your social and religious groups about **MMI, Inc**;

- Attend conferences, conventions, seminars relevant to your niche;

- Attend adult education and self-development events relevant to your niche;

- Join someone for a meal or coffee break and include a little chat about your goals for **MMI, Inc**;

- Make a point of initiating at least one networking contact every day, even if it's a short one.

And, just to be clear, networking is important even for long-term employees; all of these ideas will apply within and beyond your employers' organization.

If you don't already have a well-developed list of network contacts, now is the time to begin one. Be sure that your list includes a record of the best way to reach each contact—address, phone number, email, voice mail, Internet address, etc.

The tried and true method for keeping such a list is a Rolodex file, which makes it easy to add and change written address information. The more modern way is to keep a computerized list; there are a lot of good, simple software programs out there to keep track of contacts. The additional benefit of using a software program is that it allows you to keep track of more information, such as records of contacts and future appointments. Your file—Rolodex or computer—should be right next to where you work, and should be updated continuously with new networking leads or contacts whenever they pop up. If you use it to support effective networking, it will be worth it's weight in gold. If you'd like to develop more ideas on the subject of networking, a good resource is *Fifty Two Ways to Reconnect, Follow-Up and Stay in Touch, When You Don't Have Time to Network*, by Anne Baber and Lynne Waymon.

Gap Closer 3: Strategic Alliances And Teamwork

Strategic alliances among businesses are in the news constantly these days. Banks, media giants, computers, telecommunications—mergers and take-overs rock the markets constantly. Strategic alliances are as important at the individual level as they are at the corporate level, only they take a different form. For individuals, strategic alliances reflect the growing importance of being able to work well with other people in teams.

Teamwork has been a popular subject in business, organizational research and sociology for the past few years, because it's being recognized as a critical success factor for organizations. This is true for three reasons. First, in the information age interaction between people has become more and more central to the way work gets done. Being good at "turning the crank" to produce something is still fundamentally important in anyone's work. But with today's rapid flow of information and growing competitive pressures, good interaction skills have become the "oil on the gears" that keeps things turning easily and smoothly.

Second, we've all been in teams in the past that haven't worked well. A bad teamwork experience can leave you feeling like the team is more trouble than it's worth: you could have done it better by yourself, or someone else just took charge and you didn't need to be involved at all.

The third reason why skill in strategic alliances is so important is that, to put it bluntly, most of us aren't very good at it. You've probably never been taught, unless through the "school of hard knocks," about how to work with others in a mutually supportive way. However, you've probably been taught a lot about turning the crank to produce something, whether that means number crunching, planting corn, programming computers, child care, hairdressing, analyzing investments, cleaning a sewer, making presentations or cleaning a house. You name it, someone will have instructed, educated, trained or shown you how. But how much instruction have you ever been given on oiling the gears—understanding your interactions with others, their needs and motivations, and the most effective way to work together? Unless you're part of an organization with a truly modern outlook on customer service or selling, you've probably had no such training. Small wonder that most of us aren't great at teamwork.

Success Factors for Team Functioning

To stand out in a crowd, **MMI, Inc** will need to become very good at creating, developing and nurturing strategic alliances. Oil will flow into the gears of any work relationship, whether between two people or among many people, if these eight factors are present and working well:

- The goals are clear;

- The process for reaching the goals is clear;

- The role to be filled by each team member is clear;

- The focus of the group is on accomplishing the goals;

- The management approach is collaborative;

- People and relationships are treated with respect;

- Compatible philosophies/styles are developed and shared;

- A process to resolve differences is developed and agreed to.

Think about a situation where you've had a great teamwork experience —at work, in sports, or any group activity. How have the above eight team success factors worked to "oil" the team functioning, to help reach the team goal successfully? Contrast this with another situation you've experienced where teamwork has not worked well. Which of the team success factors was missing? How did the absence or the poor quality of the factors diminish team effectiveness and the value of the accomplishment of the team's goal?

Traits Of Successful Team Players

If the players on a team are willing and have the right skills, the eight success factors can determine how well their strategic alliance will work. But the other element in teamwork that must be reckoned with is the ability of the individual team player. All the lubricating oil in the world won't make a machine work if one of its components is rusted or broken. The team will work best if the players individually understand and exhibit these traits that support team success:

- Understand the purpose of the team;

- Agree on goals;

- Be trustworthy, and be able to trust others;

- Stay flexible and able to adjust to others' ways of working;

- Be willing to risk saying what you really think;

- Respect others' contributions;

- Agree on appropriate involvement;

- Make a commitment of time to the process.

In the good and bad team experiences you identified earlier, think about how the individual traits listed above may have helped or hindered the team functioning in both experiences. How did these traits help or hinder you and your functioning as a team member? How did these traits help or hinder the team leaders, or the person or people who you felt were the most influential team members? Do you think that creating and managing good strategic alliances and teamwork is a gap closer for **MMI, Inc**? Like the other gap closers, teamwork is a very big issue and we've only scratched the surface. If you want to get more information, a good source is *The Breakthrough Team Players: Becoming MVP on Your Workplace Team* by Andrew J. Dubrin.

Gap Closer 4: Customer Service

Successful organizations of all types—public sector and charitable groups as well as businesses—are finding that high quality, personal customer service is the only way they can assure that they get the customer support or funding they need to survive and prosper. Henry, for example, was surprised by the level of customer service he received recently at his county office. He appreciated the signs helping him find his way to the right counter and the attention he got from the workers. They really made him feel that they were there to help him. He still wasn't happy about paying for a building permit, but he liked the people and their attitude. Instead of complaining to others about the permit process, he told several of his friends about the surprisingly good service he got.

On the other side, we all have plenty of examples of being treated poorly as customers—what's your favorite horror story?

Good customer service can be hard to define. That's partly because people and their needs are different—what's good service for one person may not be good for the next. A short wait in an airline ticket line may seem fine to someone on a vacation trip, but unacceptable to a business traveler who's late for a departure. Some experts have given up trying to define good customer service, saying only: "You know it when you see it."

Which, it turns out, is a pretty good definition. To meet this definition, the service provider has to make the effort to get into the buyer's frame of reference (remember frame of reference from Step 2?) to figure out how to meet the buyer's needs and expectations.

So, you're thinking that unless you're going into a retail or service business, this doesn't have much to do with **MMI, Inc**? Guess again. Part of **MMI, Inc**'s formula for success will be knowing that your employers are nothing more or less than good, valued customers. Contrast this to the way most workers view their employers today: the powerful source and control of economic support, to be pleased, tolerated or resisted, and maybe sometimes appreciated.

There are two important points to complete the picture of the employer as customer. First, contrary to popular opinion, you don't have to kowtow to customers "who are always right." Instead, you'll develop a relationship of *equals* with customers who are members of that *selected* group of people with whom **MMI, Inc** has *chosen* to do business! Second, providing good customer service to the employer applies whether you're an entrepreneur, a temporary worker or a long-term employee of a business or government.

Whoever your future employers are, see them as customers to be served in a way that pleases them and demonstrates the value of your product. Your employer, like any customer, has the same needs we all have—to receive a quality product at a reasonable price. And don't forget that part of your role is to be sure the customer knows the real value of the product you're delivering. Remind the customer from time to time that you're there, you're doing well, you care, and you appreciate their business. Reminders can include simple things: writing thank-you notes, keeping track of personal information like birthdays and the names of family members, and following up to ask if the customer is pleased with your product or service and if there's anything you can do to improve it. Customer service doesn't need to be a major program or effort. The key in most cases is to be responsive when the right opportunity knocks.

Don't be afraid to borrow good customer service ideas. Keep your eyes and ears open and when a person or a company impresses you with their service, identify what pleased you, and ask yourself if it would also work for **MMI, Inc.** If so, add it to your repertoire of customer service techniques. In this way, you'll continue to differentiate **MMI, Inc** from others in your niche.

For example, Ron owned his own small appliance repair business. The work that paid the best was contract repairs for a large department store chain. Ron knew how to give good service to the customers whose appliances he repaired, and got more than his share of positive comments from satisfied customers. One day Ron was repairing a washer for a woman who worked out of her home taking opinion surveys, when he overheard her giving a summary of her interview results to her company office. This gave him an idea for improving his service to the department store. He came up with a short customer opinion survey which. he could easily talk with customers about while he was working on their appliances. After each service call, he'd take a moment in his truck to summarize the customer's opinion about the store in general, and their appliances in particular. Each week he sent the store's service manager a summary of what he found, including any customers who might soon be in the market for a replacement appliance. His survey results were very helpful to the store, and each week the information reminded the service manager of the quality of Ron's work. He soon became the store's first-choice appliance repair contractor, and had to employ another technician to help handle the increased work load.

How can you create an equal relationship, based on good customer service, with your present or prospective employers? Think about ways you can discover the expectations and needs of your employers for good customer service from an employee. Do you think that providing good customer service to your employers is a gap closer for **MMI, Inc**?

Just like the previous gap closers—attitude, networking and strategic alliances and teamwork—the subject of customer service is a big one. If you want help to develop more ideas, there are good resources available including *The Customer Is Usually Wrong!* by Fred E. Jandt.

How You'll Close The Gap: Goals

The idea of goal-setting has long been a basic tenet of management and self-improvement philosophies, which hold that goals are a way to subdivide the future's needs into manageable chunks to be attacked, conquered and moved beyond. The process is systematic, passionless, almost mechanical.

But recently, the whole concept of goals has received a lot of bad press. Critics charge that goals cause a person or organization to focus on pre-conceived ideas, perhaps distracting attention from the critical here and now. They can mask the need to flex, adapt, stay constantly alert and read the clues of environmental change. Goals are thought to create linear thinking, while a "systems" approach which sees holistically is more appropriate in our dynamic times.

There is a middle path between these two perspectives on goals which will create the most value for **MMI, Inc**. Taking this middle path approach will allow you to set and track short-term, "stepping-stone" goals in order to break down your journey into manageable pieces. This will enable you to continuously build, accomplish and rebuild the stepping-stone goals, which will help you in decision-making, provide tactical direction, and keep track of and celebrate your progress as milestones are passed.

Using this approach, you'll stop short of developing long-term, sweeping goals. Instead, for the big picture you'll be able to rely on your vision for **MMI, Inc** to provide an overarching sense of direction, motivation and inspiration. This middle path for goal setting will allow you to keep one eye on your vision, and the other on current issues, trends, and changing relationships as they ebb and flow around you.

You can now bring your gap analysis to a close by developing, in concert with your vision, your first set of stepping-stone goals. To be useful, the goals you set should be **SMART**:

S   Specific—The result is clear.

M   Measurable—The end point is determined, and incremental progress can be measured.

A   Achievable—It is generally possible, can really happen.

R   Realistic—It is personally possible, I can really do it.

T   Time-oriented—A deadline for closure exists, and provides appropriate motivation.

Here's an example of a **SMART** goal, based on the starting point: "I don't feel good about the way I look."

S   Specific: I am going to lose weight.
M   Measurable: The amount I will lose is twenty pounds.
A   Achievable: Is it possible for someone my size and age to lose the weight? I do a little research, talk to my doctor, and answer, "Yes."
R   Realistic: I have no health, psychological or other reason that truly keeps me from losing the weight, and I've made a decision to do it.

T   Time-oriented: I will lose the weight by November 15, to look and feel my best for the holiday season.

The original statement, "I don't feel good about the way I look," is so unfocused that it doesn't allow for any action; instead, it just causes anxiety. After you've turned a desired outcome into a SMART goal, you'll have the information and motivation you need to succeed, and you'll be able to measure your progress.

Keiko, whom we met earlier in this Step, was forced to update her stenographic skills to become a court reporter when she lost her secretarial position. Because she was new in her field and not well known she was low on the list of court reporters to be called by law firms and as a result her income fluctuated. She viewed this uneven cash flow as a gap which she could fill by providing better customer service than any of the other court reporters. She developed a SMART goal to determine what her customers—law firms—wanted in a court reporter, and to find a way to exceed their expectations so that she'd be on the top of the list to be called.

Keiko's goal looked like this:

S   I will be among the top three court reporters in town.
M   I will have work to fill 80% of my available hours.
A   I will determine what the top ten law firms consider to be outstanding customer service from a court reporter, and develop a specific list of things to do to provide the best service to each firm.
R   My skill, capability and motivation are high, making this goal realistic. I will develop a short survey and visit each of the top ten firms to determine their needs as part of my networking program.
T   I will complete my survey in two months, and reach my goal in six months.

You now have the information you'll need to set short- to mid-term goals for closing the highest priority gaps you've identified, using the SMART criteria. As you develop your goals, consider what you'll need to start, stop, continue and/or learn in order to accomplish each. If you've identified gaps and set goals which leave you feeling a bit overwhelmed, keep these points in mind:

- You now have a clear picture of what you need to do to fulfill your vision. That's much more powerful than being in the dark because you have a basis for taking positive action, starting with a "glass-half-full" attitude.

- No one expects instantaneous achievements on all fronts—unless it's you. Instead, you're creating a plan based on your vision, with specific activities and carefully thought-out ways to make steady progress over a period of time, which will result in a successful future.

- The process for you to become **MMI, Inc** is now organized and can be managed using the SMART, stepping-stone goals you've created.

- You'll be able to set priorities for your goals, which will help you make progress without trying to do everything at once. Some tips for setting priorities are included in Step 9.

Based on the goals you've developed, what personal issues will you face as you work toward them? Think about ways you can address each of the issues. Compare your competitive advantage as **MMI, Inc** in your niche today with what your competitive advantage will be when you have completed your goals.

The work you've done up to this point provides a strong foundation for launching yourself on a successful journey into the molecular marketplace. The remainder of the book will focus on how to resolve the specific issues you'll face in creating **MMI, Inc.**

Case Studies

1. *Shannon*

I found thinking about personal success to be quite enlightening. For me, success means I respect myself, I can support myself, I am innovative or creative, and I'm acknowledged by others. On the other hand, the comments about failure helped me see that, as a skill (!), I'm not very good at it. I don't mean that I don't like failure—I don't suppose anyone does—but that I don't deal with it well at all. It drags me off track from my goals and stops my progress. So I'd have to say one way for me to improve my "competitive advantage" is to get better at dealing well with failure.

Once I got into the personal work of this Step, I hit some speed bumps. It started when I did the Success Factor checklist. As I thought about which success factors would give me an advantage in my chosen livelihood and niche, I checked that I needed all but 2! Then I thought about how many I actually have now—nowhere near that many. It started seeming like a lot of work to get where I want to go.

And, of course, that was the next section I got to—the gap. If the success factors checklist was informative, the gap analysis was scary. My gap is huge! Since my livelihood and niche are newly-chosen, I need more things than I already have. By the time I made even a partial list of gaps to fill, the whole process seemed insurmountable. The instructions in the Step did acknowledge that this could be heavy-duty, and suggested that I choose a "few key" gaps to close. I came up with four major ones: a degree, some experience with ESL students, better presentation skills, and money to make it possible to change careers. No easy path here.

I felt frustrated to leave my own huge list of specific gap closers and read about still more things I needed, according to the authors. But once I got into attitude, I was extremely impressed with the information presented. When I hear the topic "attitude," I expect to hear the usual little pep talk: get a good one, or "just say yes." This is the first time I've seen an honest attempt to define how attitude works and how to improve it. I especially liked the chart listing the symptoms of bad attitude and some possible ways to fix it. Taking a practical approach to working with attitude really appeals to me; I think my attitude is generally pretty good, but when it's not, I'll have some specific techniques to try for improving it. I have to say, though, that as I finished reading this attitude adjustment process, I wondered if I have enough time in my life to try using all the processes suggested in these 10 Steps!

I guess the best part of this Step for me was the fact that the four "gap closers" included in this Step are thrown around by people all the time: have a better attitude, do teamwork, use your network, practice good customer service. But they're rarely fleshed out as to what they mean, much less how to do them. So both the explanations and the references to other books make them more tangible. After reading about the four gap closers, I think strategic alliances is the most challenging for me, so I've added it to my list of gaps (I guess one more can hardly hurt at this point!).

And then I tackled goals. Based on my big list of gaps, the goals process was another huge one for me; I have *so* far to go. I took the four "key" gaps I'd come up with earlier, and ranked them: I first need to figure out where the money will come from, then I can begin getting experience and working on my degree, and later I can improve my presentation skills. Realizing that I wasn't going far without resolving the financial issues made me think more seriously about possible sources for money: a second job, loans, etc.

In hindsight, I'd say that I'm glad I had to do this step, though it seemed for a while like it made my livelihood choice seem even less possible. The first list of "to-do's" (gaps) was tough to deal with, but laying out the pieces helped me get a handle on my new livelihood and niche; now I finally feel like I can begin to make some headway. Before, I called teaching ESL "the impossible dream"; now it seems like hard work, but imaginable.

2. *Brent*

The idea of competitive advantage through personal excellence has always appealed to me—no surprise, as I'm an incurable perfectionist. I've always found rewards in maintaining the highest achievable quality even when there is no direct and immediate reward. As an example, my colleague Hank, a twelve-year veteran of the electronics industry and an acknowledged expert in the field, took on a quality assurance role which he soon tired of because it was extra work without extra pay. Starting as a novice, over time I learned enough from him and others to build a reputation for the highest quality work in the office, and to also step into Hank's quality assurance role. In fact, I'd just been chosen over Hank for a quality-oriented managerial position when my organization was dissolved in the merger downsizing.

I found the section on gap analysis difficult. It required a lot of serious introspection to critically assess the needs of **MMI, Inc** and the shortcomings in my personal abilities. For a new livelihood the *real* requirements for success can't be known for sure until you actually *do* the job, and assessing one's untested skills against an unsure set of minimum requirements is frustrating. It is necessary, however; taking a first shot at closing the gap makes you competitive for the job, and closing the remaining gaps as you get closer to your goals ensures your success.

Networking is important, but I'm not good at it. It always feels to me like imposing or intruding, especially if I'm only calling to keep up a contact. I much prefer making and sustaining friendships, but that implies we have a lot in common to begin with rather than only being a convenient business contact. I would rather build a reputation for doing a great job than just talk to others about it. The dilemma is how to spread that reputation outside one's insular work group. This is one of my gaps, and I'm planning to buy the suggested reference book for new ideas.

Teamwork used to be a problem for me. I tend to become abrasive, especially with people who don't agree with me. My supervisor pointed this out a year ago, so I've been working hard to change, and I think I have. By being more thoughtful in my relationships with others, everyone seems to be more cooperative. One manager from another department and I both had rationally thought-out opinions that often were diametrically opposed. I changed my attitude toward her, becoming more understanding and less critical, and her attitude toward me changed as well. The big boss took me aside a few months ago and said, "Lynne told me she's had a great time working with you the past few weeks. What did you do?" It's nice to know that it shows.

I've always found that small goals, taken over time, are more effective than huge sweeping goals. They're easier to manage, and provide a better sense of completion. I've taken a stepping-stone approach to the goals I've set for **MMI, Inc.**

3. *Emily*

The success factor in Step 6 that is most relevant to my development of **MMI, Inc** right now is attitude. I found the general discussion about attitude to be a helpful, different approach, and can see specific areas in my life where I can benefit from shifting my attitude from negative to positive. Here's an example.

As part of my student work at the community college, I spent a couple of weeks observing a Master Teacher in a particular counseling class. Then I was given several sessions alone with the students to present my own information and to hold a discussion.

Because I am so new at the process of teaching, I like to come into the classroom with a very well-prepared and thought-out approach. I write down exactly what I will say to introduce the subject, choose an experience to get the students involved in the topic, and think out a precise time frame for the class discussion.

As a result of preparing thoroughly, my attitude when I first went into the classroom was quite rigid. I knew what should happen and I was very well prepared for directing it to go that way.

Unfortunately for me, I had not taken into account the varieties of things that might intrude on the best-laid plans. For instance, in the first class I had on my own, where I had carefully prepared materials for the 50 minutes, a bell began ringing after a few minutes into the class signaling a fire drill, so everyone trooped out, stood around for 10 minutes, and then trooped back in—cutting 20 minutes out of my prepared 50 minute class time. And at the next class, again carefully planned, I found more then half of the class gone for a field trip. I was frustrated and upset with these changes in my plans and had no idea what to do. I felt angry at the disruptions and blamed others for my frustrations.

The ideas in Step 6 about how to change my attitude made sense, so I decided to try them. I knew feeling angry and blaming others was not doing me any good and was certainly not doing the students any good either. The idea of looking at my expectations and thinking through different possible outcomes seemed to be a good idea. So, before the next class, I thought through as many possible disruptions as I could, including fire drills, field trips, sickness, bad weather, teacher strikes, earthquakes, and student absences. As the semester proceeded, I found that I was more able to deal with unforeseen situations and I was able to incorporate the attitude-changing ideas into my classroom curriculum as a way to help the students learn how to anticipate and prepare for unforeseen circumstances in their own lives.

4. *Forrest*

As I prepare to end my second short career as an employee of a consulting group and begin a third career as an independent, I worry about "working without a safety net" for the first time. Do I really understand competition and enjoy it like I thought I did? Can I really make it through the tough times? Most of all, can I learn to effectively sell my services and still keep a positive attitude?

Having taken a good look at who I really am and where I am going in Steps 2 and 3, I can see that I'm in pretty good shape on the six success factors. The one that still gives me pause for concern is marketing; I'm happy that there's another Step coming which deals with marketing.

My personal gap analysis showed me that my attitude is generally positive and that I'm good—an expert, in fact—at customer service. I gave a lot of thought to the issue of strategic alliances, and realized two things. First, I've worked a lot on teams, but usually they were set up by others so I was a member, not the team leader. In my new role, I'll need to be good at picking people for teams, setting them up, and working on more than one at once. The second realization was that I'll probably need to work more closely with others than I'd realized, both to bring in lots of resources for a project, if needed, and to bring in some skills where I didn't feel personally strong, like accounting and billing systems.

These insights have helped me decide to incorporate my business and find two or three other good people to affiliate with to have easy access to the broad set of skills needed to launch a service center project. The ideas on how good strategic alliances work have helped me develop a screening interview for people I might want to include on my future teams.

The insights also helped me set my initial goals for launching **MMI, Inc** as a consulting company:

- Complete the process of incorporation of business within 60 days.

- Attend a seminar on marketing professional services within 3 months.

- Interview other consultants and select at least five to affiliate with for larger projects; complete informal agreements with affiliates within 3 months.

- Obtain second client contract within 120 days.

- Schedule one week next summer to assess first six months of consulting work and create detailed plans for development of my long-term niche.

- Schedule one week for vacation with my wife, to relax.

I completed my work on this Step with a strong feeling of confidence that I could be successful in my new work by standing out in the crowd.

Step 7

Develop A Financial Strategy

Matt, a successful 34-year-old pharmaceutical sales representative: *There's been a big change in employees' expectations and sense of security where I work. The company recently merged with a giant international drug firm, and the company culture has changed for the worse. There is a lot of turnover among sales reps. I'm not happy here anymore, so I've decided to look for a position in the business of leasing big-ticket medical equipment. But meanwhile, my wife and I have a family, a mortgage, and a lifestyle to support, and eventually we want to retire comfortably. How do you find financial security with this new way of working?*

Matt's question introduces another perspective on the process of creating **MMI, Inc**. It's great to know about yourself, to plan for what you will do as **MMI, Inc**, and to develop ideas to be sure you're successful. But the snappiest concepts in the world are neither realistic nor relevant if you can't make them work on a daily basis. What about the universal, practical obstacles that confront you everyday, that keep you focused on the here-and-now when you want to reach for the stars? We call them "challenges," and financial concerns almost always top the list. What are the practical challenges that you personally face as you develop **MMI, Inc**?

Your personal list of challenges will be unique to you, but from previous experience, it will probably include items like those below.

Not having enough income
Planning far enough ahead
Managing money
Gaining support of partner
Keeping up with the pace
Competing successfully
Saving for retirement
Knowing job market trends
Dealing with emotional ups and downs
Knowing employer's work plans
Balancing my life, fearing work will
  dominate
Understanding business planning and
  processes

Marketing **MMI, Inc**
Making network contacts
Dealing with family concerns
Feeling stressed
Planning for benefits
Planning for or avoiding relocation
Managing time
Updating skills
Working as a team member
Keeping my sense of identity
Not having enough savings to get
  through a change

It's true—there are a lot of challenges! However, if the march toward the molecular marketplace is inescapable, then you'll need to find practical solutions to these challenges and incorporate them into your plan. While they may loom large, the good news is that none of these challenges are insurmountable. They can be addressed by gaining new knowledge or skills, including the skill of making a start by taking small, consistent actions toward your goal.

Notice that the above list contains two basic types of challenges: practical (how do I do it), which stem from the DO side; and emotional (how do I feel about it), which stem from the BE side. This Step and the next will address the most universally pressing DO challenges, finances and marketing. We'll wrap up the challenges in Step 9, which focuses on dealing effectively with emotional, or BE, issues.

If Money Is The Root,
Then Why Doesn't It Grow On Trees?

It's not too surprising that money ranks high on almost everyone's "worry list." As a culture, Americans have a tendency to assume that money will take care of itself. An Asian-born counselor who works with people with credit problems remarked, "Standing outside the American culture, it is very clear: Americans don't talk about money." As a result, there's often a discrepancy between inflow and outflow. Errol Flynn spoke for many Americans when he said, "My problem is trying to reconcile my gross habits with my net income."

This tendency to hope that ignoring the financial problem will make it go away results in what one financial planner called "financial illiteracy" in an article in *The Futurist* magazine: "Fear of the future is one consequence of an increasing financial illiteracy among Americans. It's becoming more widespread, and it cuts across all strata of society. Millions of Americans in every income category live on the brink of financial disaster." And the changes that the molecular marketplace is bringing will only add to the problems described.

So what's the good news in all of this? First, it doesn't take a financial wizard to manage finances. The counselor quoted above found that there was a very accurate and simple way to predict whether a person was likely to have financial problems: whether or not he or she balanced the checkbook. It's not that there's magic in the act of adding and subtracting numbers, but balancing the checkbook immediately communicated to the counselor that the person was unwilling to stay in a fog about money. He or she had gotten past the foremost American myth about money: "If I ignore the problem, it will go away."

There's another American myth about money: "Save everything, spend nothing," based on the belief that you can never have enough. This myth is less common among younger people, but it's often believed by the generation who lived through the great depression of the 30's. Many younger people have parents or grandparents who believe this myth, which helps to explain today's tendency toward free spending as a form of rebellion against the frugality of the older generation.

Sid was in his late 40's; his parents were in their 70's, both retired civil servants. They'd always lived on very little money, and Sid grew up with no frills. As it became more difficult for Sid's parents to maintain their home, they expressed interest in moving into a retirement home, which required a big up-front fee and a complete accounting of their finances. They asked Sid to help them decide what to do, and he called in a financial advisor. When the accounts were organized, Sid was amazed! His parents had investments worth over $500,000, though they'd always lived on less than $15,000 per year. Sid thought it was great that they had more than enough money to move to the retirement home, but also realized how his parents' cautious money attitudes had kept them preoccupied with money, preventing them from doing many of the things they enjoyed—traveling, attending musical performances and being in nature.

Sid gave the situation a lot of thought. He was sad for his parents that their belief in an ultra-conservative myth about money had kept them from enjoying life more—they'd worked hard and saved enough, and deserved it. But he also began to think about his own retirement. Sid and his wife reviewed their own financial situation with the financial advisor and found that they weren't saving enough to retire with their preferred lifestyle until they were well into their 70's. After taking some time to reflect on their goals, they developed a plan to reduce their spending in order to retire earlier.

There are many other American myths about money, falling somewhere between the extremes: "If I ignore the problem, it will go away" and "Save everything, spend nothing." If your approach to money is based on a myth, how can you dispel it? By learning to manage your money.

If you're a person who does balance your checkbook, you'll probably say that a balanced checkbook isn't all there is to managing money. Of course, you're right, but it is a starting point. The counselor cited earlier swears that she still has clients whose response is, "What do you mean I'm overdrawn? I've still got checks."

So if you don't balance your checkbook, that's the first action for you to take in managing your finances. Beyond that, your success in the molecular marketplace will correlate closely with the financial management skills you'll develop in the course of completing this Step. These skills will bring your finances under control by helping you to prioritize your spending and, when necessary, to stretch your dollars. You'll be more aware of income, spending and the net result. You'll know how to use the good times to save for the lean, and how much to save. You'll avoid impulse spending, but not lose the enjoyment of using your money for what pleases you. And, very importantly, you'll manage your credit.

As an added benefit, financial management skills are transferable, and as **MMI, Inc** you'll bring them into your workplace to add value to your niche.

Old Versus New Money Assumptions

Learning to manage your money starts with thinking clearly about the role that money will play in your life. Thinking clearly about money can be difficult, partly because the role of money in our whole society is changing as the industrial age gives way to the information age. Many assumptions about money which were once perfectly valid have now become obsolete. Being obsolete unfortunately doesn't mean they've gone away, just that they don't work well anymore.

To be clear about the role of money in your life, you'll need to look carefully at your own assumptions. Below are four common obsolete assumptions about money that arose during the industrial age, along with their information age counterparts and implications for personal action.

Obsolete Assumption	Contemporary Assumption	Personal Actions
Consumption and spending are the major goals.	Productivity and investment are the major economic goals	Invest in a competitive MMI, Inc to make money.
Income increases each year until retirement with a pension	Income will change based on many variables, retirement is not automatic.	Plan for variable income, not stability; save for retirement.
Buy now; pay later.	Manage debt.	Keep as current as possible on your debts; pay cash.
A fair day's work earns a fair day's pay.	Continuous improvement is required to compete.	Create competitive advantage to stand out in the crowd.

In general, the obsolete assumptions about money are based on spending an ever-increasing income, while the contemporary assumptions are based on saving in order to compensate for a fluctuating income and to invest in improving the future.

At a personal level, the underlying difference between the obsolete and current assumptions is that you can no longer count on an employer to guarantee your income and help plan your financial future—you have to do it for yourself. This difference will require that you plan, take initiative and exercise self-management—the same new skills you used to develop your niche and create competitive advantage.

Here are three common, specific financial issues which will make it necessary for many portfolio workers to exercise more financial self-management:

Qualifying for a pension versus planning for retirement

Under the old assumptions, you found a good job, stuck with it and your employer took care of you with an adequate pension for life when you retired. As **MMI, Inc**, you'll be less and less likely in the future to work for a single employer until you retire. Perhaps the government will legislate that more portfolio workers are covered by pension contributions, and that the funds set aside for pensions are portable from employer to employer. And perhaps the government will find a way to keep Social Security solvent. But the government may never take these actions, and at best they could be a long time coming. So for the foreseeable future, you'll need to save in order to have a comfortable retirement.

Employer health care benefits versus your own coverage

With health care costs rising every year, a good health care plan is important. But, as with retirement, the transient nature of employment in the molecular marketplace means employers can't or won't provide health benefits for a lot of people they employ. Unless you're certain of working for an employer who will pay for health care over the long haul, expect to pay for some or all of your health care yourself. For example, Raul left a government job right after his first child was born to work on his own as a contractor. The new position provided a reasonably good health care plan for him, but the coverage for his wife and baby would have been substandard and costly. So he enrolled in his employer's health plan as an individual, but got a separate private policy for his wife and baby which better met their needs.

Self-employment taxes versus payroll withholding

An employer pays a share of the social security and Medicare taxes for every employee. When you're self-employed, you have to pay the employer's share of these taxes and sometimes additional self-employment taxes. Not every worker in the molecular marketplace will be self-employed or start a business, but it's quite possible that at some point you'll find self-employment to be your best option. When considering self-employment, be sure to get expert advice on the tax consequences. Paying the additional social security and Medicare taxes can be a rude shock if you're not prepared.

So how do you prepare yourself to successfully face the increased financial opportunities and risks of this brave new world? The answer is to plan for it.

Your Financial Plan

Most people assume a financial plan can only be prepared by an expert and is relevant only for wealthy people. But using the following five financial planning steps, you'll be able to prepare your own basic plan to assure that your finances are in order and supporting the success of **MMI, Inc.**

Step 1: Determine your average monthly expenses.

If you're a person who balances the checkbook, perhaps you also keep track of what you spend your money on. If so, look back at the last three months (or longer if you have the records) and determine your average monthly spending including all expenses and taxes. If you don't have records of your spending, you have two other options for developing your monthly spending figure using the Monthly Expenses Worksheet below. You can reconstruct your spending over the last three months from receipts and your checkbook, or you can start now and keep track for three months to determine how you spend your money. One easy way to keep track of personal spending is to use personal financial management software (such as Quicken) on a home computer.

Step 2: Determine your minimum monthly financial needs.

Now that you're aware of what you are currently spending, review the information to decide what your absolute minimum spending level would be, in a crisis. Assume that you won't go further into debt, which means making minimum payments on whatever you now owe. In addition, assume you won't do something extreme, like selling major assets such as your home or car. Look closely at the categories where you have a choice about what you spend, such as dining out, gifts, recreation/travel, vacations and clothing to see what spending could be eliminated, if necessary.

Monthly Expenses Worksheet (over the course of 3 months)

Deductions	Month 1	Month 2	Month 3
Medical/Dental			
Property Taxes			
Deductible Interest			
Charitable Contributions			
Unreimbursed Bus. Expense			
Miscellaneous Deductions			

Household

	Month 1	Month 2	Month 3
Child Support/Day Care			
Clothing			
Dry Cleaning/Laundry			
Groceries and Sundries			
Homeowners/Renters Insur.			
Household Maintenance			
Mortgage/Rent			
Utilities			

Transportation

	Month 1	Month 2	Month 3
Auto/Transportation Expense			
Auto Insurance			
Auto Payments/Replacement			

Discretionary

	Month 1	Month 2	Month 3
Club Dues/Vacation Homes			
Recreation/Travel			
Dining Out			
Education			
Home Furnishings			
Personal Allowances			
Personal Gifts			
Savings/Invest/Debt Reduction			

Other

	Month 1	Month 2	Month 3
Life/Disability Insurance			
Umbrella Liability Insurance			
Income/self employment taxes			
Other major expenses:			

TOTALS

AVERAGE MONTHLY TOTAL $_____

(Based on information from Bert Hughes and Associates, Certified Financial Planners.)

Step 3: Plan for savings.

At a minimum, you should save 10% of your pre-tax income (your total gross income *before* deducting withholding or self-employment taxes). Anything less will simply not provide the level of flexibility you'll need to support your plan for **MMI, Inc**. Saving 20% is recommended by many financial advisors.

Step 4: Determine your buffer.

Based on the minimum monthly needs you developed in financial planning step 2, determine the amount it would take for you to survive at that minimum level of spending for six months, the period recommended for employment transitions in the molecular marketplace. This buffer amount is what you'll need to be sure that **MMI, Inc** has the financial flexibility to change employers, niches or livelihoods when necessary.

Step 5: Determine your investment strategy.

How and where you invest your money depends on your individual situation. If you have a severe current debt problem, for the moment it may not be possible to do any more than pay down your debt. But this is also investing—it's investing in **MMI, Inc** by getting you into a position where your head is above water, and you can begin to develop a positive financial future.

If you're not in a debt crisis, you should be investing some money in savings and paying off your debt at the same time. When you begin investing in savings you'll have lots of options, and how you'll invest will be determined by your goals. Your first goal will be to create your buffer. When investing in your buffer, the money should be put into accounts where it is available quickly if you need it, and where it is very secure. Good investment opportunities for this money would be a bank or credit union savings account, savings bonds, or a money market account.

Once your buffer amount is safely set aside, your investment goals will change, focusing on longer-term needs like education or retirement. There are nearly unlimited opportunities for investing money, and many sources of information and advice about how to invest. The investment pyramid below shows the basic kinds of investments available and how they match up with the different investment strategies that might be right for you.

Investment Pyramid

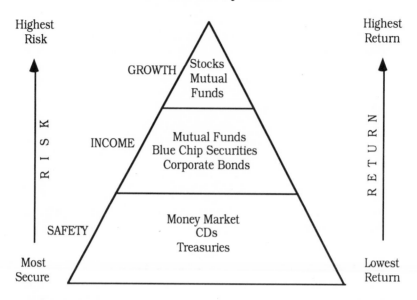

The investment pyramid shows the three different investment objectives: safety (protect the investment); income (steady stream of money coming in); and growth (keep up with inflation, increase the investment). It also shows examples of investment options which fall into each category, and the relationship between these three investment objectives and their relative risks and returns. Ideally, you'll create diversification among several types of investments, which will allow you to minimize short-term risk in some parts of your investment portfolio while maximizing long-term return in other parts.

When you've met your buffer requirement and are ready to move on to serious investing for your long-term financial future, there are lots of resources to help, including books, publications, bankers, brokers and financial advisors. To develop the investment strategy that's right for you, start by meeting with a financial professional to set your direction. Once you've developed your initial strategy, you'll have a choice of continuing to meet regularly with an advisor to get ongoing expert advice, or launching out on your own.

To find out more about the advantages of meeting with a financial planner or to find one near you, contact:

The National Association of Personal Financial Advisors (NAPFA)
355 West Dundee Road, Suite 107
Buffalo Grove, IL 60089
1-888-333-6659

(NAPFA is solely for financial advisors who are "fee only," who are paid for their advice directly by you, not through commissions on securities they sell to you)

or: The Institute of Certified Financial Planners
       7600 East Eastman Avenue, Suite 301
       Denver, CO 80231-4397
       1-800-322-4237

You can now use the five financial planning steps to prepare you own personal financial plan for **MMI, Inc**, which should include:

- average monthly spending;
- minimum monthly needs;
- planned rate of savings;
- buffer amount;
- how you will create your buffer;
- how you will invest in savings beyond your buffer;
- when you will begin doing so.

Just This Once: Avoiding Temptation

Your financial plan will give you information about your money—income and expenses—and guide you to creating a surplus for investing in savings. Once your financial plan is set up, the flow of information and the mechanics are pretty straightforward. But what *can* be very difficult is sticking with the plan you've created for spending on things beyond your basic needs.

Managing credit responsibly is a requirement. The easy availability of credit today can be an insurmountable temptation to spend. If you know this is true for you, or if you're already in hot water with credit before you start on your plan, then you should get help. You can get help in learning how to manage credit by contacting The National Foundation for Consumer Credit at 1-800-388-2227. They'll refer you to an office close to you for information or to schedule an appointment with a credit counselor.

Once you've got control of your credit, you'll take the further action of finding a way to motivate yourself to stay on your plan. Sticking with your plan will be necessary to properly launch and support **MMI, Inc**, which in turn will be your ticket to a secure economic future. But that might be a little hard to remember at the moment you confront your personal "great temptation:" the perfect new outfit, the incredibly fast PC, the radical sports car or the wonderful new gourmet restaurant. The question is, what about your plan will be powerful enough to keep you on track when you're tempted to splurge "just this once?"

It's not that splurging is a bad thing in and of itself; in fact, rewarding yourself for an accomplishment can be good psychology. But the rewards or splurges should be built into your financial plan, or should come if you receive a windfall like an unexpected bonus or overtime pay. If you splurge or reward yourself not as part of your plan but in spite of it, some part of your goals for financial progress are going to be delayed, and that hurts your future.

But we're all human, and everyone's "fallen off the wagon" occasionally. If that happens to you, it's a waste of energy and counter-productive to become angry with yourself, or to decide that your financial plan will never work. Instead, your new financial management skills will help you reconnect with your motivation in order to pick yourself up, dust yourself off, deal with the consequences and continue with your plan.

The best motivation is always internal—you stick with your financial plan because you believe in it, you believe in yourself, and you believe in what your plan will ultimately bring to you. What aspects of your vision statement are powerful enough to keep you on your plan, even in the face of your great temptation? Motivation from another person can also be very helpful to you in sticking with your plan, especially when your great temptation shows up. Someone you're close to and care about, who would be willing to give a little "tough love" advice when you're tempted to spend too much, can be worth their weight in gold.

Matt, the pharmaceutical sales rep we met at the beginning of Step 7, and his wife found that creating their financial plan was a real eye-opener for them. Matt was planning to change his livelihood to another medical-related sales position, and they wanted to take stock of their financial situation and to begin thinking about retirement. They'd always lived pretty comfortably on about $60,000 a year, including Matt's income and several thousand dollars a year from his wife's part-time earnings. Their debts consisted of their home mortgage of $90,000, on which they paid $1050 per month including taxes and insurance, an auto loan of $12,000, and credit card balances of $5300. They had about $7500 in a savings account which was earmarked for the education of their two children.

In addition, Matt had a 401k plan at work with a balance of $28,000 which they assumed was a good start toward their retirement nest egg. Since Matt was thinking about resigning, he checked the fine print on his 401k plan. His balance included $16,000 in stock contributed by his employer which was not yet "vested" as Matt's money; if he resigned during the next three years, the money wasn't his to keep. The portion of the 401k that he'd receive if he resigned now was only $12,000.

Matt and his wife set out to develop a financial plan that included saving 12% of their gross income, $7200 per year or $600 per month. But they quickly found that they didn't have $600 per month left over after monthly spending! On top of the bad news about the "shrinking" 401k, this was a shock.

As their initial surprise wore off, they decided it was time to get their finances in shape. With a deeper resolve they looked again at their monthly spending, and found there were several areas where they could spend less without making major changes in their lifestyle. Matt agreed to sell the hot rod he was restoring but didn't particularly enjoy anymore, and to drop his plans to replace their slow but otherwise adequate home computer. His wife agreed to purchase fewer, less costly clothes. Together they decided to cancel the private music lessons that their kids complained about anyway, and to take the family out to eat only once a week. With these reductions in non-essential spending, they'd be able to save 10% of their gross income, or $500 each month, which they decided was an acceptable target for the moment. At that rate of savings, in eight months they'd have an additional $4000. When added to the amount available in Matt's 401k, this would give them the buffer they'd need to feel comfortable with Matt resigning his position. After he was established with a new company they'd continue to save at least 10% and start a serious retirement account. Here are the highlights of their financial plan:

	Current	Planned
▪ Average monthly expenses (including all taxes):	$3500	$ 3050
▪ Minimum monthly financial needs:	?	$ 2500
▪ Savings per month: (plan to increase to 10% of gross income = $6000/year, $500/month)	$170 (401k)	$ 500
▪ Buffer, 6 months x $2500 (minimum monthly needs):	?	$15000

Investment plan: Save $500 per month for 8 months in savings account in credit union to build buffer, including an extra $1000 to pay tax penalties, if required, on early withdrawal of money from the 401k. At the end of eight months, Matt will make a job change. Start saving again as soon as possible after job change to rebuild buffer in savings account. When buffer is rebuilt, consult an advisor to open a diversified account to build up funds for education and retirement.

The insights they'd gained about their financial affairs and how to reach their goals gave Matt and his wife a strong sense of shared purpose for sticking with their financial plan. They both knew that they'd support each other as the temptations loomed. Matt was concerned that their financial plan could lead to friction when one of them wanted to spend money on something the other didn't agree with. They solved the potential problem of disagreements by deciding that each would have an allowance which didn't require any explanations to the other; beyond that, any expenditure which exceeded the monthly budgeted amount for its category would require the other's consent. This additional agreement helped them keep their relationship supportive while they created a successful financial future for their family.

Like many other aspects of work in the molecular marketplace, the process of securing your financial future is often cyclical. You create a buffer, perhaps use it up during a transition, and then rebuild it again as soon as possible. And even when your buffer is secure, the cycles continue: for example, you save money for a house and college costs and are out of debt; then, when the house is purchased or the child goes to college, you find yourself saving little and maybe even going back into debt. But when the cycles occur in a way and at a time you've planned for, it's reassuring to see where you're going and why.

Building a successful financial future can be challenging and at times frustrating, but it will also be one of the great rewards of creating **MMI, Inc**. The most important purpose of your financial plan is to create flexibility so that you're not bound to a job, but can benefit from employment opportunities wherever and whenever they arise in the molecular marketplace.

If you'd like to learn more about how to work effectively with your money, a good resource is *Your Money Or Your Life*, by Joe Domingues and Vicki Robin.

Case Studies

1. *Shannon*

I have to admit that it felt like injury after insult to move straight from making my huge list of gaps and goals to listing the rest of the challenges I would face! I wasn't sure how much more bad news I could face, but I did notice that some of the things on the challenges list were items I'd already come up with for myself in Step 6. Some challenges are certainly inevitable, and I'm sure that not thinking about and dealing with them now just makes them more deadly later on. I suppose the thinking behind these 10 Steps is to use the first few steps to get a firm grasp on the positive things about yourself and **MMI, Inc**, and then deal with the issues after that.

And there's no question that a discussion of finances was exactly what I needed next, since financing my new livelihood and niche was the top goal I set in Step 6. Fortunately, by nature I'm not a person who likes to be "in a fog" about money, so I have a head start there. Yes, I do balance my checkbook regularly! I think that having been financially self-sufficient forces you to pay some attention to money—either that or wind up on the street or with really high credit card debts.

Looking at the chart of obsolete vs. contemporary assumptions about money, I realized that I still strongly hold the obsolete assumption that income increases regularly. If not, how can I have the new cars, bigger houses, and gradually more prosperous lifestyle that I'm "supposed to" (in other words, that my parents had)? Not to mention retirement, though at 27, that's not a very immediate concern for me. The honest answer is obviously that it's not all going to happen automatically for me; I'll have to plan ahead to make it happen.

Getting started on my own financial plan, I had some raw numbers for monthly expenses, but I decided to keep track of the expense categories listed for one month to have a basis for comparison. The bottom line was that I spend more than I expected on "discretionary" items. I don't feel like I live extravagantly, so I was surprised at how much of my money goes to recreation/entertainment, dining out, clothes, etc. On one hand, it's great to be single and independent; on the other, I have very little savings right now, so it's time to make a shift. Because of my high optional spending, my minimum monthly needs looked very different from my average spending now.

As far as saving 10%, that's a great goal *once I'm in my liveli-hood/niche*. But in order to get there, I'm going to have to take some steps like using savings and perhaps even getting loans. I understand why savings will eventually be important, and I think the buffer idea is a great one; if I had done that before, I'd be in a position to move toward teaching ESL immediately. So I modified my buffer to have savings of four times my minimum monthly needs before I start into the degree and training I'll need for my new livelihood. Once I'm doing the work, then I'll be ready to build up savings and think about investing. Right now, my goal is to invest in me!

I feel very motivated to stick with my financial plan, since career-wise I'm now going somewhere that's important to me. I'll try to reduce the traveling, eating out, and clothing temptations; I can't guarantee that I'll always succeed, but I think my new goals will help put me back on track.

2. *Brent*

Step 7 was the easiest of all for me, because most of the work was already done. I'm one of those who always balances the family check-book, and I've used personal financial and budgeting software since 1990. The software keeps track of everything we spend, and produces reports on monthly spending with the push of a button. Having the money details close at hand has helped us see where to save money or spend more carefully, and that's why we've been able to actually increase our savings even though we don't have much extra every month.

The software helps a lot at tax time, too. Taxes are the toughest part for me to keep an eye on. I've never fully recovered from the shock of how much additional tax I had to pay when I worked as a contractor a few years ago. I took a contractor job that paid a lot more per hour than my previous salaried position, but after paying the self-employment taxes and the extra social security, I actually had less money to take home.

We're now saving for our financial future, but not as much as I'd like. We're saving about 9%, with about 5% going into a company matching retirement account and 4% into mutual funds for the children's education. It's less than the 10% recommended, but it actually should build up fairly fast since the company matches a portion of the 5% in the retirement account. I also have a company-paid pension benefit, which I don't have to contribute to, which will add a lot in the long run if I continue to work for this company. I guess the rate we're saving will do for now; at any rate, it's the best we can do at this point.

My wife is currently working without pay to help start-up a new company, which is a great experience for her and has a chance of bringing in a good income in the future, but right now she's not bringing in any extra income for all the time she's spending there. I hope that changes and she starts getting paid soon; that would help us save more and maybe make some progress toward building up our six-month buffer. Right now, facing a job change, I'd be a lot more comfortable if we had a six-month cushion, and it would be great if I didn't feel I have to accept my next job offer quickly whether or not it's right for me, just to keep the income stream going.

3. *Emily*

You can't work for long around counselors and teachers at a community college without talking about money. Many of these people are working on a part-time basis and feel they're discriminated against financially. As part-timers, they have no benefits, are paid an hourly wage that is quite low, and generally are looked down on by full-time professionals. In the past, the goal for most of the part-timers was to get a full time position, but now many of them have actually chosen this part-time approach in order to develop variety as a portfolio worker. Many of them have very interesting portfolios, which include work at a community college, contract work for corporate employers, as well as doing some private practice counseling.

This approach to work, with a lot of variety, definitely appeals to me, but I can see that not having a regular, dependable salary to contribute to the family finances will be difficult. Rick, my husband, is beginning to think about retirement from a 25-year career in health management with a pretty decent pension. We find ourselves at very different places in the progress of our livelihoods, with Rick looking toward the end of his career and me at the beginning. But, in order to allow him to retire while I continue developing my career, we definitely need to look closely at our financial situation.

What we found is that with the children on their own, and with planning to move into a smaller house where the two of us can live comfortably, our expenses will drop considerably. This move won't happen for about 5 years, after Rick actually retires, but we need to make plans for it now. I plan to work in my chosen livelihood for 10 to 15 years before I retire.

One future expense we foresee that will be different from past needs will be travel, since we both enjoy seeing new places and I definitely want to continue to broaden my perspective on life by meeting people with backgrounds different from mine. So we'll need to plan for travel to be included in our budget.

Our immediate course of action, having completed the five elements of our financial plan, will be to meet with a certified financial planner to discuss our current situation and to work up an investment plan to help meet our future needs.

4. *Forrest*

I thought I understood money and had managed it pretty well over the years. But after developing my financial plan in Step 7, I found there were two areas where my thinking about money was flawed.

The first area where I was thinking wrong had to do with holding unconsciously to the myth that my regular income would continue to increase until retirement. When the company offered me an early retirement it was a surprise, not something I'd planned ahead for. It was a shock to lose the regular paycheck I'd had for 30 years, and replace it with a monthly retirement check of about $2000. After I got started working regularly as a consultant I relaxed a little, because I could see I still had some earning power, even though I didn't get paid if I didn't find projects to work on. I've found that I look at the world a lot differently now that I don't have a regular paycheck each month.

The other area where my thinking hadn't been clear was saving for retirement. When I was an employee I had a good pension plan, completely paid for by the company. I could contribute if I wanted to, but it was optional. I was able to make some contributions in the years before the kids went to college, and built up a nice little nest egg of about $150,000 on the side. I felt very comfortable with my nest egg, believing that it would supplement my company pension to provide all the income I'd need for retirement, with a little extra thrown in from social security (if the social security system survived!).

Now that I'm actually getting a pension check each month, I realize how small an amount it really is. To live the way we want to, we need at least $35,000 per year more than the amount of my pension. What I learned from creating my financial plan is that the $150,000 nest egg can provide some income, but to keep the principle amount intact I should only expect to take out about 8% per year—or $12,000 per year—in income from it. That means I still need another $23,000 in annual income after I completely retire to live on. That was a surprise to me.

Fortunately, I figured all this out while I was still making money as a consultant, and I'm now saving as much as I can to increase the nest egg. I have to use a little of my savings to start my own consulting business, but my plan is to then build up the nest egg with a carefully diversified portfolio of mutual funds. By continuing to work and save for about five more years, my investments, along with my pension, should provide what we need for retirement income. Then I can retire for the second—and hopefully last—time, in order to do the things I enjoy without the need to make money. That will be a wonderful time for me.

Step 8

Market Yourself

Juan, a 42-year-old educator: *I've been an elementary school teacher for 20 years, so my work life has always been helping people. I like teaching, and enjoy my special niche as coach of the high school wrestling team. I think my job is secure, at least for now, and I have no desire to change anything about my work. The whole concept of marketing makes me uncomfortable. Marketing seems like it's based on getting someone to buy something they don't necessarily need by using fast talk or tricks. Why would I want to learn to do that?*

The Bad News: You Have To Sell Yourself

Unless you're one of the lucky ones who already know how to market your services successfully, learning how to sell **MMI, Inc** is one of the most important changes required for success in the molecular marketplace. We all know a few people for whom selling appears to come easily. They seem so self-confident that people just accept that they're competent and that they deserve to get what they want. The rest of us watch in admiration most of the time, and try hard not to resent them.

The ability to market yourself is one of the six most important characteristics, described in Step 6, for a successful worker in the molecular marketplace. Unfortunately, for most of us, the transformation to being good at marketing is a tough hill to climb. Maybe you're asking: "Why can't somebody else do the selling and let me do what I like, what I'm *good* at?" The answer is: "In the molecular marketplace, there is no one else to do

165

it—you're an independent economic entity, and if you don't do it, it won't get done."

Why is marketing so important anyway? It's been said that selling is the most fundamental of business skills: if you can't get someone else to buy your great product, then there's no point in having one. And since in the molecular marketplace you *are* the product, and as **MMI, Inc** you wish to draw a livelihood out of this marketplace, then you have to be able to get buyers to spend money for your product. Once again, this isn't true just for people who have their own business; every successful worker, even a long-term employee, needs to learn how to think and act like a small business—especially in terms of marketing.

Len is a good example. He'd sold insurance as an outside rep with the same company for eighteen years, and was a consistent million-dollar producer. Despite his strong performance, he felt that everyone in the company, and especially his boss, took him for granted. To boost his visibility, Len started a simple process of compiling a summary of his achievements—not just his sales but his community involvement activities and his "above and beyond" customer follow-up visits. At the end of each quarter he now makes an appointment with his boss to review them. Len's marketing effort—which is no less marketing just because it's focused on an "internal" customer, his boss—helps him feel recognized and independent, and makes his boss much more aware of his value.

Using either your current position or your most recent past position, think of simple ways that you could "market" yourself or your accomplishments. The audience for your marketing effort might be co-workers, a boss, or outside customers; the point is to find ways to get the word out about what you're good at. Possible marketing ideas include starting or expanding a newsletter, setting up a system for office birthday cards, taking a course to increase your expertise in office technology, doing a "brown-bag" presentation on a subject you know and setting up a Weight Watchers lunch meeting group.

Marketing And Sales

Since the terms "marketing" and "sales" are often used interchangeably, let's introduce some simple definitions. Selling usually refers to actually contacting customers to get them to buy something. Marketing is a term that includes selling, but which also includes other aspects:

- planning for a product and how to sell it;

- developing, preparing and improving a product (**MMI, Inc**) so it better meets customers' needs;

- doing research on customers and markets; watching trends to be ready for future changes in buying habits;

- communicating with potential customers about the features and benefits of the product;

- and convincing customers to buy (this is the actual selling part).

As **MMI, Inc** you'll first complete the *marketing* research and planning necessary to be a success, and then use this information to sell your product.

The Good News: You're Already Pretty Good At It

For many people, the subjects of marketing and sales trigger feelings of distaste. You can start to ease the queasiness a bit by recognizing that you actually market and sell all the time. Have you ever done any of these things?

- Explained your project, company, job or profession to a group?

- Been asked to do training in something in which you are an expert?

- Been chosen as a presenter or guest speaker to a group?

- Recruited volunteer workers, or someone to work on a task with you?

- Talked someone into going to (or staying away from!) a movie?

- Persuaded people to use certain companies or services?

- Given someone an idea about how to do their job better?

Of course you've done some of these things, which actually makes you an experienced marketer. Each of these activities involves talking, showing, persuading, influencing, or doing volunteer work, all of which are forms of marketing.

We often do these things without thinking, and doing them doesn't usually get us all worked up the way the idea of "marketing" or "selling" does (with the possible exception of speaking to a group). If you have negative feelings about marketing, it may not be so much that you don't know *how* to do it, as it is a problem with your *attitude* about marketing. Later, you'll learn some techniques and skills to increase your marketing capabilities, but first let's focus a bit more on the attitude you may bring to this touchy subject.

The Seven Dwarfs Of Selling

Imagine yourself in a situation where someone is pushing you hard to buy something. How do you feel about pushy sales people and strong-arm techniques? When this question is asked in a group of people, participants often become perversely gleeful as they develop a long list of negative characteristics about sales people and the experience of being sold to. Many of the negative terms that pop into people's minds start with the letter "S," offering a little comic relief by describing the "seven dwarfs" of selling: Slick, Sleazy, Slimy, Sneaky, Shifty, Sly, and Speedy.

Americans even have a cultural icon for the occupation which most closely embodies the seven dwarfs all in one role: used car salesman. With apologies to Walt Disney for the dwarfs and to car salesmen everywhere for the bad press, we nevertheless have to recognize that the vast majority of words representing our feelings about sales are negative. Why is this true?

How You Can Feel Good About Selling:
Your Value Proposition

Probably the biggest reason you have negative feelings about marketing and sales is that, when someone is selling you something, it's often not really being sold to meet *your* needs (even though you're usually told that it is). Mostly, in our materialistic culture, things are sold for the *power* that the sale brings to the seller. Sometimes that power is financial—in a sense, the seller is stronger because he or she is wealthier as a result of the sale. As a customer, you can understand that, and so long as you get what you want from the purchase, you probably don't mind enriching the seller as a result.

But there's another kind of power that can motivate a salesperson: the sense of psychological power over a buyer. This type of power play probably does bother or offend you, even if you're not aware of it at a fully conscious level. You might experience it with a pushy or rude salesperson, or when you're being coerced into buying something you don't need, maybe even just to get rid of the seller. When you think about the popular sales method of telephoning at dinner time, part of the frustration is the feeling that your private or family time is interrupted; you are being manipulated.

Sometimes outright lying is involved in this kind of psychological power struggle during a sale. But more often you just experience unwelcome pressure from someone who has carefully thought through and practiced a pitch that is designed to overcome or wear down your objections, and who is forcefully working to get you to agree, whether you want to or not. What is completely missing from this kind of power play is a *value proposition*.

The concept of a value proposition in selling is relatively new. It was formulated by business people and researchers studying what was *effective* in marketing, and how to market with integrity so that customer loyalty was built and retained. A sale based on a value proposition is entirely different from one based on power, because the seller, who wants to maintain a continuing relationship with the buyer, bases the transaction on the value of the product to the buyer.

For example, Virginia is an older woman who lives alone. She has some physical disabilities, so a friend helps her with housekeeping chores two or three days a week. Virginia decided a dishwasher would help her be more independent. She called a national store with a good reputation for appliances and said she needed a machine. The telephone sales person quickly convinced her she needed the "Premiere" model, with lots of fancy features. An installer from a local contracted service company (a portfolio worker!) came out two days later to put it in. The installer assessed the situation, and suggested to Virginia that an economy model would be more than adequate for a single person's two or three loads a week, and would save her over $150. She quickly accepted. The transaction left her less trusting of the big store, but if she needs appliance repairs she won't hesitate to call the installer from the local service company who helped her get good value from the deal.

Unfortunately, most of us probably still experience more power plays than value-based selling in our daily lives, especially in situations where we're one-on-one with the seller. So it's no wonder if you have a generally negative attitude about selling, and if you therefore dread the idea of selling your own product. A good tool for helping you change your attitude about selling is the realization that you are marketing **MMI, Inc** based on a valid value proposition. You understand and intimately know the value of what you are selling. And you're aware enough of the potential buyers' needs that you know what you're selling has value for them. So you can feel very honest and genuine about trying to help the buyer become aware of the value that they will receive from your product. This may not necessarily mean you always make the sale, but it will certainly help you feel better about selling.

Of course, it's sometimes true that a buyer is not aware of his or her needs; then the seller, who knows the product and the value it can bring in a given situation, has to convince the buyer to make a purchase. Do negative pangs about selling begin to well up when there's talk about convincing? Look closely at how this works in a value proposition: so long as it's true that the buyer will benefit from the decision to buy, then the seller is actually bringing value by helping to convince the buyer.

For example, Glenda, a successful counselor in private practice, is by nature a shy and introverted person. She says that she's able to effectively market her services to clients "...simply because marketing is the means by which I can continue to do what I love: help people." She knows her work is valuable and that it makes a great difference to her clients. Those benefits—to herself *and* to her clients—motivated her to learn how to market, and moved her beyond her natural reluctance to take the initiative with people.

The Four Keys To Marketing Yourself

If you're going to be successful in the molecular marketplace, you'll eventually face the need to convince someone to buy. Selling **MMI, Inc** effectively is the subject of the Marketing phase of the Livelihood Cycle, which was introduced in Step 5.

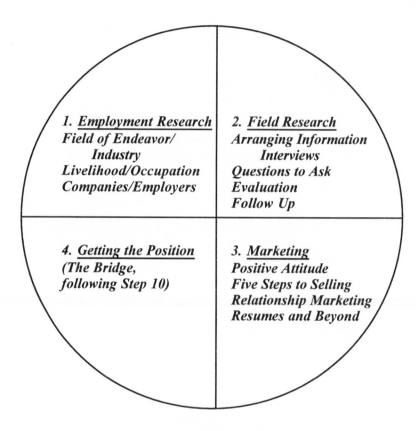

The Livelihood Cycle

In the Marketing phase of the Livelihood Cycle there are four keys to marketing yourself; the previous sections of this Step focused on the first key, having a *positive attitude*. The following sections of this Step deal with the remaining three keys: having a technique such as the *Five Steps to Selling* to practice and perfect your selling skills, understanding and using *relationship marketing* effectively, and using materials and documentation—*resumes and beyond*—to maximum advantage. The final phase of the Livelihood Cycle, Getting the Position, is discussed in "The Bridge", following Step 10.

The Five-Step Sales Technique

Clearly the biggest obstacle to successfully marketing **MMI, Inc** is attitude. But it's also important to have the skills of selling—like any skill—down cold. So the second key to successful marketing is to understand and be proficient in the techniques of selling. There are many techniques for selling, and most of them have been packaged and sold as "the greatest thing since sliced bread." Out of the numerous options available, many people have found the following simple five-step framework to be useful in getting started.

The first step to selling is *enthusiasm*. You've certainly experienced the difference it makes when someone is excited about what they're doing or selling. They put a lot of energy and feeling into what they communicate about it. At the very least, this energy and feeling draws your attention, even if you don't think you have an interest in the product. After all, how many people come to the county fair to buy a Veg-O-Matic? Probably not very many; yet the salesperson, through relating enthusiastically to the audience, usually can draw a big crowd. Enthusiasm plays to the entertainment value of the interaction, encouraging participation and opening doors to a deeper dialogue.

The second step to selling is a *needs assessment*. This step sounds long and arduous, and it can be if you're in "the sale of a lifetime" situation. But it can also be a simple and brief process of identifying the specific needs of your potential customer related to your product. It may take research, but it also includes keeping your eyes and ears open during conversations, looking at what's on someone's walls or desk for clues to his or her interests, and above all going to the source and asking.

The third step to selling is determining the *unique benefits* that your product can bring to the customer, based on the needs you identified earlier. Again this could result in an elaborate proposal if the situation warrants, but it can also be very spontaneous. The two keys are to know your product well, and to have gained enough information and insight during your needs assessment to relate to your customer's specific needs.

Notice also that in this third step you're describing *benefits*, or what your product can do for the customer. Don't confuse benefits with *features*, the characteristics of your product. For example, the features of a briefcase might be that it is leather, 21" long, and contains several pockets. But the benefits include rugged good looks to compliment any attire, the prestige of the label, and assistance in organizing your life. Customers care a lot about benefits, while they often don't care much about features, except to know how those features will benefit them by meeting their particular needs.

The fourth step to selling is to learn how to *overcome objections*. It can be difficult for an inexperienced salesperson to do this, in part because of the bad experiences many of us have had of being coerced. But once you've gotten past your own mental limitations and focused on the value proposition, you'll be able to work with objections as one way of bringing value to **MMI, Inc** and to the customer as well.

Generally, you can count on the first thoughts of potential customers to be why they *don't* need or want your product—after all, they've been bullied by sales power trips all of their lives, too. If you're going to bring them value, you need to have thought through their likely objections in advance and have an honest answer to counter them. Your answer will help defuse their natural reluctance and re-focus their thinking on the value your product can bring. Objections may very well occur in several cycles in the course of a sale, as you lead the customer closer and closer to accepting your value proposition.

The fifth step to selling is to actually *ask for the sale*. In some ways, this is the toughest step to take, because it carries the ultimate risk of rejection, and the unpleasant feelings we human beings all have about being rejected. It's not uncommon for someone to wonderfully execute the first four steps to selling, but then hesitate in actually asking for the sale.

And the rejection you feel from a "no" answer can be all the more acute when it involves **MMI, Inc**—which is to say, you personally. But the molecular marketplace, like any marketplace, has many, many potential transactions, only a small percentage of which are ever actually consummated. Remember, even the best sales people don't make all their sales; rather, they choose their prospects carefully and approach them with a positive attitude. And don't forget the power of vision; many successful sales people set time aside to imagine the best possible outcome before each sales call.

But there's no question that to sell effectively, you will have to learn to live with and move past rejection. The key is learning to detach from the result—which is much easier said than done—so that you can move on with enthusiasm and a positive attitude to the next potential customer. To make the next sale successful, it's important to focus energy ahead to the potential transaction; that energy can be unproductively sapped if there is lingering resentment toward the potential customer who didn't buy.

One of the most important aids in maintaining a good attitude in the face of a lost sale is the ability to separate the value of the product, and your own value, from the response. After being turned down, be sure to acknowledge that both you and **MMI, Inc** remain valuable to a buyer you'll soon find. Some people find it helpful to create a quick mental checklist of good qualities that they can review. Another technique for detaching from resentment uses the lost sale as a motivational tool; the goal is to create a frame of mind that says "Thank you for that 'No;' it brings me one step closer to my next "Yes."

Practice Selling Exercise

It's important to understand your attitude toward marketing, to see how valuable it is to develop marketing skills, and to learn the five steps to selling. But it's equally important to practice the five steps by selling something tangible and simple. One way to do this is to select an item of value to you, and prepare to practice selling it to someone else.

You can do this by involving someone who's willing to help you—a friend, co-worker, or someone close to you. Think of something you can practice selling to the other person; it should be something simple, so the experience is focused on learning the five steps to selling, not on describing a complex product. Set up a time with the other person when you can have 15 minutes or so without interruptions. And if the other person really wants to help you, give him or her the five steps of selling and ask him or her to also practice selling something to you, so you can see another example of how the five steps to selling work.

Think about how to be *enthusiastic* and energized about what you're going to sell. The natural edge of embarrassment you may feel about setting up this artificial situation can itself provide a lot of energy! But try to move beyond that by thinking about how you're actually developing a critical skill set. Practice an appropriate level of enthusiasm and energy by focusing on what you know will be required to properly represent the incredibly valuable product that you will be selling later, for real: **MMI, Inc**. Ask the person to whom you choose to sell to treat the situation as serious training by playing the role thoughtfully, and moving beyond embarrassment to help you.

Perform a quick *needs assessment*. What needs does the other person have which might be met by what you're selling? Are there any needs that can only be met by your product? Or needs which can best be filled by your product? Are there needs you can think of that the buyer has, but doesn't know he or she has? If you don't have a lot of specific information about this buyer's individual needs, think of examples of needs that people generally would have.

What are the *unique benefits* of your product? How can the needs you identified be met by something with the unique characteristics of your product? What's the difference between your product and alternative ways the buyer might meet the needs? Think of examples of specific situations in which the buyer could have used your product.

Using your ideas about needs and benefits, think through what *objections* the buyer might raise to buying your product. If you have already thought about the objection and can answer it yourself, you're much less likely to be thrown off track by something the buyer brings up. Develop responses that are positive, rather than "objecting to the objection" with more and more detail. Try to bring the discussion back to the needs of the buyer, and how the features and benefits of the product will help meet those needs. In this practice session the situation is contrived, the product is relatively unimportant, and you haven't prepared in a lot of detail, so you may not feel passionately that your product will meet the buyer's needs. All this can make overcoming objections feel like a "hard sell." But keep in mind that the goal is to build your skills in preparation for the time when you'll actually sell **MMI, Inc**. At that time, you'll be selling a superior product, confidently overcoming the buyer's objections to bring value to both of you.

Finally, practice how and when you will *ask for the sale*. As discussed earlier, this fifth step to selling can be difficult. There are two helpful points to keep in mind. First, practice is important because timing is critical. Over time, experienced sales people gain a sense of timing, neither "overselling" or "underselling." To develop timing, you have to be experienced—which means practice. In your practice session, try to ask for the sale before your "buyer" (who's already on your side) says: "OK, you've sold me!" And be sure you don't just end things by assuming you made a sale without getting firm agreement from the buyer. You should literally have in mind the words you'll use, such as "I'm sure this sounds good to you; would you like one?" or "Can I put you down for an immediate delivery?"

The second important point to keep in mind is a willingness to risk rejection. Practice may also help here, but rejection probably will always hurt a bit. What will help the most is always keeping in mind the sure knowledge that what you're offering is valuable, and that you're offering value with dignity, skill, and integrity. Beyond that, you've done all you can do, and the outcome is up to the buyer. In your practice session, it will be helpful to practice getting both "Yes" and "No" answers. If you make a sale on the first try, try to set up another role-play situation with a negative outcome to practice how you'll handle it.

The Five Steps To Selling MMI, Inc

Enthusiasm

As you create **MMI, Inc**, you're building a natural sense of enthusiasm about your product. As you recall your product definition statement from Step 3 and the competitive advantage of **MMI, Inc** from Step 6, what are the elements of your product that create the most energy for you? Drawing on these sources of energy will help you clearly and confidently convey your belief in your product.

Needs Assessment

What are the needs, including currently unmet needs, in your field that **MMI, Inc** could fill? For example, are there positions just being developed due to technology or other changes? Or is there some way you could offer your expertise to combine two traditional positions into one, thus eliminating the need for extra hiring? Thinking creatively may help you identify needs that even the employer isn't aware of.

Unique Benefits

How will you translate your competitive advantage into unique benefits for your customers? It's important to remember that this step to selling requires that you move beyond your own frame of reference—your competitive advantage—to see the benefits from your customer's frame of reference. Then you should be able to simply and persuasively state the benefits that your customers will receive from **MMI, Inc**.

Overcoming Objections

Seeing the selling situation from your customer's frame of reference will also be very helpful in the process of anticipating the possible objections and preparing in advance to overcome them. What are the objections you're likely to encounter to selling **MMI, Inc**? Examples might include: "I don't need the service right now"; "The service is too expensive"; "You don't have enough experience"; or "I'm not really the decision maker". What ideas can you develop to be prepared to counter these objections?

Asking for the Sale

There are two important aspects of preparing for this step to selling. The first is what you've been doing in the process of creating **MMI, Inc**: understanding your product and developing confidence in your ability to provide a quality service. The second important aspect is practice. Through practice, you'll develop a natural sense of the flow and timing of a selling interaction and, perhaps most important, the courage to ask for the sale. You'll also be able to determine how best to prepare yourself in advance to be alert and ready to make your move at the right moment, and to know exactly what you'll say. When the moment is right, how will you ask your customer for the sale?

Pricing Your Services

As **MMI, Inc**, sooner or later you're likely to work as an entrepreneur, contractor or consultant. When you do, you'll need to figure out how to price your services. Here are some guidelines for determining what to charge. The price for your services should be:

- high enough to imply value for the product/service;

- low enough to be reasonably close to your customers' expectations;

- within the range of other similar products/services;

- high enough to make a profit.

If you're going to be working in a situation where you'll set a price for your services, the employment and field research you did in Step 5 should provide data to use with the guidelines above to determine the optimum price for your service. There are many resources available to help you with pricing decisions, including *The Contract and Fee-Setting Guide for Consultants and Professionals*, by Howard L. Shenson.

Before you quote a price to a potential customer, be sure you know if **MMI, Inc** has any flexibility in what it will charge and if so, within what range. You'll know this by answering two questions: Can you afford to do it for less? Will you be able to sell your services for more somewhere else?

If your work situation requires it, think about the optimum price of your services, your flexibility range, and what options will you offer for payment (for example, base plus bonus, performance-based, hourly, daily, cost per unit, completion bonus, cost plus, or profit sharing).

Relationship Marketing

The third key to marketing **MMI, Inc** successfully is knowing who your customers are, and treating them well. The marketing required to make **MMI, Inc** successful will usually not involve reaching retail or mass market consumers. With the goal of selling your combination of skills, knowledge and experience, you will more often be approaching a certain number of possible employers, perhaps more than once and maybe even regularly. In situations like this, the most effective marketing is based on building quality relationships.

Relationship marketing, currently a hot topic in business circles, begins with being clear about who your customers are—the circle of people who know about **MMI, Inc**, or who make decisions to employ, retain or refer people in the area of your niche. Marketing in this way means listening carefully to your customers, and then using what you learn from them to create business opportunities while maintaining a strong reputation and a wide group of contacts.

A couple of things distinguish relationship marketing from traditional, high-pressure marketing. First is the belief that the best and most efficient form of sales is by referral, meaning that people happy with your services recommend you to others. If that's true, it certainly pays to keep your customers not just happy with your product, but also feeling good about you. Second, relationship marketing also involves developing strong and honest ongoing relationships with people, rather than just "using" them to get a sale. The more you treat clients as people, the less they'll think of you as just a commodity and more as a valued acquaintance, or even friend. A good resource for further exploring the value and techniques of relationship marketing is Don Peppers' and Martha Rogers' book, *The One-To-One Future: Building Relationships One Customer At A Time*.

Melinda, a self-employed graphic designer, offers a great example of the difference relationship marketing can make. She had done several freelance jobs for one department of a major electronics company, but she also knew that they had other designers available to them. Her work for the company had been satisfactory, but she still wasn't sure how to make herself invaluable to them.

One day, while speaking to the in-house designer with whom she worked, she found out that they were having some trouble getting signs made for the annual company picnic in two weeks. Melinda offered to make up some basic signs at no cost and bring them to the event. Providing a "freebie" was Melinda's first great marketing ploy, but the best part came later. Once she arrived at the event and dropped off her signs, Melinda was invited to stay for the picnic. She not only met many of the people she'd worked with over the phone, but she ate and laughed with them, creating real relationships for the first time. And, as Melinda says, "they now say they feel like they know and like both my work and me, so why would they go anywhere else?"

Learning to market your product, demonstrate your value proposition and make the sale is crucial. But creating the *opportunity* to sell is equally important. The most important factor in creating marketing opportunities is the relationships you have and maintain with others. Those relationships will strongly influence who will give you the opportunity to present your value proposition in the first place. Using the networking list you developed in Step 6 is a great start toward relationship marketing for **MMI, Inc**.

Once again, selling is not just for entrepreneurs. Presenting and gaining acceptance of your value proposition can be just as important for an employee in a business or group. And for a long-term employee, networking can be an extremely important way to keep aware of what's going on in the organization, and to maintain a strong reputation.

Resumes And Beyond

The fourth key to effectively marketing **MMI, Inc** is documentation. When you can't be there in person to speak for **MMI, Inc**, or when someone says "Don't tell me, *show* me!" documentation speaks for you.

Your Business Card

Your business card is documentation for **MMI, Inc** in its simplest form. Traditionally, only employers issued business cards, and only to employees who met customers or the public. Like almost every other tradition in the workplace, this one has also changed. In the molecular marketplace, everyone should have a business card. If you're a portfolio worker who changes employers often, or if your employer doesn't provide a business card for you, have your own cards printed up. They don't cost much, and they're a quick and easy way to convey a key image or message about **MMI, Inc**. Many printing shops and copy stores have samples of business cards that you can review for creative ideas.

You never know when you may find it useful to have a simple marketing tool available at a moment's notice. If the chatty stranger in line at the supermarket turns out to know a key person at the place where you've always dreamed of working, *voila!* With your business card, you have available just what you need to "seize the moment."

Your Resume

A resume, something most of us have prepared at one time or another, is actually a very good basic marketing tool. It can be used to send information widely to a lot of people at the same time, as part of a search for work. It can be used more personally, in a discussion with your employer about your accomplishments or your skills. Your resume should always be kept up-to-date for two important reasons. First, it keeps you current about the history, skills and characteristics of your product, **MMI, Inc**. Second, even if you only use your resume to show someone you know—even yourself!—how impressive you look in print, the boost in self-confidence will be worth it. The details of developing a dynamite resume will be explored in The Bridge, following Step 10, which focuses on your search for employment.

In the past, a resume was about the only marketing tool anyone needed or used to get a job. Now that the concept of "job" is becoming obsolete, however, the resume has become only a good starting point. What else is needed?

Beyond Your Resume

The other piece of documentation you'll use in the process of marketing **MMI, Inc** is your achievement portfolio. What's an achievement portfolio, and why is it important?

Your achievement portfolio is a compilation, in one place, of examples of your work and/or the opinions of other people about your work. It supports your resume with tangible evidence of your capabilities and accomplishments. Artists and writers have always used portfolios because it's difficult to summarize their work without seeing samples or examples. Many employers, when hiring, are now insisting on seeing evidence of accomplishments because the faster-paced work environment means new employees have to be immediately productive.

Your achievement portfolio will contain evidence to support your accomplishments, which reflect both your general transferable skills and your unique work-specific skills. What you'll use as evidence of these skills will depend on the type of work you do, and what documentation is available. Good examples of evidence in support of skills include diplomas, certificates and licenses; thank-you notes, awards, commendations and letters of recommendation; records or photos of extra-curricular and community involvement activities; and documentation of work-specific skills. If you create ideas at work, document the results for your achievement portfolio. If your work is designing something tangible, you can include a sample or a photograph. In The Bridge, following Step 10, you'll find more specific information about how to develop your achievement portfolio as one of the tools to support your search for employment.

Your achievement portfolio is important because it performs several critical functions, depending on your personal circumstances. It

- supports your resume with convincing evidence, but doesn't replace your resume;

- demonstrates your skills objectively;

- reflects your professional growth as you move from niche to niche, reflecting changes in your capability and value to employers;

- provides a simple way to visually review your progress over time;

- may be useful documentation for getting a loan to start a new business;

- may support getting educational credit for work experience;

- improves the chances for **MMI, Inc** to land the right position during an employment search.

Your achievement portfolio will be there whenever you need to demonstrate the competitive advantage of **MMI, Inc**.

But Selling Myself? Your Promotion Plan

Reading about marketing and practicing selling may have eased some of your concerns, but most people will still feel uncomfortable about their ability to market. And whether you're a "natural" at selling or someone struggling to improve your selling skills, it's always hardest to think about selling yourself. Even the implications of the phrase "selling myself" are none too savory. But marketing is critical to your success in the molecular marketplace, and the concepts in this Step will provide the basic tools you need.

Often the best approach to getting started is to take one small self-marketing action, rather than trying to do it all. The best action to start with is to develop a 30-second speech about **MMI, Inc** that you can deliver with no advance notice on the street corner or in an elevator. Get your talk exactly right by practicing it in front of others; you may want to memorize it. Make it tight and to the point, highlighting skills and accomplishments, and focusing on the value of **MMI, Inc** to the customer. Answer the question "What can I do for you?" Find an opportunity at least once a week to give your talk—to someone where you work, a prospective employer, a network contact, or even in a social situation.

Armed with new ideas, motivation and techniques for marketing yourself, you can now pull it all together into a promotion plan for **MMI, Inc**. Your plan will be very personal, depending on your livelihood and niche. If you're going to start a business or be a consultant, your promotion plan for **MMI, Inc** will be fairly complex; you'll need to think about things like publicity, advertising and logos. There are many resources on this subject, including *Marketing Your Services: For People Who Hate to Sell*, by Rick Crandall.

If you plan to be a long-term employee or contractor, your promotion plan may be more simple—but you should still have one. Certainly you should consider how you will promote **MMI, Inc** to a new employer, when and if necessary. But don't neglect the benefits of marketing your competitive advantage to your present employer, who is your current customer. As an example, consider how you might regularly remind your employer of your value, perhaps with a monthly list of your accomplishments.

Juan, the teacher we met at the beginning of Step 8, was initially uncomfortable with the idea of marketing. He could see no point to marketing his services, but as he learned more about marketing he became convinced that teachers—like everyone else—need to develop and practice good marketing skills. He could see that the security of his teaching position wasn't absolutely certain, and in fact there had been some rumblings about declining enrollment in his school district which could bring a reduction in teaching staff. And he knew that his extra work as wrestling coach at the high school could disappear if funds were cut, or if wrestling were to drop in popularity among the students and their parents.

Juan developed a promotion plan with three elements. First, he decided to assemble and maintain a complete achievement portfolio of his accomplishments as both a teacher and a coach. At his next discussion with the principal, he'd use his achievement portfolio to demonstrate the value he brought to the school. He also knew his achievement portfolio would be a great help in getting work in another school district in the future, if a change ever became necessary. Second, Juan knew that his work was valued both as a teacher and as a coach, but by two separate customers—the elementary school where he taught, and the high school where he coached. He invited the principal of the elementary school and the athletic director of the school district to join him for lunch, to discuss his schedule for the next school year, but with the added intent of making each aware of his contributions to both schools. Finally, he decided to create a flyer, featuring this year's successful wrestling squad in pictures and stories, which would be distributed to present and incoming students. He enlisted the help of one of his wrestlers to create the publicity piece as a project for a journalism class. Juan knew the flyer would generate interest and help to keep the wrestling program viable and growing, which would increase the stability of his coaching position.

Consider the unique elements to be included in your promotion plan for **MMI, Inc**. As things change and you learn more about working in the molecular marketplace, you can revise and update your promotion plan whenever necessary.

Case Studies

1. *Shannon*

My limited product sales experience comes from childhood magazine selling contests and a brief attempt at multi-level marketing. I didn't do particularly well in either case, mostly because I feel very uncomfortable taking advantage of a relationship to advance my own financial interests. It's very embarrassing, no matter how much I believe in the product; I'd always rather just relate to the person without feeling the pressure to "make the sale."

But in my various jobs and positions, I've had plenty of chances to practice selling my own abilities or talents. Strangely enough, that's never seemed as difficult as product sales. There are two big differences for me: first, I'm usually not looking for a job from friends, so I don't feel like I'm risking a relationship; and second, I know the employer/client has a need that I feel I can meet, so I'm selling with more confidence.

Still, it's true that some weird issues come up when you're "selling your work self." The amount that you value yourself becomes critical to success: do you truly believe that you are a valuable and appropriate "product"? Trying to "sell myself" always reminds me of starting a relationship: there's that feeling of leaving oneself vulnerable to real pain if the person approached says "no." It feels like you're risking a lot by putting yourself on the line.

As I went through the five steps presented in the marketing chapter, I recognized some of the issues I've experienced with each when selling **MMI, Inc**. For example, the first step is to have enthusiasm for your product. But think about it: enthusiasm about yourself, in our culture, comes across as arrogance. How many of us were encouraged to speak well about ourselves or our abilities?

As far as doing a needs assessment, for me that starts with really knowing the field and livelihood you're dealing with. This is where I have my work cut out for me, since I'm starting into a brand-new livelihood.

My "unique benefits" as **MMI, Inc** come from transferable skills, although I know that specific work skills are often the first requirement for getting into a position. In one job interview I did, I know that the ad executive had seen several people with desktop publishing experience; I convinced him that I was also efficient and a perfectionist, and he told me later that my approach was what landed me the position.

With my work history, I always know that the first objection people have is to the number of jobs I've held, and my short average length of stay. "If you've left every other job after one or two years, won't it be the same here?" So I have learned exactly what I need to say to address that concern: I've left in the past because other events took place (moving, international traveling) or because I became aware that the work was not right for me. I also always add that I've never been fired, and in fact in all but one of my previous positions I've been asked to stay.

It's hard for me to get very specific about how I'll market **MMI, Inc** in the ESL teaching market, since I'm still learning what that market is and how I'll fit into it. But I definitely feel better prepared by what I've learned about marketing both from my past experience and from Step 8.

2. *Brent*

I guess I'm pretty typical, but I don't like marketing. I'm sure it's partly my father's values talking, but I feel you should do a good job and be recognized for it. Not only shouldn't you have to sell yourself, but it even seems like it's impolite or antisocial to toot your own horn, like boasting.

I know that I have to be able to get the word out about who I am and what I can do as **MMI, Inc**, and I actually feel I do that pretty well one-on-one, like in a job interview. I once set up an information interview with a company that built life-sized, animated models of dinosaurs, just to find out what they did and how one might work in that field. At the interview, I found they had an immediate need for the services of a mechanical engineer for a short-term project, and I signed up to help them on the spot. While I enjoyed working on the short project with them very much, unfortunately they couldn't pay me enough to live on, and the company later went bankrupt. But that's the way I prefer to market myself—one-on-one, not a lot of fireworks, never having to directly ask for the sale, just quietly finding a match between someone's need and my skills.

When we were first married, my wife and I lived for a year in Tokyo teaching English. I felt really comfortable with the Japanese style of networking and relationship marketing. I think relating to people in the Japanese way, more subtly and with a lot of formalities and etiquette involved, helps me to see what's going on in others' heads and stay one step ahead of the objections or questions that they may be thinking about.

Using my resume as a marketing tool is fundamental, and has worked very well for me in the past. Once you've sent a resume, you've actually already asked for the sale, so when you find yourself with an opportunity for an interview, you don't have to pop the question in the same way as if you're on a normal sales call—I like that better.

The idea of an achievement portfolio also sounds good to me, and it's something I'm going to develop. I already knew I needed a more extensive portfolio of examples of my computer graphic renderings to demonstrate my ability to move into that field, and the other parts of an achievement portfolio sound like good additions. The more the work of marketing **MMI, Inc** can be done by documentation and materials, the better I like it.

3. *Emily*

The idea of seeing myself as a product, working through the process of identifying the elements, and then thinking through how to sell it is very new to me. Generally, my approach to life has been more laissez-faire— what happens is what happens. Up to this point in my life, I haven't needed to think about selling my wares or skills, so this challenge makes me quite uncomfortable. Thinking through my approach now will be of great help when I complete my education and am actually out looking for a way to enter the world of work.

The work of setting up a Product Definition Statement in Step 3 has given me a good basic sense of confidence in my product. I know what I am skilled at, where my values fit in, and what work environment best fits my personality type. I also feel good about the niche I have identified, that of working with teens with learning problems, and feel strongly motivated to actually be out there helping this population. But I am still faced with actually selling myself as an educational resource specialist.

I asked Sarah, a close friend who is in my Master's program, to role play the five-step sales technique with me. Since she feels a lot like I do about marketing and faces the same challenges herself, it was a helpful experience for both of us. In the role play situation, I asked for an internship position at a local education resource center. I had no trouble bringing enthusiasm to the process, both because I am eager to begin to participate in the work environment and also because I know this particular arena of counseling will be of great help to teens like my niece.

The needs assessment phase entailed doing research into the several resource centers in my area, and identifying one or two where there is a need for a specialist in teen learning problems, or where that is a gap in what they offer.

The unique benefits I can bring to a center without a teen specialist will be my ability to fill that niche. I will also bring the maturity of my years of life experience which often count for more than having taken specific classes to meet some graduate requirement. And, perhaps most importantly, I bring personal experience of having been with a teen with learning problems and am intimately aware of the many concerns, from educational to emotional, for the teen and for the parents.

In the role play, Sarah brought up the objection: "We just can't afford to take on a new specialist at this time." I countered with: "This is a one year internship I am proposing, without pay, so essentially you are getting fresh ideas and a lot of enthusiasm for free." She suggested that there is not really a need for a teen specialist in this geographical area, to which I responded: "From research I have done, many teens are being tested inadequately within this particular school district, leaving both teens and their parents feeling frustrated and without any direction to pursue."

To close the deal, I presented a well thought-out proposal, including a time frame, exactly what I would do, how I would benefit their program, and where I would locate clients. Sarah, of course, agreed to the plan and said, based on all the work I had done, that I looked like I would be a great asset to the center.

This wasn't a real situation, or one where I was asking to be paid, but it's very like what I think will be my first step after I finish my degree. And it sure helped me feel more prepared for the real thing when it comes.

4. *Forrest*

Like most people, I don't relish the idea of selling. My first experience wasn't very positive. I was six or seven years old, into reading comic books, and I was completely captivated by ads showing the things you could own if you just helped some nice company sell a few things that everybody wants and needs—in this case, "White Cloverine Brand Salve."

I'm sure my parents would never have let me have the BB gun anyway, but it was sure what I wanted. But then again you had to get lots of points to get a BB gun, so I set out on an intermediate goal of a water pistol. I eagerly sent off for my starter supply of White Cloverine Brand Salve. And I believed the ad which said that I'd sell stuff to my friends and family, maybe even people on my block, and they'd all thank me for bringing them this great stuff (whatever it was). And they'd ask me for more again the next time I called!

Well, they didn't. I sold a few cans, but it took some doing. We had unsold little tins of White Cloverine Brand Salve around the house for quite a few years! My bubble was burst. It was hard selling something, especially when people said "no." The dream of tons of good stuff coming my way was badly tarnished amid a sea of unsold cans of salve.

As I grew a bit older I had some chances to speak to groups, did pretty well in a college speech class, and helped out in fundraising activities. As time went on, I realized that all these were marketing activities, and found I really didn't mind them too much, and actually got pretty good at them.

There were some things that seemed to help gradually reduce my aversion to selling (or fundraising.) First, doing it with others made it much more fun. Second, I believed in the value of what I was promoting. Third, working with others who also believed reinforced me and helped me through the discouraging moments.

As a consultant with a larger firm, the "maturity" of my product and the red-hot employment market in my field of telecommunications have meant that I've had to do relatively little cold-call or face-to-face selling. Now, as I plan to branch out and open my own consulting business, I'll probably face the need to do more selling, especially at the beginning. But the product I'm building into **MMI, Inc** now has lots of solid strategic alliances and networking to support it, a pretty broad telecommunications skill and experience portfolio, and a generally positive track record. All of these things have as much to do with marketing as any sales call.

So even though selling isn't my favorite activity, I now realize that I can happily market something I believe in, and it helps to be doing it with others with the same objectives. For the success of **MMI, Inc**, this is a good thing to know.

Step 9

Integrate Your Work And Your Life

Lynn, a 32-year-old legal secretary and "soccer mom": *When I was working full time our two latch-key kids tended to get into trouble. Although my husband is a lot of help, he's away on business three nights a week. I arranged with my law firm to work fewer hours, so I could be home with the kids after school. But there are a lot of demands at work; I often bring my laptop to soccer games to try to keep up. In fact, the firm is pushing me to come back full time. Sometimes I feel like I need to be three places at the same time—with the kids, at work, and with my husband when he's home. I feel like there isn't enough of me to go around.*

Like Lynn, you may feel the pressures arising from work are overwhelming, ready to consume the rest of your life and dominate your existence. No one, even the most dedicated workaholic, can remain effective over the long term under this kind of pressure. The question is: "What can you do to keep pressures from work manageable, so that all aspects of your life are in balance and working together smoothly?"

You'll function at your best—meaning you'll be happy, productive and have healthy relationships—when the BE and DO aspects of yourself are in harmony, bringing fulfillment and meaning to everything you do. Among other things, this means that the demands and rewards of your work life will be integrated and balanced with the rest of your life.

The Pressure Cooker

The most important way to find and keep balance is to be able to deal effectively with the emotional issues that come up all the time. One persistent source of emotional issues for people today is the tension, concern, worry or anger that they feel as they realize they're facing a change in their relationship to work.

These emotional issues are expressions of natural human responses—the same ones we all have when we're afraid or frustrated. They're caused by the fact that we're surrounded by a swirling sea of contradictory demands as the old employment social contract—everything we thought we knew about jobs and employment—is being transformed in the molecular marketplace:

- you're worried about the future of your job.

- you want to get or hold a job for security, but full-time positions are going away;

- you worked hard to get an education, but you still don't have the experience to work in the field you desire;

- your ideal job requires that you move to a place you hate;

- you work hard to get a position with a good company, only to find that the company has been taken over by another firm;

- you've sacrificed to meet the minimum standards for your chosen livelihood, only to find there are no opportunities available;

- you consciously sought out new opportunities to expand your skills, only to have someone question whether you're able to hold a steady job;

- you've settled for a job that isn't ideal but works for you, and then find you're at risk of being displaced by someone else;

- you really just hate you job (or your boss).

Of course, emotional issues also arise from pressures and contradictions that develop in other areas of your life besides work. Causes of emotional issues can include relationships, health, concerns about other people, the environment, the state of the world, and on and on. Any contradiction in your life, from whatever source, can bring up emotional issues because it will be a source of cognitive dissonance.

Cognitive Dissonance

Understanding more about cognitive dissonance, which was introduced in Step 1, is helpful in learning how to deal effectively with emotional issues. Cognitive dissonance, which occurs when two or more opposite ideas seem true at the same time, may leave you feeling that you need to respond but don't know which way to turn. It may leave you wishing you could escape to a tranquil place to figure things out and reorder your life, but you know you have to deal with the situation right now, because it won't go away.

Any change in your life—especially a big change like marriage, birth of a child, death of someone close, divorce, relocation, illness, loss or threat of loss of a job—will cause cognitive dissonance, even if the change is positive. Cognitive dissonance causes stress, and stress creates emotional issues. The art of balance in life requires that you have an effective way of dealing with the emotional issues that develop—a process that helps you manage the transition.

Dealing Effectively With Transitions

Most of us don't know how to deal very well with changes in our lives, so we try to ignore them and the emotional issues they cause. It's helpful to know that there is a transition process that you will go through with any change. Using knowledge of the process to effectively manage transitions in your life is an important skill for **MMI, Inc**. William Bridges, in his book *Transitions: Making Sense of Life's Changes,* outlines a three-phase model which will help you deal with transitions, including those caused by employment-related changes.

Phase 1: Endings

> To effectively manage a transition, the place to start is not with the beginning, but with the end. When something changes, we usually want to quickly focus on what's ahead. For little things, that may be the right response. But for the big things that throw you headlong into the disorientation of cognitive dissonance, it's best to consciously stop trying to solve future problems, and first deal with the ending of the old, whatever that may be. By focusing first on what is ending, you can begin, over time, to understand that the loss of the old may have changed everything for you. It may feel like the underpinnings of your life are giving way, that the familiar roles you've played are changing, and that your whole identity is threatened.
>
> When something ends that's important to you, your response may be directed outwardly, inwardly or both. Outwardly, you may find yourself being very emotional, perhaps angry, expressing it physically or psychologically: kicking the dog, hitting the table, lashing out at people around you, or even at yourself. Your inward expression of emotion may take the form of fear or apathy. You might withdraw

into a private emotional space, perhaps still doing normal everyday activities, but inside you are not fully participating. In this mode you may find that you actually sabotage positive activities to which you've been dedicated, like losing weight, exercising, studying or spending time with your children. Perhaps you won't want to discuss feelings with others, but just to be left alone. You might go into a sort of emotional hibernation, or even a more literal form of hibernation, wanting to stay home or maybe just stay in bed.

During a transition, it's important to actually spend as much time as necessary focusing on the ending. Not taking the time to experience an ending can be like not taking the time to grieve for the loss of a loved one—the effects can spring up at a later point in life when they may be inappropriate, and much harder to deal with.

Let's follow Susan's experience as an example of the process of managing a transition. Susan experienced a negative change in her life when she lost her job as a graphic artist. The small local company where she had worked for nine years was bought by a larger firm and the local office was closed.

The endings phase was hard for Susan. She withdrew from friends and stayed home alone most of the time, not caring much about life. To make things worse, she began to put on weight. She was an optimistic person and felt sure she'd eventually move on, but there seemed to be absolutely no way she could muster the energy or motivation to do something about her state of affairs.

Phase 2: The Pit

The second phase in the process of managing a transition, called the pit, is the core period during which you psychologically begin to come to terms with the cause of the transition. It will take some time, and while the process is working you may feel as though everything is in chaos. You may experience depression or general malaise, or you may storm around being upset about even the smallest of things.

This is a time to let life happen to you, to be open, and, if possible, to avoid making decisions. You'll need to be sure you've taken time to grieve for what is being lost. While in the pit you may feel very passive, and as a result this phase is sometimes called the neutral zone. It is an uncontrolled and unpredictable time, as each person finds his or her own way to cope with the sense of loss.

The time spent in the pit provides an opportunity to re-evaluate goals, directions, hopes, fears and dreams. Spending time in the pit is essential to managing a transition, even if the change is positive. For example, a person who's used to being the primary bread winner may have mixed feelings about his or her partner getting a full-time job—it opens up new financial possibilities but also may bring a loss in his or her status, or in the amount of personal support that used to be available from the partner. A couple going through a change such as this can use the time in the pit to discuss the feelings caused by the change, which begins to form the basis for a shared vision of the future.

As Susan worked through her feelings about the ending of her job and recovered from the initial impact, she moved into the pit phase of the transition process. She stayed at home, watched TV and read, and spent a lot of time expressing her anguish and grief. Eventually, she began to regain some of her normal interest in what was going on around her. She learned to meditate, in the process getting in touch with her sense of isolation, and actually began to appreciate the time alone as the emotional healing progressed. She became more aware of her rich inner emotional life through looking at her dreams, and over time started to think about the direction her life was taking.

Phase 3: New Beginnings

When is it time to move out of the pit and focus on new beginnings? The only possible answer is: "It depends." It depends on the magnitude and importance of the transition you've faced, on your emotional health, on how many other recent transitions you've faced, and on how urgently you need to refocus on making a living or supporting others close to you. In short, it depends on you.

Most people seem to intuitively know when the time is right to move out of the pit, and you probably will, too. But if the transition is a particularly difficult one, or if you find yourself with real financial or emotional problems while you're stuck in the pit, then you may need to get professional help.

For the vast majority of transitions you'll face throughout your life, it will be clear to you when the time has come to shift your focus. Opportunities will begin to present themselves, and they will force or encourage you to move away from your internal focus and back toward fully participating in life. This is a time to trust and follow your intuition.

When you do shift your focus to new beginnings, the situation may feel unfamiliar and risky. You've been focused inwardly for awhile, and re-shifting your focus outward may not be easy. In the process, you'll move out of malaise, start the goal-setting process, and begin to make decisions and take action. This is the time to let go of the past and take on a new role or roles. Suggestions for moving forward into new beginnings include:

- stop getting ready and act;

- begin to identify with the final result of the new beginning by visualizing success;

- take things step-by-step—resist the temptation to take another route or to revert when discouraged;

- don't be preoccupied with the results, but take satisfaction in your incremental progress toward what's new.

Since Susan had created a financial buffer, she was able to survive the four months it took her to complete the transition process after the loss of her job. Eventually, the financial pressures began to build, prompting her to realize that it was time to act. She started by making calls to all her contacts in the graphics field. As a result, she found an old friend who was frustrated with her employer, and was planning to open her own office. All her friend needed was someone to share the load and give her a little encouragement. Susan couldn't help financially, but with her skills and emotional support her friend was willing to put up the money and together they opened a small graphics and printing business. This gave Susan a new beginning for a new phase of her life, which she welcomed.

Your Personal Transitions

The process of dealing with transitions will never be the same for any two people. For example, if you're an extroverted thinking type you'll often want to skip phase one and (especially) phase two and go straight to taking action. If you do that, the decisions you make will have little foundation or depth, and you'll miss golden opportunities to learn about yourself and fine-tune your product, **MMI, Inc**.

If you're an introverted feeling type, you may want to stay in phase one and (especially) phase two, and find it hard to move on to phase three. Obviously, that doesn't result in forward progress, so you might need a nudge from someone else to help you start focusing on new beginnings.

The transition process can take place very quickly or over a longer period of time, depending on the need and circumstances. It isn't always necessary or possible to "take time out" to experience the process. You probably have the strength and the skills you need to be productive at work and keep your relationships intact while you experience the process. If you're struggling with a transition and find you're really stuck and unable to move, it may be time to ask for help from a trusted friend or a professional counselor.

Think of a transition you've recently experienced. During that transition did you go through each of the three phases—endings, the pit and new beginnings? Did you leave a phase out? Did you get stuck in a phase? Exploring your past experience with the transition process may help you manage transitions better in the future.

Every one of us faces transitions, cognitive dissonance, and emotional issues all the time, and they affect us whether we're ready for them or not. If you choose to avoid understanding and managing your life's transitions, it will be impossible to make grounded decisions that will work for you in the long term. Making the transition process conscious will enable you to take care of yourself emotionally, help you make **MMI, Inc** effective in the molecular marketplace, and provide the self-knowledge you need to bring all aspects of your life into balance.

Needs, Wants And Values

You'll probably continue to work for a long time to come, so whether you like it or not, work will dominate much of your life. The challenge is to fit work and the rest of your life together in a way that is satisfying and fulfilling to you. Do you work simply to support the rest of your life? Or is your work also important in its own right?

To answer these questions you need to have a good handle on what's important to you—your values. Sound familiar? You identified your top five and bottom five values for **MMI, Inc** in Step 3, as part of defining the product you'll take into the molecular marketplace.

Now, let's take another look at values from a different perspective: not as part of developing a product, but from a whole life point of view. Looking at your values from this different perspective will help you fit your work and your life together into a fulfilling, productive whole.

Needs and Wants

While each of us has a personal, unique set of values, there are also many similarities in values among people. These similarities occur because values are based on what we need in life, and the basic needs of all human beings are quite similar. All of us have needs in several areas:

- **physical**—we all need food, air, water, space in which to live, and protection from the elements and predators to survive; to support these, we also need financial security;

- **mental**—we need mental stimulation, the ability to communicate ideas to others, and the ability to understand what others are communicating to us;

- **emotional**—we all need nurturing and love (tiny babies who are deprived of emotional contact with other human beings quickly lose the will to live); as life goes on, we need self-esteem and the respect of others;

- **spiritual**—needs in this area are experienced very individually, but there's evidence that we all need to have a sense of purpose beyond ourselves, something that draws us to our best;

- **family**—we seek a connection with other people who are close to us, and we make commitments and try to do right by them;

- **community**—most of us, as our lives progress, also find a need to extend our commitments beyond our close circle, and to do right by the larger group within which we live;

- **leisure**—we all need time for ourselves to do what we really enjoy.

The problem for many of us is that our *needs* may be fully met, but something in us still *wants* more. It's the difference, for example, between needing a roof over your head and having enough to eat, and wanting a big house on a river with a boat dock and enough money to eat regularly at gourmet restaurants.

Everyone has wants. They're not wrong, they're part of being alive. But all of us at times want things that are impossible, or destructive, or which simply lead away from what is really important to us. For example, someone with limited skills and initiative may want a private jet. But unless he or she is from a wealthy family or wins the lottery, that want is not likely to be fulfilled. Someone who is energetic and outgoing and makes a good income selling computer software to small companies may want a quiet life on a secluded ranch. In this case the want is also unlikely to be fulfilled, but for a different reason: the seclusion and modest income from ranch life won't match his or her personality type.

You've heard motivational speakers talk about getting what you want, if only you're focused and persistent. So shouldn't you just go all out for what you want? The answer is, "It depends." If what you want is aligned with what you truly value, the answer is certainly, "Yes." So how do you know if what you want is truly aligned with what you value?

Values are your deeply-held beliefs about what is right for you and for those you care about. Wants are transient; they come and go, influenced by what's going on around you at the moment. The Ferrari on the street, the gorgeous passer-by, the mansion, the boat, the movie star, the episode of "Life Styles of the Rich and Famous", the encounter with a wise person; these and a million other things can create instant wants. Pursuing all of them would be impossible.

New and old wants are with you all the time, and it's easy to dissipate your energy pursuing things that, in the end, don't really fit in with what you value. On the other hand, when your wants are aligned with what you value, the alignment of your energy and focus will give you the power to get what you want, just like the motivational speakers promise.

Values

What are your life values, those that lie beneath the values you identified in Step 3? What reflects your deeply-held beliefs about what is right for you and those around you? Here are some key points for discovering what you value:

- Your values will probably change and become more other-focused as your own needs in life are met. If your survival needs of shelter and food are met, and you have enough income to be financially secure, then you'll probably find your values more focused on good relationships with your family or community. Over time, you may find increasing value in being respected by others, in self-respect, or in making a positive difference in the lives of others.

- Different values become important depending on what's happening in your life. When your life is changed by a transition, for example loss of your livelihood, you may find yourself instantly refocusing on your survival needs. But that doesn't mean that the values you've discovered in the other areas disappear; in fact, if your life gets briefly derailed while you deal with a big transition, knowing what you value can be of immense help in working through the process and getting to a new beginning with your emotional health intact.

- You probably have some values that are selfless and some that are more focused on yourself. You may value a prominent and wealthy lifestyle and be willing and able to work for the money it takes to have it, while at the same time value helping others and be able to give large amounts of money to charities. Both selfless and personally-focused values are valid, and once clarified, should be respected.

- Your values are reflected in what you do. Sometimes it's hard to perceive your values through your own eyes. But, as you saw in Step 3, your values may be very evident to someone else watching what you do.

- When working for what you value, your energy is focused. If you're working for a want that's not aligned with your values, your energy is scattered so your effort won't be effective. You've probably had the experience of wanting something badly, and yet wondering why you weren't able to move toward getting it. That could be because what you wanted was not consistent with what you valued.

- If you have the feeling that you're wasting your time and energy and not accomplishing what you want in life, it's time to clarify your values. It may be that you've been spending your energy on your wants; if so, refocusing on your values will be a breakthrough in moving toward your goals.

Here's an opportunity for you to explore your life values by seeing how they are reflected in different aspects of your life. As you start to identify your values, if you find yourself first thinking about a goal—which is DO-based and task-oriented—ask yourself the question, "Why is this important to me?" The answer to this question will help you identify the BE-based value that lies beneath the goal.

As an example, below are the values identified by Lynn, the soccer mom we met at the beginning of the this Step.

Physical

- A body that is in good condition
- Ability to excel at some physical activity
- The financial means to support our family lifestyle with a sense of security

Mental

- The ability to solve problems effectively
- A mind that is sharp and well informed

Emotional

- Open and healthy personal relationships
- Living in the present by not dwelling on past negatives

Spiritual

- Experiencing the presence of God in every day life
- Being in touch with my inner self

Family

- Being an example of living a good life for my children
- A loving marriage that helps both of us grow

Community

- A neighborhood that is safe, secure and supportive
- Opportunities to participate with others in community activities

Leisure

- Some time off from other demands to do what I want
- Now and then, getting away to get a fresh perspective on life

Think about your most important life values in each of these areas: physical, mental, emotional, spiritual, family, community, and leisure. When you live your life based on the values you've identified, you'll feel energetic and satisfied—your life will have meaning. How can you be sure that your life is based on what you value? By developing goals to start, stop or continue doing things that will fine-tune the alignment of your life with your values. Take a moment to look back at the section on goals in Step 6. As with the goals you identified there for **MMI, Inc**, your life goals should also be useful and short term, like stepping stones, and not become too long range or global. Goals will be most useful if they meet the **SMART** criteria:

S   Specific—the result is clear
M   Measurable—the end point is clear, and incremental progress
        can be measured
A   Achievable—generally possible, it can really happen
R   Realistic—personally possible, I can really do it
T   Time-oriented—deadline for closure exists, and provides
        appropriate motivation.

Referring to her list of life values, Lynn developed the following SMART life goals:

Physical

- Continue to play coed team sports twice a week
- Contribute 40% of family's financial needs by end of this year

Mental

- Make and prioritize a to-do list each morning
- Every weekday, review current events on Internet

Emotional

- Write a paragraph in my journal every night to identify where I've held onto past resentments and how to resolve them
- Every month, schedule and go out on a "date" with my husband

Spiritual

- Use an imagination exercise once a week to reflect on my spiritual values, and write about it in my journal

Family

- Attend a parenting class with my husband in the fall
- Have a family sit-down dinner at least three nights per week

Community

- Join our block's neighborhood watch program next month
- Ask my neighbor to help me arrange a block party next summer

Leisure

- Schedule a short cruise with my husband next summer
- Each night after the kids are in bed, take thirty minutes for private reading and writing in my journal.

Based on your life values, you can now develop SMART life goals. Try to identify at least one goal in each of the seven areas of your life: physical, mental, emotional, spiritual, family, community and leisure.

Your Balancing Act

The life goals you've set complement the goals you set earlier for **MMI, Inc**. This gives you a unique opportunity to create balance in your life by looking at these two sets of goals side-by-side to see how they fit together. There will be areas where they are consistent—where your goals for **MMI, Inc** are completely aligned with your life goals. There will also probably be some conflicts or inconsistencies. To balance your goals, you'll need to identify conflicts, understand the issues that arise from them, and find ways to resolve the issues.

Lynn continued with this process and found her goals were consistent in most areas, but she did discover the conflicts below, which raised issues that she needed to resolve.

Life Goal	MMI, Inc Goal	Conflict	Resulting Issue
Attending parenting class with husband in the fall	Use evening to keep up with work in order to maintain part-time work plan	Too many evening commitments	Not enough time to do both things
Schedulae a short cruise next summer, without kids	Complete continuing education course next June	Both goals require quite a bit of money	Not enough money in discretionary budget to do both

When you compare your life goals with your **MMI, Inc** goals, what conflicts or inconsistencies do you find? What issues do these conflicts raise that you'll need to resolve? In a perfect world, where your relationships are wonderfully without friction, everyone sees things your way, and your work is well paid and matches your ideal working day, you might find that all your goals fit very well together. In the real world, you've probably identified one or two difficult issues that you, like Lynn, need to resolve to bring balance into your life and at the same time pursue your goals for

MMI, Inc. The most common issues that people identify at this point in the planning process relate to time and money.

How will you resolve these issues? It won't work to compromise your values because if you do, you'll find yourself in a non-productive cycle, dissipating your energy on activities that you won't have your heart in. Balance has to come instead through a process of grappling with conflicting issues and finding a way to satisfactorily fit things together, based on priorities. Your work in Step 7 will have helped you set financial priorities. Setting priorities for use of your time will also be important.

Setting Priorities

How do you decide between two or more very important, conflicting goals, without giving up on what's important to you? You can set priorities based on several different factors:

Importance

Are there clues from others, or from your own intuition, which clearly establish the relative importance of your goals?

Sequence

What has to happen first, in order for other things to follow smoothly?

Time

Does the time you have available fit one activity better than another? Is there a deadline involved?

Crisis

Is there a critical need or emergency that has developed unexpectedly and which establishes what's most important?

Re-evaluation

Once you've set priorities, review them often because they can change over time.

Setting priorities can help you avoid feeling overwhelmed by organizing your approach to goals. If you find that setting priorities still leaves you without enough time to create balance in your life while making progress on your goals for **MMI, Inc**, you may want to improve your ability to manage your time. A good reference for time management skill building is *Time Shifting: Creating More Time For Your Life*, by Stephen Rechtschaffen.

Lynn found that setting priorities gave her a way to resolve the issues that resulted from the inconsistencies between her goals. She discussed these issues with her husband, and together they set priorities. They decided that they would postpone the parenting class for six months, scheduling it early in the next year when the kids' soccer teams would be off-season. On the money issue, they decided that Lynn's continuing education course was so important to their financial security that it had to take priority over their desire to go on a cruise without the kids during the next year. They reluctantly agreed to postpone the cruise for a year, and in the meantime scheduled a few weekend getaways. But they solemnly promised each other that the cruise would be the top priority if they "discovered" any additional income, like a tax refund or an unexpected bonus.

If you, like Lynn, found that you have unresolved issues as a result of conflicts between your goals, you'll want to take appropriate action to resolve the issues. For example, you may want to establish time and financial priorities for goals, improve time management skills, review life goals so that you're sure that they reflect your values, review goals for **MMI, Inc** based on new insights about your values, and set one or more additional goals to provide a way to resolve an issue.

This Step has focused on BE issues: transition, life values and goals, and balance. The final section will help you assimilate all your work through a BE experience—a final imagination exercise.

The Gift Of Integration

The following imagination exercise will symbolically acknowledge and affirm the progress you've made toward creating **MMI, Inc**. It will help motivate you to keep moving toward your goals, remind you of the things you value most, and anchor your commitment to express your values in the way you live your life.

This activity is similar to the imagination exercises used to develop your personal vision statement in Step 2, and your ideal working day in Step 3. As before, if you find this type of exercise unfamiliar or difficult, keep in mind that there is immense practical value that can come from tapping your inner resources, helping you move beyond intellect and reason. Also keep in mind that using your imagination effectively takes practice, so don't be surprised if visual images don't immediately pop into you mind; keep trying.

There are three alternative ways to proceed with this imagination exercise. The best way is to have another person read the exercise to you while you listen and use your imagination. If that's not feasible, prepare by reading the exercise into a tape recorder in advance, and then when you're ready, play your tape recording while you listen and use your imagination to experience it. The final option is to read the exercise and pause each time when indicated, taking the time to experience it while you are reading. Whether someone else is reading for you or you're doing it for yourself, be sure the exercise is read slowly and thoughtfully, allowing plenty of time at each pause for the visual picture to emerge.

Before starting the exercise, create an environment that's conducive to being inner-focused: remove any distractions, such as bright lights, noises, or telephones.

Exercise:

Allow yourself to relax and to encourage your usually active mind to be at rest. Relax your body. Get comfortable in your chair and put your feet flat on the floor in order to feel grounded; keep your hands relaxed in your lap. When you feel comfortable, take several deep breaths low in your abdomen. As you breathe, be aware of places of tension in your body: neck, shoulders, jaw. Move those areas, trying consciously to relax them. Feel the tension draining out of your body. Still your mind, so that you can truly concentrate on the images your imagination creates.

(PAUSE)

In your mind's eye, you see yourself walking on a path outdoors, in a place that is very beautiful and tranquil. As you look around, you become aware that it is the same path and you are coming to the same body of water that you experienced in the first imagination exercise. What does the water look like today? Is the surface smooth or are there waves? What is your sense of the water?

(PAUSE)

As you look across the water, you are able to see the other side quite clearly. And as you look along the far shore, you see that there is a gift waiting there for you. You realize that it is symbolic of something very deep and meaningful to you, and every part of your being is motivated to get to the other side and to look at it more closely. With a strong sense of urgency you look around the area; your first impression is that there is no notice-able way to get across the water. You continue to look for a way across, aware that the special gift waiting for you on the other side is worth every effort to reach it. You know you must find a way across, so you make a plan for getting to the other side; your plan might take you across the water, perhaps over or even through the water, or maybe around the water.

(PAUSE)

You pursue your plan until you've accomplished your goal of reaching the far shore.

(PAUSE)

Once you have reached the other side, go to the gift. What is it? How do you feel about it?

(PAUSE)

You feel a deep sense of gratitude for this offering and a beginning awareness about what it means and how you will be able to use it. Do what you need to do to accept the gift and make it your own.

(PAUSE)

When you are ready come back to the present time and place.

The imagination exercise you just completed provided an opportunity for your BE side, your inner self, to communicate with you. Your inner self has the power to reflect your values clearly, because it is not encumbered by the distractions and conflicts that occupy the attention of your DO side in every-day activities. By accessing your inner side, this exercise helps align and integrate the different aspects of your life.

What was the gift you received in the exercise? What does it symbolize for you? Think about how this symbol can help you remember what's important as you work toward integrating your work with your life.

In Step 10 you'll learn how to create your Portfolio Development Plan and begin using it to guide the daily process of bringing **MMI, Inc** to life.

Case Studies

1. *Shannon*

I enjoyed doing this Step. It was refreshing to back off of the hard-core issues, lists and charts and recognize the emotional side of things. Being a DO-oriented person, I don't look at these issues automatically, so working through this Step helped me get a different perspective on **MMI, Inc** and on my life.

The initial list of contradictory demands actually touched on two of my own biggest concerns: working hard to create a niche only to find few opportunities, and getting an education but still lacking the necessary experience. Emotionally, I find these contradictions frustrating; it sometimes seems like all this work is more trouble than it's worth if I still can't do and be what I want.

When I got to the transition process, I saw that this approach to change is completely different than the way I usually do things. I suppose I go through these phases of transitions without even knowing it, at least until I reach the New Beginnings part. Since I haven't consciously spent much time in either of the first two phases—Endings and The Pit—I'm very unfamiliar with them. In the description of the Endings phase I did begin to recognize that I am more emotionally unstable and vulnerable when something is changing.

The Pit is the most uncomfortable transition phase for me: chaotic, unspecified amount of time involved, passive, and unclear when it ends.

Ugh! But taking some time off, not necessarily from doing what needs to be done, but from planning and thinking ahead, makes sense. I can see how decisions would be more integrated and focused as a result. Maybe the best motivation to try this process is getting to know myself better, since I keep feeling surprised at how much happens internally that I either don't realize or don't understand well.

My life values are another place where I've kind of gone on automatic—"of course I know what I want." But while they seem obvious, it wasn't all that easy to define them, which probably means they aren't as clear as they could be. My values in some areas (like physical and leisure) were simple to list because I think about them often; others (like spiritual and community) took more thought. I also modified "Family" to "Social/Friends" to fit my lifestyle better. I found the extended example of Lynn in this Step to be very helpful for ideas and suggestions.

As is always true for an "implementer" like me, developing goals from my values was much more comfortable for me. Having evaluated the values, the fun part is figuring out how I'll live them out in my life. The biggest challenge came next: balancing **MMI, Inc** goals, life goals, and the limited time and resources in each day. Because it feels like I have so far to go with creating my niche for **MMI, Inc**, getting on with that process takes top priority. It will mean limiting my social, community and leisure goals for now (both in regard to time and money).

I discovered in doing the final imagination exercise that I feel more comfortable using my imagination now than I did at first. For both the second imagination exercise and this one I used a tape recorder rather than trying to read it and do it at the same time, which made a big difference in my ability to concentrate. This imagination exercise was *very* powerful for me, although it's still somewhat of a shock when images just kind of "appear" out of my mind. I saw myself flying across the body of water, and then found out that the wings were in fact my "gift." Flight has always had great meaning for me personally—freedom, power, vision—so though I'm not sure what all the gift signifies, I really liked the feeling I got doing this exercise.

2. *Brent*

This Step got pretty touchy-feely for my tastes. At times I felt like it was opening a can of worms that I'd rather not get into. But I recognize that the point of this Step is to make tangible something that's pretty intangible, and in the end I think the ideas are valuable.

Specifically, as I read the material on transitions, I realized how big a transition I'm actually in at the moment, with loss of my job. I know I'll find a good job, and I've changed jobs quite a lot before, so I was puzzled as to why this transition seemed so hard for me. It dawned on me that I was actually grieving for the loss of my job, as well as for the loss of our whole unit in the company.

Then it struck me that every other time I'd changed jobs, it was because

I chose to change. This time, somebody else made the decision and I was a just a pawn, a victim like countless others. I don't like the feeling at all. But I can see, just the way it's laid out in the book, that the process is moving along for me, too. And I know from my own past experiences that there will be a new beginning with a new job soon.

The difference for me of not being in the driver's seat during this transition is profound. It underscored for me the importance of developing **MMI, Inc** as a truly independent unit, so that regardless of someone else's decisions, I'm never out of the driver's seat again.

The work on life values and goals was less important for me, not because it's less valuable but because I'd already put a lot of thought into life issues and goals when I built my vision statement. Also, I've found that for years I've had balance of work and life on my mind. Since we've been married my wife gets really upset if we don't have time together as a family, so I've always tried—and been reminded!—to make that a high priority.

But even deeper than that, I've always wanted time for myself, to pursue things that give me personal pleasure, like doing a little sculpting. I guess it's no wonder that my "gift" in the imagination exercise was free time to do the things I wanted to do.

3. *Emily*

It was quite easy to identify my life values in the seven different areas, but as I thought about how to actually change my life to better express my values, I found some problems that I need to address and resolve.

In the physical area, I value keeping my body in trim shape. Physical conditioning is getting to be more of a challenge as I get older, but I feel that I'm already doing the right thing by taking a walk of several miles every morning, which starts my day wonderfully and provides the exercise I need.

In the mental area, I highly value keeping my mind sharp and active which I am doing through the Master's program but, again as I get older, I find myself having to work harder to remember facts and names and to do the work required.

Emotionally, it is important for me to keep current with feelings: identifying and expressing fears, understanding what is making me angry, and learning why I sometimes feel so sad. My goal is to continue to share these feelings on a regular basis with Rick, who has always been a good sounding board for me and also helps me to see the feelings more objectively.

The spiritual aspect of myself is at the core of who I am and has a very high value for me. I will strengthen my relationships with friends in the spiritual community by meeting with them weekly, thereby deepening my personal connection to my inner self as well as my relationship to God.

In the area of the family, looking at my life and **MMI, Inc** values and goals made me aware that there was a growing conflict that needed my immediate attention. I found that the relationship between Rick and me was not as strong as I'd like, and it certainly was not deepening. This is true partly because I'm focusing more on myself and my livelihood path, and partly because Rick spends a lot of his spare time volunteering with Habitat for Humanity, where he plans to spend much of his time once he has retired. The conflict comes down to two issues: the first is the use of time, and the second is balancing the value of family relationships with each of our personal goals.

When I had a chance to prioritize these issues, I realized that my highest value was deepening the relationship with Rick, keeping current with emotional issues and taking opportunities to be together and just have a good time. We discussed the issue, and he agreed that this was a high priority in his life as well and that he too was missing a sense of closeness in our relationship. We agreed to spend more leisure time together, and after looking at our schedules we set aside each Tuesday evening to go to dinner, to the movies, or for a long walk together. We have already identified travel as something we want to incorporate into our life style when I begin to earn money, so we plan to set aside two times this year for a trip to a place where we have not been before.

As I was working through this Step, I looked back at the vision I developed in Step 2 and realized that they work together beautifully. Each focuses on the elements of a person: my vision is the deepest expression of what is important to me in the four aspects of myself, and this Step helped me to make concrete just how I will make manifest these values.

4. *Forrest*

I feel like I'm pretty good at surviving pressure from work, and keeping on course through good times and tough times as things change. I don't know if that's just because of my personality type, or maybe because I've worked for so many years that I've seen and survived it all. The part of Step 9 that was most helpful for me was identifying my life values and goals. After a lot of thought and prayer, here's what I came up with as my life values:

- **Physical**—Good health and personal security.

- **Mental**—Regular new challenges, to increase what I know about the world.

- **Emotional**—Ability to keep my own perspective balanced, while feeling the pain and needs of others and helping them achieve their own balanced perspective.

- **Spiritual**—A belief in God, reflected in the love I give and receive from others.

- **Family**—Loving relationships with my cherished inner circle of others.

- **Community**—Making a positive difference in others' lives.

- **Leisure**—Time for personal renewal, and to enjoy the outdoors by taking care of our family ranch property, the small part of the planet that is "mine" to watch after.

I could think of lots of life goals, so it was hard to boil them down to this short list:

- **Physical**—Stay fit with daily exercise, and weekly outdoor work on property.

- **Mental**—At the end of each day, list the most important new thing I've learned.

- **Emotional**—At the end of each day, list one way I've been helpful to another.

- **Spiritual**—Each day, use an imagination exercise to affirm one positive aspect of my life.

- **Family**—Maintain a loving relationship with my wife; see or talk with each child and grandchild at least once per week, other family members at least monthly.

- **Community**—Spend 8 hours each month doing work in my community; after next retirement, increase to 2 days per week.

- **Leisure**—Schedule one night per week for dinner or a show with my wife, and two weekends per month to work on family ranch property.

Through the process of creating these short lists, I realized that my normal tendency was to try to "do it all," without really considering what was best for the situation or most important to me. This Step helped clarify my priorities, which will help me be more effective in what I do, and closer to the other people I work and live with.

After setting priorities in order to come up with my life goals, there was only one issue left for me to resolve: how to balance my desire to do so many other things with our continuing need for income. The issue is resolved now with our plan for me to work another five years with my consulting business to assure adequate retirement income.

Step 10

Create And Implement Your Plan

Paula, a 25-year-old information systems analyst: *As I've developed MMI, Inc, I've created an incredible collection of information, insights and plans. I also know a lot more about where I'd like to go in the long run—I'd like to stay with my present employer, but become a supervisor of a group of programmers instead of sitting at a terminal all day. To get a promotion, I know I'll need to go back to school for an MBA, but how do I translate all of this into a concrete plan to make it happen?*

The final Step in creating **MMI, Inc** is to create your Portfolio Development Plan (PDP). This final activity is a powerful way to synthesize all your ideas, insights and effort into something tangible that will guide and inspire you on your journey to success and fulfillment.

For some of us, creating a plan sounds like a difficult activity. The good news is that as you completed each of the previous Steps, you also considered many of the components for your Plan. The first part of Step 10 will address the final three components you'll need for your Plan. In the remainder of Step 10 you'll complete the documentation of your Plan using the PDP template provided, and celebrate the completion of the process.

These are the last three components in the planning process:

- Turning your goals into concrete milestones for your life as you make a commitment to complete each key goal in a specified *time frame.*

205

- Looking honestly at your goals to see what attaining them will
  cost, and make a commitment to support the *financial requirements* that they create.

- Developing a list of the remaining *"nitty-gritty" items* that you
  will need to work out in order to get started.

You Want It When?

Considering your work in Step 9 and earlier, you can now decide which are
the current highest priority goals for **MMI, Inc**. Some of your high-priority
goals can be accomplished in a relatively short time frame. For these, you
can simply plan a start and completion date. Other high priority goals for
MMI, Inc may be much more complex, requiring a longer time frame for
completion. For these more complex goals, you can break them down into
stepping stones, and plan a start and completion date for each stepping
stone.

For example, Pete's first goal was a simple one that could be accomplished quickly. He was about to graduate from a trade school as a
machinist, so he set an **MMI, Inc** goal to identify and call on all of the
potential employers/customers within a fifty-mile radius of his home. He
wanted to call on each of them to determine the current prospects for a
machinist position. Pete's friend Jan had a much more complex first goal.
She worked for a local car dealer as a receptionist, but wanted a better
paying position, so she decided to complete her four-year college degree at
night while working full time. Jan divided her goal into a series of stepping
stones. The first was to enroll in the next term of classes which started in
three weeks, and complete her first class three months later. Pete and Jan
shared their goals with each other, and agreed they'd both start working on
them the following day. Pete committed to complete his simple goal in thirty
days, while Jan's commitment was to finish the first stepping stone in her
goal to get a college degree at the end of the school term.

Your **MMI, Inc** goals will include some that are simple and others that
are more complex; for the complex goals, you'll need to divide them into
manageable stepping stones. After you've reviewed your **MMI, Inc** goals
and developed the stepping stones required to complete them, decide what
will be the start and completion dates for each goal or stepping stone. Be
realistic about when you will be able to start, and how much time will be
required to finish each goal or stepping stone. But don't be too soft on
yourself, since accomplishing these goals is the route to your success as
MMI, Inc.

After you've set time frames for your high priority goals, you'll want to
regularly review the dates you've set and update them with actual start and
completion dates. No one developing a plan can ever see everything in
advance, so adjustments are always needed as your plan moves toward
implementation. Along the way, you too will find that you have to make
some adjustments:

- You may find that your original dates were too ambitious. If so, change the dates to make them more realistic but still challenging.

- You may be meeting completion dates sooner than you planned. If so, take a minute to enjoy the feeling of success; then, set your next completion dates realistically based on your accelerated accomplishments.

- At some point you'll find that your original goals no longer apply, or that others have become more important. When you find your goals are no longer quite right, revise them based on your latest information and continue the process of setting time frames for completion of the new or revised goals.

Whenever you make an adjustment in a goal, stepping stone or date, note in your PDP what caused the change. Over time, these notes will give you an interesting record of your progress. More importantly, the notes will help you anticipate what may be ahead when you make the next revision to your Plan.

And It'll Cost How Much?

All of your goals for **MMI, Inc** will take time and effort to accomplish. Some, but not all of them, will also require money. Goals that you may be able to accomplish without extra money include self-paced study, research, self-improvement, networking, and marketing **MMI, Inc** through resumes, the Internet or direct contact with potential employers/customers in your area. Goals that will probably require extra money include taking organized courses leading to a license or college degree, setting up an office, making an exploratory trip to investigate a work opportunity, or working as a volunteer or intern instead of taking a salaried position to gain experience or credibility.

So what can you do if your future is based on accomplishing a goal that requires extra money and you don't have the money available to start pursuing the goal? As you might expect by now, the answer is to make a *plan* for getting the money and accomplishing the goal. You'll want to be able to answer these questions:

- Which of your goals or stepping stones will require additional money to accomplish?

- How much more money do you estimate will be required?

- Do you have the funds to pursue this goal now? If not, when will you have the money?

- Where will you get the money?

- Is the required amount of money included in the financial plan you developed in Step 7?

Answering these questions may give rise to another goal, or to a change in your expected completion date for a goal; that's OK, and in fact it's normal in a planning process as important as this. Keep your vision for **MMI, Inc** in mind whenever you meet obstacles or start feeling discouraged because your success in the end will be worth it.

The Nitty-Gritty

Based on the niche you've chosen and the goals you've set, you'll certainly face some additional "nitty-gritty" items. These items will vary greatly depending on whether you're planning to launch a new business, remain an employee, or become a contractor or consultant. Below are a few details which you might need to consider.

- Status as employee, contractor, temporary, or self-employed

- Tax implications

- Alternative versions of resume to fit more than one niche

- Business or professional group membership

- Mentor(s) for guidance in your niche

- Office space, home office

- Business telephone, mobile telephone, fax line

- Computer and software (database, word processing, financial)

- Internet access/home page

- Bookkeeping, records management and storage

- Business calendar

- Business cards/stationery

- Business or professional logo

- Advertising or marketing materials

- Rolodex or software file for network contact management

The Power Of Your Plan

Look back over all you've done in the process of creating **MMI, Inc**. Think about all the things you've learned about yourself and all the skills you've gained to help you survive and prosper in the molecular marketplace. Feel the power of the self-confidence you've gained about **MMI, Inc**, and your prospects for success based on your thought and preparation.

How will you use this information and skill to successfully enter the molecular marketplace? By summarizing the key insights and goals for creating **MMI, Inc** into your Portfolio Development Plan (PDP). Your PDP will be a great way to anticipate what's around the corner, guide the decisions you'll make at key intersections, and inspire you to hold the course when the going gets rough. It will also be an important way to communicate with others about **MMI, Inc** and the product you're bringing to the economic marketplace. Finally, it will be a major component of your achievement portfolio, which you'll prepare in the following chapter, The Bridge.

If you're someone who fears or dislikes plans and planning, keep two things in mind. First, if you personally considered the issues and answered the questions in the previous Steps, you've already done most of the hard thinking work. Second, when you've completed the documentation, your Plan will have great value as a guide and inspiration for you. The effort of the final push to completion will be well worth it. Paula, whom we met at the beginning of Step 10, discovered how valuable it was to have a plan during a crisis in her work life.

Paula had taken the time and effort to translate everything she'd learned from working with the 10 Steps into her PDP. She felt good about the livelihood and niche she'd selected, and the progress she was making toward her goals. Her selected niche was to become a supervisor of computer systems analysts with her present employer. Through research she found that she'd need at least five years' experience and a master's degree in business. Paula's top goal was to get her MBA, so she took night classes, planning to complete the degree about the same time she had the required five years' experience.

When she was just a year away from completion of her degree, Paula's plans were suddenly upset by events at work. Her company announced a downsizing of the information technology (IT) department, and several of the supervisors—whose ranks she wanted to join—were laid off. She felt as though her world was coming apart before her eyes. She recalled the transition process from Step 9, and effectively moved through the first two phases. As she came to the third phase, New Beginnings, Paula was glad she had completed her PDP. She started to update it with the idea that she'd have to completely change her goals and probably move to another company.

However, as she reviewed her PDP, she realized that she strongly preferred to stay with her present employer to avoid relocation, and that realization prompted her to discuss her situation with some friends in other departments. Through them, she learned that despite the downsizing in the corporate IT department, some expansion was occurring in the smaller IT groups in the company's line departments. After selecting the department that she thought fit her best, Paula researched its IT needs and plans, got to know the departmental management team, and established some good network contacts. She was able to help the department with some small projects and provide advice on IT questions; they learned of her many capabilities, including her intense focus on providing good service.

Before she graduated from her MBA program, Paula received a job offer from the department for a management position, supervising a group of analysts who coordinated the development of their IT systems. The position turned out to be everything she'd hoped for. Looking back on the dark days of the IT department layoffs, Paula was happy that she knew about the transition process, she'd kept her plan updated when conditions changed, and she hadn't given up on her vision.

Your Portfolio Development Plan

The last activity in completing your Plan is to document the work you've done in a way that's concise, understandable, and easy to update regularly. Documentation will involve answering the questions in the previous Steps, if you haven't already done so, and transferring the appropriate information, insights and goals from your answers to your PDP document, using the following template. If you want to put your PDP into another format that works for you, by all means do so. The template on the following pages has worked well for others as a format for documenting their PDP, and can be copied and enlarged, if you prefer.

Portfolio Development

Plan

Prepared By:

_____

Date:_____

in conjunction with

Me, Myself and I, Inc: 10 Steps to Career Independence.

Purpose: create a "future-proofed" relationship with work to enable the author to prosper as an independent economic entity in the emerging molecular marketplace for employment.

This plan will be maintained at its peak effectiveness through regular review and update every six months to one year.

Date of next planned review and update:

_____

Portfolio Development Plan

Contents

1. The Changing Work Environment. Purpose: To summarize your personal reasons and motivation for preparing this Plan.

    Reasons for preparing this Plan: *[Include both "carrot" and "stick" reasons, drawn from Interaction 1.1, Interaction 1.3, and your insights from the 10 Steps.]*

2. MMI, Inc Vision. Purpose: To impart motivation, inspiration and direction by envisioning oneself as a success.

    The Vision for **MMI, Inc**: *[From Interaction 2.18]*

3. Product Definition. Purpose: To define the portfolio of skills, knowledge, attitudes, abilities and experiences which you take to the marketplace as **MMI, Inc**.

> **MMI, Inc**'s product definition: *[From Interaction 3.7]*
> *Personality Type* _____
>
> *Top 5 Skills*
>
>
>
>
> *Top 5 Values*
>
>
>
>
> *Essential Elements of Ideal Working Day*
>
>
>
>
> *Product Definition Statement*

4. Field of Endeavor and Livelihood. Purpose: To describe the chosen sphere within which **MMI, Inc** will deliver its services in the molecular marketplace.

Field of Endeavor and Livelihood for **MMI, Inc**: *[From Interaction 4.7.]*

Areas where the chosen Field of Endeavor and Livelihood do not fit well with the Product Definition of **MMI, Inc**: *[From Interaction 4.8]*

5. Niche. Purpose: To understand the competitive environment within your chosen Field of Endeavor and Livelihood, to identify the attributes of people who perform well in that livelihood, and to define a unique way to specialize **MMI, Inc**.

Current market demands, market trends, pay and benefit expectations and potential target employers for **MMI, Inc**: *[From Interaction 5.1]*

Attributes that make workers today successful in **MMI, Inc**'s chosen livelihood: *[From Interaction 5.3]*

Attributes that could set **MMI, Inc** apart from others in the same livelihood in the future: *[From Interaction 5.3]*

The Niche for **MMI, Inc**: *[From Interaction 5.4]*

6. Competitive Advantage. Purpose: To determine the specific success factors and actions needed to assure that **MMI, Inc** is a top performer in your chosen niche.

Knowledge, skill and ability gaps for **MMI, Inc** (including gaps in areas of attitude, networking, strategic alliances or customer service): *[From Interaction 6.6]*

Goals for closing gaps: *[From Interaction 6.13]*

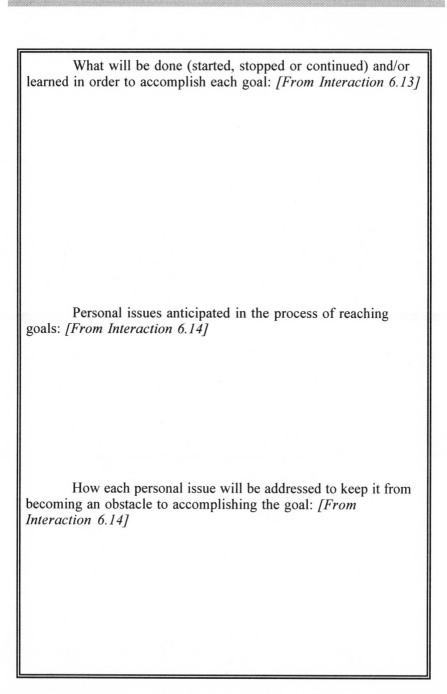

What will be done (started, stopped or continued) and/or learned in order to accomplish each goal: *[From Interaction 6.13]*

Personal issues anticipated in the process of reaching goals: *[From Interaction 6.14]*

How each personal issue will be addressed to keep it from becoming an obstacle to accomplishing the goal: *[From Interaction 6.14]*

The competitive advantage of **MMI, Inc** in its Niche today: *[From Interaction 6.14]*

When the above goals are accomplished, the competitive advantage of **MMI, Inc** will then be: *[From Interaction 6.14]*

7. Financial Strategy and Plan. Purpose: To take responsibility for your finances so that you create a secure financial base from which to pursue your goals.

Minimum monthly financial needs: *[From Interaction 7.4]*

$_____

Minimum monthly savings percentage: *[From Interaction 7.5]*

_____%

Six month buffer: *[From Interaction 7.6]*

$_____

Investment plan: *[From Interaction 7.7]*

Tactics to ensure that you stick to the financial plan for **MMI, Inc**: *[From Interaction 7.8]*

8. Marketing and Promotion Plan. Purpose: To assure that **MMI, Inc** can successfully reach its customers/employers, and obtain and retain their business, in order to meet its goals.

How **MMI, Inc** will implement the five steps to selling: *[From Interactions 8.4 through 8.8.]*
Enthusiasm

Needs Assessment

Unique Benefits

Overcoming Objections

Asking for the Sale

Pricing plan for sale of services: *[From Interaction 8.9]*
Optimum Pricing

Flexibility Range

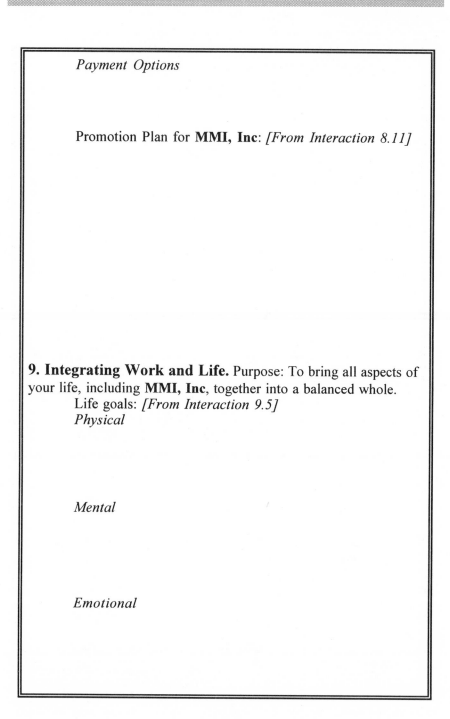

Payment Options

Promotion Plan for **MMI, Inc**: *[From Interaction 8.11]*

9. Integrating Work and Life. Purpose: To bring all aspects of your life, including **MMI, Inc**, together into a balanced whole.
Life goals: *[From Interaction 9.5]*
Physical

Mental

Emotional

Spiritual

Family

Community

Leisure

Comparing **MMI, Inc** goals with life goals: *[From Interaction 9.6]*
Inconsistencies

Issues Raised

Resolution Plans

10. Implementing Your Plan. Purpose of Implementation: To put your plan into action.

Time Frame: *[From Interaction 10.2]*

Goal	Activity	Start Date	Comp Date	Revision/ Comments
___	___	___	___	___
___	___	___	___	___
___	___	___	___	___
___	___	___	___	___
___	___	___	___	___
___	___	___	___	___
___	___	___	___	___
___	___	___	___	___
___	___	___	___	___
___	___	___	___	___

Financial Implications: *[From Interaction 10.3]*

Item and Estimated Cost	Funds Avail.?	If not, When?	Source	Included in Fin. Plan?
___	___	___	___	___
___	___	___	___	___
___	___	___	___	___
___	___	___	___	___
___	___	___	___	___
___	___	___	___	___
___	___	___	___	___

Logistical, "nitty-gritty" issues, with plans to address each item: *[From Interaction 10.4.]*

Additional points, reviews and comments:

Keeping Your Plan Current

While you're working hard to accomplish your initial goals, you'll want to refer to your PDP often—at least a couple of times each month—for inspiration and updates. Keep it close at hand, easily accessible for regular review and additions, such as new ideas for customer service or updates to your progress on goals.

Once you've fully established **MMI, Inc** as a key contributor in your niche, you probably won't be updating your PDP as often as you did initially. That's fine, but keep in mind that your niche or your livelihood could change dramatically. To be prepared, you'll need to continue reviewing and updating your PDP regularly throughout your working life. Every six months, even if you feel nothing much has changed, pull it out and go back through your work.

Like Paula, you may well run into a tough period and feel like you're unable to make progress toward your vision. If you feel bogged down, that's a very important time to go back to review and update your PDP. Whether your review is prompted by a need to reestablish your vision or by the fact that six months have passed since you last updated your PDP, each review will turn up valuable new insights and ideas to revitalize your work life.

Do I Hear A Fat Lady Singing?

How do you usually celebrate the successful conclusion of a task or a project? Do you go out to dinner, buy something to commemorate the event, take a short vacation or have a party? There are many ways to affirm the successful completion of a task, to tell the world "I've done it!"

You've just completed a critically important process, creating a Plan for **MMI, Inc** that's appropriate for you. You deserve to celebrate this major accomplishment, and below are two suggestions to conclude your work on the 10 Steps in a positive way. Your efforts included both DO and BE activities, and both these suggestions will continue to strengthen the balance between your BE and DO sides, which will help to assure the success of **MMI, Inc.**

The first way to celebrate is creative and artistic and will produce the final component for your Plan which captures the spirit of your accomplishment—its cover. Your Plan has plenty of words in it already, so balance them with a creative expression that pulls all the concepts and insights together for you: make a collage of pictures, use a favorite photo or take a new one, draw a picture of your own, write a poem, or compose a piece of music. You may want to relate this BE activity to the gift you received in the imagination exercise in Step 9. This is a private activity which you'll never have to share with anyone else unless you want to, so don't worry about how it will appear to others; make it just right for you.

The second way to celebrate is ongoing: each day, take time for an imagination exercise on your own. Many people find great benefit in daily inner activities. For example, Scott Adams, the creator of the popular cartoon strip *Dilbert*, was quoted in *USA Weekend* on the subject of "affirmations" that he did many times a day: "Wish good things for yourself that are not overtly bad for someone else...Amazing things will happen."

In doing the imagination exercises as part of the 10 Steps you'll have developed a way to prepare for them that works best for you. Choose a time each day, perhaps early morning or in the evening before you go to bed, when it will be quiet and you will not be disturbed. Once you have stilled your mind and are able to focus your attention, imagine a picture or scene in which **MMI, Inc** is successful. You are performing at your best in the place that is just right for you. Develop the scene as it would play out for you, always seeing yourself being and doing what is ideal for you.

Congratulations! You've completed the 10 Steps. As **MMI, Inc** you can revisit what you've learned as often as you like until you've mastered the 10 Steps as your secret for success. You can come back to the concepts or to your own work in each Step for clarification or fresh ideas if something isn't working well for you. Keeping your PDP regularly up to date is the surest way to keep current as conditions change, keep your outlook fresh, and keep building toward your vision for **MMI, Inc.**

The last section of the book deals with how to apply the skills, knowledge and ability you gained in creating **MMI, Inc** to also master the employment search—getting the position.

Case Studies

1. *Shannon*

At first Step 10 felt like I was re-hashing the same old material, and I have to admit that I didn't spend much time on the timing and nitty-gritty sections. I felt like I'd done most of the basic work on planning already, and I also wasn't inspired to dive back into the details after finishing Step 9 with such a good feeling. I did use the financial section to begin finding out how much getting my degree would cost, and to list the options I've thought of for financing my change in livelihood.

After the financial questions, I felt tempted to skip the rest of this Step. But in looking ahead, I realized when I found the actual plan template that there was some value to reviewing my findings. For example, although I know that my vision and product definition statements were supposed to be guiding my decisions throughout the 10-Step process, it had been a long time since I'd even looked at them. So filling out the spaces in the plan gave me a worthwhile opportunity to examine the pieces of **MMI, Inc** all together.

I was surprised at what a feeling of accomplishment I got from seeing the plan put together—it made sense! As I went through each Step, many of them were so busy that I couldn't tell if I'd made much progress. But now that I can see the whole picture, I know that I've come a long way in my view of work and where I want to go, from just kind of "hanging out" to having a direction and some ideas on how to make it happen. **MMI, Inc** has a business plan, which wasn't something I would ever have known how to do on my own.

I did decide to copy the plan and put it into a nice folder where I can get access to it easily. The idea of drawing a cover wasn't very interesting to me, since my artwork leaves something to be desired. But as I thought about it, what impresses me most about this plan is that it gives me and my work a level of professionalism and importance that I've never felt before. So, using my computer skills, I created a very classy and professional-looking color design for the front of my plan folder. I took it to a copy shop and had a high-quality color reproduction made. Putting that on the front of my plan made it even more personally significant to me, and I enjoy seeing it sitting on my desk.

I guess I'm most impressed and surprised by the fact that, although all of the information came from me, the result is new direction and motivation. Whatever happens next, I'll be better prepared to handle it after the 10 Steps than I would have been before. I can't say for sure at this point how successful **MMI, Inc** will be in the molecular marketplace, since I'm still creating it. But I can definitely say that I've gotten further in my work planning and goals by doing the Steps in this book than I have in my previous 27 years. I'd say that's a pretty good result from a few weeks of reading and writing.

2. *Brent*

Far and away my highest priority goal at the end of the 10 Steps was finding and getting settled in a new job, since my company's given us 60 days to find work before we're off the payroll. It would be great if I could use this unpleasant event as a springboard to change my field to computer graphics or animation, but that's just not practical now. I need to keep my income at the same level and, since we don't have a big buffer, make sure that I don't have a big time gap between jobs. That means I'll almost certainly end up in another job in a different group at my company, which will be OK but not ideal. The time frame for completing this goal is dictated by the situation: 60 days.

My second **MMI, Inc** goal is to improve my strategic alliance/teamwork skills. In my last performance review my boss said that was my weakest area, and since I've got some free time during the job search I'll take advantage of the company-provided training center to schedule myself for a teamwork seminar before I start another job. My time frame for this goal is 30 days.

My third goal is to create a portfolio of images and concepts I've rendered on the computer, which will be a necessary part of getting a position in the field of computer graphics and animation in the future. This is a pretty long range goal, but one I'm motivated to work on because that's the livelihood of my dreams. My completion date for this goal is one year.

None of these goals will require money to pursue. I'd love to have better computer software and hardware at home to build my graphics portfolio, but the simple fact is we can't afford it, and I can do the work on what we have already, just not as quickly or as well.

It was a little hard to muster the energy to complete the PDP document, because I felt I already had all the answers I needed about my future from the work I'd done on the 10 Steps. But with a little encouragement from my wife, I finished my PDP, and was pleasantly surprised to find how good it felt to be able to turn to one small document to review everything that was important about my work and life. I'm really glad I finished it.

I know my first review and update of my PDP will happen as soon as I'm settled in my new job. Then, for the next year, while I'm building my computer graphics portfolio and learning more about how to move into that livelihood, I'll update it at least every three months. Perhaps after I'm settled in the new livelihood, updating my PDP once every six months will be OK. One thing is certain: I've put too much into this Plan and gotten too much out of the work on the 10 Steps to walk away from it all and let it gather dust on a shelf somewhere. It's the story of my life, and there are a lot of chapters yet to write. I wonder what they'll say?

3. *Emily*

At the end of Step 9, I felt as though I had come to a completion point in the 10-step process. I am particularly drawn toward the BE-type activities and, after finding a special gift during the last imagination exercise, I felt inspired to go out and begin to put the process as a whole into action.

When I saw that this Step involved creating a Portfolio Development Plan, I felt deflated, like I was back at ground zero with all of the work I had just completed adding up to nothing. So my first thought was to skip this whole Step and just take my new insights and enthusiasm out into the world. But I knew that every one of the preceding Steps were of value, so I decided to read forward a couple of sections to see just what was involved. I soon began to feel more at ease, especially when it was suggested I had done most of the work already. I decided to read on and complete this last effort.

As I read about setting time frames, I could see that developing start and completion dates would help make my previous decisions more concrete; it would move them from being fairly esoteric to being fully and clearly developed. A large part of my timing was pre-determined by my Master's degree program, which will end in June of next year. At that time I will need a couple of years to complete my Master's Thesis, which I will do while working or going through an employment search. Because the degree program is rigorous, I want to put my full attention on it until the course work is completed, which means putting my other goals on hold for now.

Financially, we've ear-marked some extra money for education needs. We'll probably continue to include this item in our budget even after I complete my degree, since we're beginning to see how important education is for growth both in a work setting as well as for our own personal development. We see the investment in my education as being an investment in our eventual retirement. Rick continues to work and still brings home a nice pay check on a regular basis and by the time he retires, I'll be bringing in money to continue to support our needs and interests.

As I started to complete my Portfolio Development Plan, I was surprised and gratified to find myself feeling a strong sense of accomplishment. Actually seeing so much of my hard-won efforts put together into one place brought me a great feeling of success, and I can see how the Plan and what I've learned about putting it together just might come in handy in the future.

As I came to the close of the Step, I loved the idea of imagining myself as a success on a daily basis. This exercise fits nicely with the goal I committed to early in this process to continue to deepen my spiritual base by daily active imagination exercises. I'll just begin the process with this new aspect of visualizing success, and since I deeply believe in myself as well as in the power of the BE side, I have no doubt that success will come for **MMI, Inc.**

4. *Forrest*

I really enjoyed seeing all my work on the 10 Steps come together in one place in my PDP. Setting dates for my goals was easy for me, since I'd been doing planning at work for years and automatically think of dates and contingencies whenever I set a goal. Other than the financial impact of starting my own business, which I'd already considered in my financial plan, I had no goals that required any significant money.

Thinking about the "nitty-gritty" items was very relevant to starting my own consulting business. Before working with Step 10, my head had been full of the things I'd need to do to, but similarly to my approach to life goals in Step 9, I hadn't focused and prioritized my ideas, so they were pretty undeveloped. I now have short-term, stepping stone goals to get started: incorporate my business, convert the spare bedroom to a true office, buy and learn to operate bookkeeping software, and develop some dynamite marketing materials.

I think about my situation compared to younger people who are just starting out. I've worked hard for a lot of years and paid my dues, but I can't help feeling grateful for what I have which was mostly the result of a past when jobs were more stable. I'm a "mature" worker with a lot of transferable and job-specific skills, some exciting goals, a well-developed product (not to mention a regular small pension!) in a growth industry. To my way of thinking, that makes me pretty lucky.

The Bridge

Putting The 10 Steps To Work

In the molecular marketplace, all of us are portfolio workers—temp-oraries, contractors, consultants, even long-term employees. Most of the time we'll either be looking for work, or planning to look for work when our current assignment ends. Staying alert to opportunities is part of making a living in the molecular marketplace. But if you're a long-term employee, you may think you'll never again need to look for work. You're probably wrong.

If your employer runs out of work for you for any reason, you'll be looking elsewhere. You may also decide in the future to change your livelihood and move on for your own reasons. But even if you're the exception and you keep working for one employer until retirement, that still may not be the end of the story. Many healthy retired people find that they want to—or have to—work, at least some of the time, as a portfolio worker. Their reasons include making ends meet, keeping active, having a little extra spending money, and meeting people. So the issue is not *if* you go looking for work, but *when*.

In a way, getting the position could be called Step 11 of the process of creating career independence. But even after **MMI, Inc** is well established in a successful niche, you'll probably go through the employment search process often, so it's not so much a Step as it is a recurring event in your working life. Therefore the skills involved in getting a position are the connection between the product—**MMI, Inc**—and the marketplace, and therefore gaining those skills is like building a bridge. Hence the name of this last chapter of the book.

The Livelihood Cycle: Getting The Position

To prepare for the next time you look for work, look again at the Livelihood Cycle that was introduced in Step 5 and further developed in Step 8. Let's complete the Livelihood Cycle by focusing on Phase 4, Getting the Position.

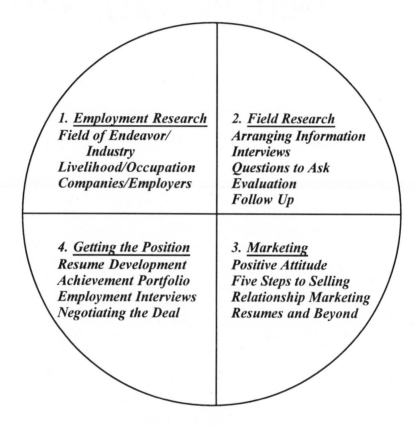

The Livelihood Cycle

The first step in getting a position is having in mind a position to get. If you're already working in your chosen field of endeavor and livelihood, then you're probably aware of the employment situation in that field: possible positions, good and bad employers and who's hiring. If you need to find other potential employers in your field, you probably have a network of contacts with whom to brainstorm ideas.

If you're newly entering the world of work or changing your field of endeavor, you're more likely to embark on a full-blown employment search. In this case, the research you did in Step 5 will have given you good ideas about who employs workers in your field, livelihood and geographical area. Your first activity will be to contact people within your network who can help generate leads for positions with these potential employers. Other sources for leads include the Internet, job or career fairs, college placement offices, private and state employment offices and the old stand-by: want ads.

On the Internet, you can start with web sites of employers you know and see if they have jobs available. Or you can start with one of the big six job boards on the web which were listed in Step 5. To learn more about conducting an employment search on the Internet, a good resource is *The Guide to Internet Job Searching* by Margaret Riley.

Once you've identified one or more possible positions you're interested in, you'll do additional research to investigate potential employers and gain the specific information you'll need to customize your resume, prepare fully for an employment interview, and negotiate details of your employment.

Whether you have a specific position in mind or plan to search broadly to see what turns up, your next task is to get a top-notch resume into the hands of potential employers.

Resume Development

Your resume is one of the most important marketing tools for **MMI, Inc.** As discussed in Step 8, a resume has many potential uses, including opening the door for an employment interview, which almost always precedes an employer's hiring decision. This means your resume is usually the first impression that an employer has about **MMI, Inc**; the challenge is to make sure it's not also the last. With so much riding on your resume, it's important to be sure that it represents you effectively. To do this, your resume should be structured in an appropriate format, be grammatically correct and accurately portray a match between you and the employer's need.

There are two basic formats that can be used for your resume: chronological and functional. The traditional resume format is chronological, with work experiences listed in reverse chronological order, including employers, job titles, duties and dates. Today, a chronological format may be best if you've stayed in one field of endeavor and progressed into related positions with more responsibility.

In contrast, a functional format is often more appropriate in the molecular marketplace, where portfolio workers tend to have a variety of positions, sometimes even simultaneously, which use different transferable and work-related skills. A functional resume highlights your best skill categories and lists specific accomplishments that demonstrate the variety and depth of those skills. In addition, your employment history can be summarized in a short section following the presentation of accomplishments and skills.

Depending on the employer and the position you're targeting, you'll want to highlight different accomplishments and skills. Therefore, you'll start with a basic version of your resume which you'll customize for each employer before you send it.

Following are examples of the basic chronological and functional formats. These are used with the permission of Yana Parker, author of *"Ready-To-Go Resume"* software, which is a good source of ideas and additional examples for preparing your resume (See the Suggested Resources list for details).

Chronological Resume Format

YOUR NAME
Street Address
City, State, and Zip
(xxx) xxx-xxx

Objective: Position as

SUMMARY OF QUALIFICATIONS

- Number of years experience in the field or line of work.
- Relevant credentials or training or education.
- An accomplishment* that directly relates to the objective.
- A quality* or characteristic* that supports this goal.
- Another accomplishment*, or another characteristic*.
  reflected in the details below, of course

RELEVANT EXPERIENCE & ACCOMPLISHMENTS

1990-present   **Job Title**   WORKPLACE, City, State
- Accomplishment/one-liner, from this job, that's relevant to the new job objective.
- Accomplishment/one-liner, from this job, that's relevant.
- Accomplishment/one-liner, from this job, that's relevant.
- Accomplishment/one-liner, from this job, that's relevant.

198x-8x   **Job Title**   WORKPLACE, City, State
- Accomplishment/one-liner, from this job, that's relevant.
- Accomplishment/one-liner, from this job, that's relevant.

198x-8x   **Job Title**   WORKPLACE, City, State
- Accomplishment/one-liner, from this job, that's relevant.
- Accomplishment/one-liner, from this job, that's relevant.

EDUCATION & TRAINING

Degree or classes or whatever
Some credentials, maybe

Functional Resume Format

YOUR NAME
Street Address
City, State, and Zip
(xxx) xxx-xxx

Objective: Position as

SUMMARY OF QUALIFICATIONS
- Number of years experience in the field or line of work.
- Relevant credentials or training or education.
- An accomplishment* that directly relates to the objective.
- A quality* or characteristic* that supports this goal.
- Another accomplishment* or another characteristic*.
  reflected in the details below, of course

RELEVANT EXPERIENCE & ACCOMPLISHMENTS

ONE RELEVANT SKILL
- An accomplishment* that illustrates or documents this skill.
- Another accomplishment* that illustrates or documents .
- Another accomplishment* that illustrates or documents .

ANOTHER RELEVANT SKILL
- An accomplishment* that illustrates or documents this skill.
- Another accomplishment* that illustrates or documents.

ANOTHER RELEVANT SKILL
- An accomplishment* that illustrates or documents this skill.
- Another accomplishment* that illustrates or documents.

* Where possible, mention where this happened; link to Employment History.
  NOTE: "Relevant" means relevant to the job objective.

EMPLOYMENT HISTORY
1990-present	**Job Title**	COMPANY NAME, City
198x-8x	**Job Title**	COMPANY NAME, City
197x-7x	**Job Title**	COMPANY NAME, City

EDUCATION & TRAINING
Degree or classes or whatever
Some credentials, maybe

Nothing can destroy a first impression about you faster than a misspelled word or a punctuation error! Once you've created the perfect resume for the position you want, have someone else read it to check spelling, grammar and punctuation, and to be sure that it communicates clearly.

Employers with many resumes to screen will commonly use a computer to scan them for key skills or experiences, or even for specific words or phrases, in order to quickly select a short list of candidates for employment interviews. A clever or artistic presentation is irrelevant if your resume is to be scanned by a computer. Instead, what counts is the way you portray **MMI, Inc** as exactly matching what the employer is looking for. You can call a prospective employer and ask if scanning is used in the selection process; if so, the following suggestions may improve your chances of getting on the short list.

- Use white or light-colored 8½ x 11 inch paper, laser printed on one side only.

- Don't staple pages.

- Use an easy-to-read type face, for example Helvetica or Times.

- Use a font size of 10 to 14 points for text and headings; your name can be up to 32 points.

- Use boldface and/or capital letters for section headings as long as the letters don't touch each other.

- Avoid vertical and horizontal lines, graphics and boxes.

- Use a single column format.

- Use more than one page if necessary for legibility.

- Place your name at the top of each page on its own line.

- Use a standard format for your address, below your name.

- List each phone number on its own line.

- Date ranges should be on the same line.

- Load your resume with key words—nouns or short phrases describing your knowledge, skills, abilities and experiences.

If your resume is likely to be scanned, you should consider creating two versions of your customized resume—one for a computer to scan with detailed information, and the other to be read by the prospective employer with a more creative layout and enhanced typography on high quality paper. Send the "computer" version to the employer with a cover letter, and carry the "people" version to the employment interview.

The cover letter you'll send with your resume will convey an important first impression and serve as an introduction for **MMI, Inc**. Your cover letter should point out the reason you're sending the resume; for example, you're answering an ad, responding to a referral, or initiating a contact because of a need you perceived. It should also include a clear and brief statement of how you will fill the prospective employer's need, a description of your unique competitive advantage as **MMI, Inc**, and a request for a personal interview. Keep the following points in mind as you prepare your cover letter.

- Address your letter to a specific person, if possible.

- Be certain that spelling, grammar and punctuation are perfect.

- Keep it to one page maximum.

- Include specific skills and achievements that meet the employer's need.

- Briefly describe how you created a unique niche in a previous position.

- Clearly communicate your goal.

- Be assertive but not aggressive; express interest in the position as a challenge, and as a way to broaden your skill base.

Now that you've prepared your resume and cover letter, you'll need to get them into the hands of the prospective employer. The best alternative is hand delivery to the right person—the decision maker—but since this often isn't possible, you may have to submit your resume along with everyone else's and wait for a response. A growing number of employers—especially high-tech companies—are *requiring* that resumes be submitted via the Internet.

However you've submitted your resume, if it's well done it will be working on your behalf while you're waiting for a response. If your resume is to be scanned, loading it with key words will help it make the short list. Then, when your resume is actually read by a person, the quality of the content and presentation will give you an edge when the decision is made about which candidates to invite for an interview.

Your Achievement Portfolio

The term "portfolio" is interesting: "port" is from a root word that means portable or movable, and "folio" suggests a collection of essential things in a package. In the molecular marketplace, most of us are—or will be— portfolio workers, able and willing to transport our skills and experience to a new work environment when necessary. Similarly, your achievement portfolio is a compact collection of information about **MMI, Inc** which substantiates your resume information with objective evidence, and shows how you will effectively bring unique benefits to a new employer.

Your achievement portfolio will contain many pages, possibly even oversized folders or envelopes for photos, drawings or samples. It will include your PDP or selected items from it, but will consist primarily of examples, samples and other objective evidence supporting the information about **MMI, Inc** on your resume.

Several purposes for preparing an achievement portfolio were discussed in Step 8. One of the most important is to improve the chances of getting the position you want. The Center on Education and Training for Employment conducted research among personnel managers in the late 1980's which suggested that applicants who prepared portfolio demonstrations for employment interviews gained at least a 10% advantage over others. If you're preparing an achievement portfolio for the first time, or updating it to prepare for an employment interview, a suggested structure is shown below. The items listed on pages 247 & 248 are general examples which you can customize to fit your situation. Include any additional evidence that may help strengthen the case for an employer to hire **MMI, Inc**. Exclude items that may not portray your achievements in a positive light.

Put your achievement portfolio into a package that's easy to update and customize, like a loose-leaf binder or a set of folders in a briefcase. Before you take it with you to an employment interview, use what you've learned about the employer from your research to customize your material by including items of particular interest for this employer. Also, have in mind a few selected items from the portfolio that you can quickly refer to as support for the claims in your resume.

Employment Interviews

Getting the opportunity to meet a prospective employer for an employment interview is a major milestone. It means you've met the basic requirements and are now competing with a small number of highly qualified candidates. The interview is your big opportunity to display the competitive advantage that you will bring to the employer by pointing out how **MMI, Inc** stands out in the crowd.

Preparing for the interview is critical since your preparation—or lack of it—will be quickly evident to a skilled interviewer. Being prepared shows that you're taking this opportunity seriously and that you've done your homework, which can help you make a connection with the interviewer. You should prepare carefully in three areas:

The employer

- Learn as much as you can about the organization you've targeted.

- Request an annual report, brochure or other informational material.

- Learn as much as you can about the person doing the hiring through your networking contacts.

Yourself

- Review both the transferable skills and the job-specific skills you'll bring to the employer.

- Be able to clearly articulate how these skills have made you successful, and how they will meet the employer's need.

- Update your achievement portfolio so it is current and be prepared to display a few key items in support of your skills and accomplishments.

- Using a friend to play the role of the interviewer, practice holding the interview in order to feel secure in your answers to questions.

Your appearance

- The interviewer reviews not only your answers to questions but everything about you—including your appearance—so dress accordingly.

- Dress one level up from the way you would if you had this position (for example, if people doing the work dress in jeans, wear slacks; if people wear slacks, you should wear a business suit or jacket—you don't want to feel out of place, but it's better to be overdressed than underdressed.)

- Ask someone else to check your appearance before you leave for the interview.

During an interview, being well prepared is the best way to be relaxed and comfortable. An interview is a stressful event at best, but below are some ways to help you deliver a high-quality, genuine performance.

- Keep in mind all the work you've done to understand and improve your attitude in preparing your PDP—it will come across to the interviewer, and strongly support your "fit" for the position.

- With a responsive attitude, you'll express a sense of sincerely caring about the targeted organization, which is an important foundation for a good interview.

- Your thorough preparation will help you present yourself with a sense of confidence.

- Focus on being genuinely interested in the interviewer, not preoccupied with yourself or how you're coming across, which will enable you to truly listen to the interviewer's comments and questions.

- Take the initiative by making a connection with the interviewer, with a warm handshake and a bit of personal small talk, if appropriate.

- Above all, be yourself; don't try to be someone or something you aren't.

The interviewer has a job to do and a limited amount of time to get a lot of information and form an opinion about you, so the key questions will probably be very much like those on the list below. If you can answer these questions well, you'll go into the interview with a sense of self-confidence. The interviewer may try to throw you off guard with a question you don't expect to see how you respond; if so, the important thing is to keep your cool and give a short, honest response. Other than practicing and being ready for the questions, the most important things to remember are to tell the truth and to keep your answers short.

Questions that will typically be asked by an employment interviewer include:

- Tell me about yourself—your personality, background and other interests.

- Why did you leave your last position? (In your answer, be sure to avoid badmouthing, misrepresenting or over-explaining; keep your answer to one or two sentences.)

- Why are you interested in this position? (Here's a great opportunity to display the benefit of the research you've done.)

- What are your accomplishments? (This is the heart of most interviews; include some success stories to show that you can accomplish results, and be sure to provide some specific details and numbers to support them.)

- Describe a work situation where you faced a problem and explain how you solved it.

- What are your strengths? (Be objective and brief.)

- What are your weaknesses? (Be honest in describing an area of weakness, preferably outside of the work environment, and your successful efforts to overcome it, learn from it and move on.)

- What salary do you expect? (If asked during the interview, return the question by asking about the salary range of the open position. If asked when a position is being offered, it's time to begin negotiating, based on the research you've done.)

Interview questions should come from both sides; after all, you have a lot to learn about the employer and a lot more at stake than the interviewer. Asking your own questions reflects the fact that you're taking an equal role in a business discussion, and that you have the skill to take 100% responsibility for a situation. You may want to ask questions like these:

- What are the overall strengths of the organization?

- What is the organization's most pressing problem at the moment?

- Where is the employer most vulnerable?

- What has been the turnover in the past few years? If the turnover has been high, can you tell me why?

- To whom does the position report?

- What is the offered salary or salary range for the position?

- Can you tell me what benefits are offered?

- Does the employer support employees in the area of _____? (Be specific; for example, work-life balance, child care, continuing education, flexible working arrangements, telecommuting.)

- What are the major challenges in the position—immediately, and also long term?

- Which of my skills, experience and achievements are well-matched to this position? Which are less well-matched?

- Will this position provide me the opportunity to grow my skills and capabilities in the area of _____? (Be specific.)

- Will you personally be making the hiring decision? If not, can you tell me who will?

- When will the hiring decision be made?

- Will you let me know your decision? By when?

The final activity associated with an employment interview is often neglected—the follow-up. *Always* send a thank-you note the following day, which can accompany any additional documentation or information that may have been requested. If you don't hear back by the date promised, keep the initiative by contacting the employer to find out why. Ask if the position has been filled; if so, it's a fair question to ask why you weren't selected. But be sure your attitude is positive and professional so you don't close future doors and so you can learn as much as possible about how you could have been even more competitive. You can also ask if there are other similar positions available.

The employment interview may be the most important opportunity you'll ever have to market the services of **MMI, Inc**. Because as you saw in Step 8 practice is so helpful in being able to sell effectively, it's a good idea to practice holding an employment interview with a friend playing the interviewer role.

The employment search process can be emotionally draining. Preparing a resume—or a lot of resumes—and waiting for a response is bad enough, especially if you need an income. But if you're not selected for a position you really wanted after an employment interview, you could experience a letdown and a strong personal sense of rejection. You might even find yourself back in the pit, the second phase of the transition process described in Step 9. If so, keep the transition process in mind to help you move through to phase 3, new beginnings.

In fact, each employment interview is a new beginning, which makes it critical to remember what you've built as you created **MMI, Inc** and your PDP: a competitive and resilient independent economic entity with a set of valuable skills and experience. There are a lot of places out there where this combination will be a prized member of a workplace team; you haven't found one yet, but you will.

Practice keeping a responsive attitude, which will be the single most important factor in any employment interview situation. Managing your attitude in a disappointing situation is one of the key new skills you possess as a result of mastering the 10 Steps. Other new skills you're building through the employment search include marketing **MMI, Inc**, interviewing, communicating, building confidence and handling stress.

Negotiating The Deal

When your employment search bears fruit and you're the person selected for the position, your final task is to negotiate the deal. Often, especially if you're just starting out and don't have a long work history, it's a pretty simple matter of agreeing to work under the conditions offered. Sooner or later, though, you'll face a situation where there's enough at stake for both **MMI, Inc** and the employer that negotiation will become necessary.

How do you know when you've reached the point where you shouldn't just accept what's offered, but should begin to negotiate for something better? Negotiation is appropriate when the employer needs something you have that's in short supply or that's unique, like your well thought-out niche for **MMI, Inc**. If you're asked what the price of your services or your salary requirement is, that's your first cue to negotiate. If you're going to be offered a contract for services or as an employee, that's another cue.

Even if you're offered a standard contract with an established pay scale, it's worth trying to negotiate if there's some part of the offer that you can't live with. It won't hurt anything to make your own counter proposal in order to see how the employer will respond. Most people feel intimidated by the prospect of negotiating an employment contract, which means that employers often get a better deal on a great new employee than they'd be willing to settle for if pushed.

The most important preparation for a negotiation is the research you've done about your livelihood and about this employer. Through your research you know a lot more about the employer than he or she knows about you, including the working conditions of others who work there. That's a huge advantage for you in the negotiation. The employer has different advantages, including holding the purse strings and having lots of negotiation experience. All in all the advantages offset each other to make this a negotiation of equals, which can set the stage for a win-win solution.

Keep the points below in mind when you enter the ranks of workers who command the power to negotiate a contract for what they want.

Preparation For Negotiation

- Enter your negotiation armed with information on comparable pay and benefits; have numbers in mind based on research and your needs.

- Gather details about the position: level of responsibility, level of authority, freedom to act, flexibility, title, reporting relationships and the opportunity to personalize the way you work.

- Having an advantage through your research about the employer doesn't mean you can be inflexible in your demands; an experienced negotiator will spot a power play from a mile away, and that could sour the deal.

During Negotiation

- When both sides work toward negotiating a win-win solution, the result is often better than either side could develop separately.

- Remember to view the employer as your customer, not as an adversary.

- Try to help your customer see how you can arrive at a deal that works for both of you.

- Yes, once again your responsive attitude is critical; it brings openness and confidence to the table.

- Keep in mind what you've learned about frame of reference: see where the other person is coming from, and also be aware of your own motivation.

If The Negotiation Isn't Working

- Be willing to see the negotiation through to success, even if things get tough or take longer than you wish; unless you reach an absolute impasse, maintain your commitment to reaching a positive outcome for both sides.

- If the customer doesn't agree, don't personalize it, but look for another way to reach a win-win solution; if that's not possible, move on to the next opportunity, armed with new knowledge and confidence that you made the right decision.

- If you make a mistake, don't take it as a personal failure; re-member that you're developing a skill, which will be useful in any situation in the future including work, community activities and personal relationships.

If you're facing a major negotiation or expect to negotiate lots of deals in the future—for example, if you're going to be a consultant—you'll benefit from reading further about this skill. A good source of information is *Getting to Yes: Negotiating Agreement Without Giving In*, by Roger Fisher and William Ury. And just as you practiced for an employment interview, you can practice negotiating a deal for a position, with a friend playing the role of the employer.

Once More, With Feeling

This final chapter is called "The Bridge" because it connects the work you've done creating **MMI, Inc** with your future in the molecular marketplace. It outlines basic techniques that will help you succeed when you hit the streets to get a new position. There are numerous books available which go into more detail on each aspect of the employment search. Among the many good resources available are *Change Your Job, Change Your Life*, by Ronald L. Krannich. A practical manual for job-hunters and career-changers, *What Color Is Your Parachute?*, by Richard Nelson Bolles, *The Resume Catalog* by Yana Parker, *Portfolio Power* by Martin Kimeldorf and *111 Dynamite Ways to Ace Your Job Interview*, by Richard Fein.

The larger purpose of this book, however, is not to make you successful in getting one position, but to help you master the 10 Steps and use the molecular marketplace to your advantage. This advantage begins as you abandon traditional ideas about careers and jobs, such as expecting to get a permanent, steady job, and slowly but surely progressing to a higher-paid position with the same employer until you retire. As you've seen, the changes being ushered in by the molecular marketplace make that mode of thinking totally obsolete. Today, as a portfolio worker who wants to succeed by being in charge of your own destiny, you'll probably find yourself moving from position to position, from employer to employer and from niche to niche as opportunities develop to progress toward your personal goals.

In addition, making the most of the molecular marketplace means you understand that the employment search process is not a one-time thing, but part of the Livelihood Cycle—a cycle which continues for as long as you choose to work. In the Livelihood Cycle, as in any cycle, the end of one phase is the beginning of another. Once you're established in a position you quickly begin resetting goals and creating a new niche for **MMI, Inc**. The knowledge and information you gain in a new position may prompt you to begin research into other positions or employers. And once your next objective is clear, you begin to market **MMI, Inc** as a candidate for your next position. If you're an employee, the Livelihood Cycle may move more slowly while you take on a new position and develop the skills to be successful. If you're a temporary, contractor or consultant, the Livelihood Cycle may move more quickly, and the phases can overlap and blur if you gain and hold several positions in short order, perhaps even at the same time.

Your ultimate advantage comes from knowing the secrets of career independence and having a carefully crafted plan to guide you through the Livelihood Cycle. With this preparation, you're ready to make **MMI, Inc** the roaring success you've always dreamed of. If you can imagine it, it can happen..

Happy cycling—and recycling!

Section	Title	Included Items	Optional Items 1.
1.	Your Plan	PDP Vision Statement PDP Product Definition Statement Description of Niche for **MMI, Inc** Current resume Current resume cover letter	PDP Promotion Plan for **MMI, Inc** PDP Competitive Advantage of **MMI, Inc** PDP Customer Service Statement
2.	Education and Training —Formal and Informal	Diplomas Certificates of mastery or completion Licenses Scholarships or grants received Participation in vocational competition Transcripts or other educational records	Teachers' evaluations List of competencies mastered Standardized or formalized test results Reports of attendance at workshops, lectures
3.	General Work Performance	Letters of reference Employer evaluations Military records Examples of problems solved Records of activities in professional organizations Evidence of your leadership qualities	Employer evaluation Past job descriptions Description of experience as a consultant or temporary Earnings records

(Achievement Portfolio structure and content based on articles in *Career Planning and Adult Development Journal, Winter 1996-97, Martin Kimeldorf, Guest Editor.*)

4. "Data" Skills Documentation

Samples of your writing
Evidence of public speaking
Evidence of presentation skills
Software expertise
Software developed
Paper documents or replicas of forms, charts, printouts, budgets, plans, spreadsheets created or used

Graphs or tables produced
Documents authored or prepared
Technical reports prepared
Desktop publishing samples
Internet designs created
Grant or loan applications

5. "People" Skills Documentation

Negotiations conducted
Leadership experiences, photos or records
Organization chart showing employees or contractors supervised
Union activities
Evidence of conflict resolution skills
Mentoring, tutoring, teaching, coaching and training activities
Meetings or conferences led

Interviews conducted
Community activities, photos or records
Team member evaluation of people skills
Sample progress reports of people supervised, led, trained or coached
Projects, committees and teams served on

6. "Thing" Skills Documentation

Performance records showing speed, accuracy, productivity, complexity, sales figures

Equipment operation qualifications
Technical directions or manuals mastered
Driving records

Suggested Resources

Step One

Bellman, Geoffrey M. *Your Signature Path: Gaining New Perspectives on Life and Work.* San Francisco, CA: Berrett-Koehler, 1996.

Block, Peter. *Stewardship.* San Francisco, CA: Berrett-Koehler, 1996.

Bridges, William. *JobShift: How to Prosper in a Workplace Without Jobs.* Menlo Park, CA: Addison-Wesley Publishing, 1995.

Bridges, William. "The End of the Job." *Fortune*, September 19, 1994.

Bryne, John A. "The Horizontal Corporation." *Business Week,* December 20, 1993.

Dent, Harry S. *Job Shock: Four New Principles Transforming Our Work and Business.* New York: St. Martin's Press, 1995.

Fox, Matthew. *The Reinvention of Work: A New Vision of Livelihood for Our Time.* San Francisco, CA: Harper, 1995.

Gill, Michael and Patterson, Sheila and Gill, Mike. *Fired Up!: From Corporate Kiss-Off to Entrepreneurial Kick-Off.* New York: Viking, 1996.

Goleman, Daniel. *Emotional Intelligence.* New York: Bantam Doubleday Dell, 1997.

Hakim, Cliff. *We Are All Self-Employed.* San Francisco, CA: Berrett-Koehler, 1995.

Handy, Charles. *The Age of Paradox.* New York: McGraw-Hill, 1995.

Handy, Charles. *The Age of Unreason.* New York: McGraw-Hill, 1991.

Kanter, Rosabeth Moss. "Collaborative Advantage." *Harvard Business Review*, July/August 1994.

249

Land, George and Jarman, Beth. *Breakpoint and Beyond: Mastering the Future Today.* New York: Harper Collins, 1993.

Naisbitt, John. *Global Paradox.* New York: Avon, 1995.

Noer, David M. *Healing The Wounds: Overcoming the Trauma of Layoffs and Revitalizing Downsized Organizations.* Jossey-Bass, 1995.

Peters, Tom. *Liberation Management.* New York:Fawcett Books, 1994.

Senge, Peter M. *The Fifth Discipline: The Art and Practice of the Learning Organization.* New York: Doubleday, 1994.

Taylor, Alex. "The Auto Industry Meets the New Economy." *Fortune,* September 4, 1994.

Toffler, Alvin. *Powershift.* New York: Bantam Books, 1991.

Wegmann, Robert, Ph.D. and Chapman, Robert, Ph.D. and Johnson, Miriam. *Work in the New Economy.* Indianapolis, IN: JIST Works, 1989.

Wheatley, Margaret J. *Leadership and the New Science: Learning About Organization from an Orderly Universe.* San Francisco, CA: Berrett-Koehler, 1993.

Whyte, David. *The Heart Aroused: Poetry and the Preservation of the Soul in Corporate America.* New York: Bantam Doubleday Dell, 1996.

Step Two

Covey, Stephen R. *The Seven Habits of Highly Effective People.* New York: Fireside, 1990.

Covey, Stephen R. *First Things First: To Live, to Love, to Learn, to Leave a Legacy.* New York: Fireside, 1996.

Restak, Richard M. *The Mind.* New York: Bantam Doubleday Dell, 1992.

Step Three

Palmer, Helen. *The Enneagram: Understanding Yourself and the Others in Your Life.* San Francisco, CA: Harper, 1991.

Singer, June. *Boundaries of the Soul: The Practice of Jung's Psychology.* Anchor Books, 1994.

Keirsey, David and Bates, Marilyn. *Please Understand Me—Character & Temperament Types.* Prometheus Nemesis, 1978.

Myers, Isabel Briggs. *Introduction to Type: A Description of the Theory and Application of the Myers-Briggs Type Indicator.* Palo Alto, CA: Consulting Psychologists Press, 1987.

Tieger, Paul D. and Barron-Tieger, Barbara. *Do What You Are: Discover the Perfect Career for You Through the Secrets of Personality Types.* New York: Little, Brown and Company, 1995.

Step Four

Gelatt, H. B. *Creative Decision Making Using Positive Uncertainty.* Menlo Park, CA: Crisp Publications, 1991.

Sher, Barbara. *WISHCRAFT—How To Get What You Really Want.* New York: Ballantine Press, 1986.

Step Five

Falkenstein, Dr. Lynda. *Nichecraft: Using Your Specialness to Focus Your Business, Corner Your Market and Make Customers Seek You Out.* Harper Business, 1996.

Mort, Mary-Ellen. *JobSmart Internet Web Site*: http://jobsmart.org/

Step Six

Baber, Anne and Waymon, Lynne. *Fifty Two Ways to Reconnect, Follow-up and Stay in Touch, When You Don't Have Time to Network.* Kendall/ Hunt, 1993.

Dubrin, Andrew J. *The Breakthrough Team Players: Becoming MVP on Your Workplace Team.* Amacom, 1995.

Jandt, Fred E. *The Customer Is Usually Wrong!: Contrary To What You've Been Told...What You Know To Be True!* Indianapolis, IN: JIST Works, 1994.

Sher, Barbara. *I Could Do Anything If I Only Knew What It Was: How to Discover What You Really Want And How to Get It.* New York: Bantam Doubleday Dell, 1995.

Viscott, David, MD *Emotional Resilience: Simple Truths for Dealing With the Unfinished Business of Your Past.* Crown Publishers, 1997.

Step Seven

Domingues, Joe and Robin, Vicki. *Your Money or Your Life: Transforming Your Relationship With Money and Achieving Financial Independence.* Penguin USA, 1993.

Lerner, Joel. *Financial Planning for the Utterly Confused.* New York: McGraw-Hill, Inc., 1994.

Quicken personal financial management software, by Intuit.

QuickBooks small business financial management software, by Intuit.

PeachTree small business accounting software, by PeachTree Software.

Step Eight

Crandall, Rick. *Marketing Your Services: For People Who Hate to Sell.* Chicago, IL: Contemporary Books, 1996.

Peppers, Don and Rogers, Martha. *The One-to-One Future: Building Relationships One Customer at a Time.* New York: Bantam Doubleday Dell, 1997.

Shenson, Howard L. *The Contract and Fee-Setting Guide for Consultants and Professionals.* New York: John Wiley & Sons, 1990.

Step Nine

Bridges, William. *Transitions—Making Sense of Life's Changes*. Addison-Wesley, 1980.

Rechtschaffen, Stephen. *Time Shifting: Creating More Time For Your Life*. NewYork: Doubleday, 1996.

Step Ten

Abrams, Rhonda A. *The Successful Business Plan: Secrets and Strategies*. Oasis Press, 1993.

Jenkins, Michael D. *Starting and Operating a Business in (Your State): A Step-by-Step Guide*. Oasis Press, 1995.

The Bridge

Bolles, Richard N. *What Color is Your Parachute? A Practical Manual for Job-Hunters and Career-Changers*. Berkeley, CA: Ten Speed Press, Revised annually.

Fein, Richard. *111 Dynamite Ways to Ace Your Job Interview*. Manassas Park, VA: Impact Publications, 1997.

Fisher, Roger and Ury, William. *Getting to Yes: Negotiating Agreement Without Giving In*. Houghton Mifflin, 1992.

Kimeldorf, Martin. *Portfolio Power: The New Way to Showcase All Your Job Skills and Experiences*. Princeton, NJ: Peterson's Guides, 1997.

Krannich, Ronald L. *Change Your Job, Change Your Life!* Manassas Park, VA: Impact Publications, 1997.

Parker, Yana. *The Damn Good Resume Guide: A Crash Course in Resume Writing*. Berkeley, CA: Ten Speed Press, 1996.

Parker, Yana. *The Resume Catalog: 200 Damn Good Examples*. Berkeley, CA: Ten Speed Press, 1996.

Parker, Yana. *Ready To Go Resumes* Software. PO Box 3289 Berkeley, California 94703. $29.95. Telephone: (510) 658-9229.

Riley, Margaret F. and Roehm, Frances and Oserman, Steve. *The Guide To Internet Job Searching*. Lincolnwood, IL: VGM Career Horizons, 1996.

Index

Want More Information About the 10 Steps to Career Independence?

The authors operate WorkVantage, an innovative training and consulting group dedicated to helping people improve their lives by changing the way they work. It was founded in 1995 as a family business by Shirley and Keith Porter, and Christine Bennett.

WorkVantage has provided seminars and consultation to a variety of employers—public and private, large and small—who recognize the bottom-line benefits of helping workers reinvent themselves. Workers ranging from blue collar employees to executives have transformed their work lives using the 10 steps to career independence.

WorkVantage offers:

- A variety of materials to guide and motivate people to deepen their exploration of the 10 steps to career independence;

- A seminar called *MMI, Inc: Preparing For a Future Beyond Jobs* which uses an exciting group process to engage participants in the 10 steps to career independence;

- Courses bringing a new perspective to the job search process, including resumes and cover letters, interview preparation, negotiation skills, and innovative new achievement portfolio;

- Individual counseling using the 10 steps to career independence.

If you're interested in learning more about WorkVantage and the services offered by the authors to workers and employers—or to give them feedback on your experience with the 10 steps to career independence—please contact the authors directly at:

WorkVantage, Inc.
1865 Ridgeland Circle
Danville, CA 94526
Tel. 925-838-4498
Fax 925-838-3289
e-mail: *ksc@workvantage.com*

Or meet them online at their Website:

www.workvantage.com

CAREER RESOURCES

Contact Impact Publications for a free annotated listing of career resources or visit their World Wide Web site for a complete listing of career resources: ***http://www.impactpublications.com***
The following career resources are available directly from Impact Publications. Complete this form or list the titles, include postage (see formula at the end), enclose payment, and send your order to:

IMPACT PUBLICATIONS
9104-N Manassas Drive
Manassas Park, VA 20111-5211
Tel. 703/361-7300 or Fax 703/335-9486
E-mail: impactp@impactpublications.com

Orders from individuals must be prepaid by check, moneyorder, Visa, MasterCard, or American Express. We accept telephone and fax orders.

Qty.	TITLES	Price	TOTAL
Career Planning and Job Search			
___	Best Jobs For the 21st Century	$19.95	___
___	Change Your Job, Change Your Life	$17.95	___
___	How to Succeed Without a Career Path	$13.95	___
___	Me, Myself and I, Inc.	$17.95	___
___	The Pathfinder	$14.95	___
___	Up Is Not the Only Way	$28.95	___
___	What Color Is Your Parachute?	$16.95	___
Resumes			
___	100 Winning Resumes For $100,000+ Jobs	$24.95	___
___	1500+ KeyWords for $100,000+ Jobs	$14.95	___
___	Dynamite Resumes	$14.95	___
___	High Impact Resumes and Letters	$19.95	___
___	Internet Resumes	$14.95	___
___	Portfolio Power	$14.95	___
___	Ready-to-Go Resumes	$29.95	___
___	Resume Catalog	$15.95	___
___	Resumes & Job Search Letters For Transitioning Military	$17.95	___
___	Sure-Hire Resumes	$14.95	

Cover Letters

___	201 Dynamite Job Search Letters	$19.95 ___
___	201 Winning Cover Letters For $100,000+ Jobs	$24.95 ___
___	Dynamite Cover Letters	$14.95 ___

Interviews, Networking, and Salary Negotiations

___	101 Dynamite Answers to Interview Questions	$12.95 ___
___	101 Dynamite Questions to Ask At Your Job Interview	$14.95 ___
___	101 Dynamite Ways to Ace Your Job Interview	$13.95 ___
___	Dynamite Networking For Dynamite Jobs	$15.95 ___
___	Dynamite Salary Negotiation	$15.95 ___
___	Interview For Success	$15.95 ___
___	What Do I Say Next?	$20.00 ___

Skills, Testing, Self-Assessment, Empowerment

___	7 Habits of Highly Effective People	$14.00 ___
___	Discover the Best Jobs For You	$15.95 ___
___	Do What You Are	$16.95 ___
___	Emotional Intelligence	$13.95 ___
___	I Can Do Anything If I Only Knew What It Was	$19.95 ___
___	Your Signature Path	$24.95 ___

SUBTOTAL -- ___

Virginia residents add 4½% sales tax ___

POSTAGE/HANDLING ($5.00 for first
title plus 8% of SUBTOTAL over $30) $5.00

8% of SUBTOTAL over $30--- ___

TOTAL ENCLOSED ------------------------------------- ___

NAME _____

ADDRESS _____

_____

_____

❑ I enclose check/moneyorder for $ _____ made payable to
IMPACT PUBLICATIONS.

❑ Please charge $ _____ to my credit card:

❑ Visa ❑ MasterCard ❑ American Express

Card # _____

Expiration date: _____/_____

Signature _____

The On-Line Superstore & Warehouse

Hundreds of Terrific Career Resources Conveniently Available On the World Wide Web 24-Hours a Day, 365 Days a Year!

Ever wanted to know what are the newest and best books, directories, newsletters, wall charts, training programs, videos, CD-ROMs, computer software, and kits available to help you land a job, negotiate a higher salary, or start your own business? What about finding a job in Asia or relocating to San Francisco? Are you curious about how to find a job 24-hours a day by using the Internet or what you'll be doing five years from now? Trying to keep up-to-date on the latest career resources but not able to find the latest catalogs, brochures, or newsletters on today's "best of the best" resources?

Welcome to the first virtual career bookstore on the Internet. Now you're only a "click" away with Impact Publication's electronic solution to the resource challenge. Impact Publications, one of the nation's leading publishers and distributors of career resources, has launched its comprehensive "Career Superstore and Warehouse" on the Internet. The bookstore is jam-packed with the latest job and career resources on:

- Alternative jobs and careers
- Self-assessment
- Career planning and job search
- Employers
- Relocation and cities
- Resumes
- Cover Letters
- Dress, image, and etiquette
- Education
- Telephone
- Military
- Salaries
- Interviewing
- Nonprofits
- Empowerment
- Self-esteem
- Goal setting
- Executive recruiters
- Entrepreneurship
- Government
- Networking
- Electronic job search
- International jobs
- Travel
- Law
- Training and presentations
- Minorities
- Physically challenged

The bookstore also includes a new "Military Career Transition Center" and "School-to-Work Center."

"This is more than just a bookstore offering lots of product," say Drs. Ron and Caryl Krannich, two of the nation's leading career experts and authors and developers of this on-line bookstore. *"We're an important resource center for libraries, corporations, government, educators, trainers, and career counselors who are constantly defining and redefining this dynamic field. Of the thousands of career resources we review each year, we only select the 'best of the best.'"*

Visit this rich site and you'll quickly discover just about everything you ever wanted to know about finding jobs, changing careers, and starting your own business—including many useful resources that are difficult to find in local bookstores and libraries. The site also includes what's new and hot, tips for job search success, and monthly specials. Impact's Web address is:

http://www.impactpublications.com